Castles Made of Sand

The Life and Music of Jimi Hendrix

James Court

NEW HAVEN PUBLISHING

Published 2025
First Edition
www.newhavenpublishingltd.com
newhavenpublishing@gmail.com

All Rights Reserved
The rights of James Court as the author of this work, have been asserted in accordance with the Copyrights, Designs and Patents Act 1988.
No part of this book may be re-printed or reproduced or utilized in any form or by any electronic, mechanical or other means, now unknown or hereafter invented, including photocopying, and recording, or in any information storage or retrieval system, without the written permission of the
Authors and Publisher.

Cover design©Pete Cunliffe

Copyright © 2025 James Court
All rights reserved
ISBN: 978-1-915975-18-8

Forward

It was in Minneapolis, of all places, that this book became a mission to complete. I was on a pilgrimage for Prince, I was in his home city in April 2023 during the 7th anniversary of his death. A lifelong fan and follower of his work I had previously written and released his biography and was intrigued and fascinated by Minneapolis, an incredible city and one I intend to return to. The city was alive with tribute shows and fans, immersing themselves in everything purple. I visited all the iconic sites associated with him, as well as First Avenue, a music venue forever associated with Prince in his early years. I'd joined a tour of his recording complex, a little further south in Chanhassen, a fascinating place emersed in originality, ingenuity and artistic eventfulness. It stood as a musical playground free from restriction or filter, where jam sessions and musical freedom could be played at any time, whenever the creative urge would arise. During a tour of the vast complex, we entered the belly of the beast, the recording studio itself, known as studio B. An Iconic creative space, where the actual recordings were made.

This space, like many from the past, has great significance. With Prince this was of course Paisley Park, and after such an incredible visit, I wondered what other recording studios would be as iconic, I could name a few, but one seemed to stick in my mind, Electric Lady Studios in New York. I was a huge admirer of guitarists, and as a guitarist, Hendrix was the greatest ever, there never was and never has been, anyone better. His songs, albums and live performances were etched in my mind, like millions of others who watched and listened to his genius. I had written about Hendrix previously, I had released The 27 Club, a book dedicated to the musicians within the infamous club, those that died at age 27. The book celebrated the lives of the most famous six, Brian Jones, Janis Joplin, Jim Morrison, Amy Winehouse, Kurt Cobain, and of course Jimi Hendrix. Because of the subject matter I only briefly touched on Jimi and always wanted to write a book that was solely dedicated to him.

Paisley Park however, although a creative space for one artist, was not the first. Years earlier in New York, Jimi Hendrix embarked on creating his own studio complex, one that could truly encompass everything he was, not just musically but morally and philosophically. After an incredible few days in Minneapolis, following iconic venues and places where Prince performed, I decided to do the same for Jimi Hendrix, two key Cities sprung to mind; New York and London.

I landed at JFK and made my way to the city. I visited Birdland on West 44th Street, a quintessential place harboring an historic encyclopedia of Jazz greats from the past; the likes of Charlie Parker, Dizzy Gillespie, Bud Powell, Miles Davis and John Coltrane, to name a few. I watched a superb performance by The John Pizzarelli Trio and could only have imagined what clubs like this would have been like watching someone like Jimi Hendrix in the late 1960s. The dark club was a window to the past, a time when it would be full of smoke and packed with music lovers until the early hours. Within the club were dark corners, people as shadows moving around, some of these clubs in the 1950s and 1960s were run down, neglected and shabby, the thick smoke and darkness hiding their threadbare interiors.

This venue located within the Theatre district was not the original club, that started back in December 1949. The original Birdland was located at 1678 Broadway, just north of West 52nd Street in Manhattan, sadly due to spiraling costs it was forced to close its doors in 1965. It was at this venue that the infamous beating of Miles Davis occurred from a New York Policeman on the sidewalk outside on August 25, 1959, during a performance. I also visited the infamous Apollo Theatre in Harlem, an area that Jimi became acquainted with in his early days arriving in the city, he quickly blended into its nightlife, performing at any club he could, with any band that would have him. The Apollo is located at 253 West 125th Street in the Harlem neighborhood of Upper Manhattan, Jimi famously won an amateur night competition at the club.

The visit to these two iconic venues celebrated the early years of Jimi, giving an insight into just how these places operated, a time when Jimi was coming through, travelling from band to band, performing nightly in any of the variety of clubs scattered around, perfecting his craft. It was a completely different world, an underground circuit, quite literally, of bands and performers rotating around the various venues. Performers of the highest order where the live performance was far more valued than anything that could be recorded; it was a different time. That said Jimi came through this circuit, rising to the top to become infamous for his ingenuity, originality and prowess. Music in these clubs though, despite how brilliant they were stayed predominantly live, rarely recorded, the transition from stage to studio was something I wanted to explore, and something that I wanted to examine more closely.

Many musicians and bands over the years can be associated with certain recording studios. The Beatles is an obvious one with the forever connection to Abbey Road, few though have truly made a studio their own, in the literal sense. With Jimi Hendrix he was one of, if not the first of note, to truly do so. Similar to Prince, who would rise later in the 1980s with Paisley Park, Jimi wanted it to be more; this was freedom; a freedom he would consistently crave while playing restricted alongside various bands. Here he could be truly emancipated in his own creative space where anything can happen, musically or otherwise.

It was in 1968 that Jimi Hendrix and his manager Michael Jeffery bought the Generation, it stood as a defunct nightclub in New York's Greenwich Village. It was a popular joint for Jimi, a place where he attended jam sessions frequently, he also jammed and welcomed many others to the venue, the likes of Big Brother & the Holding Company, B.B. King, Chuck Berry, Dave Van Ronk, Sly & the Family Stone, and John Fahey.

Originally Jimi wanted to resuscitate the nightclub, and to leave it as just that, but was persuaded by advisors Eddie Kramer and Jim Marron to convert the space into a professional recording studio. His studio fees for the lengthy Electric Ladyland sessions had been astronomical, with Jimi's constant prolonged jamming sessions the cost would spiral out of control, it meant Jimi was constantly in search of a recording environment that suited him.

Jimi was so taken by the project it ran over in many ways and took nearly twice as long as initially planned plus almost double the budget that was set. There were delays in permits as well as freak weather conditions which flooded the site. The location was also discovered to be above an underground river so soundproofing had to be installed.

The studio was constructed specifically for Jimi, he gave instructions for round windows and a machine to generate ambient lighting in myriad colors. It was designed to have a relaxing feel, a climate of calm enabling creativity to flourish freely. He commissioned it in 1968 and by 1970, it was ready. It was designed by architect John Storyk and audio engineer Eddie Kramer. Jimi's time here was short, but the impact was immense, he would spend just over two months recording in Electric Lady.

His last studio recording was a new solo demo for 'Belly Button Window', which was recorded on August 22, 1970. The last mix session with Eddie Kramer took place on August 24th of that year on 'Freedom', Night Bird Flying', 'Dolly Dagger', and "Belly Button Window". An opening party was held on August 26, with the plan for Jimi to return at will, to create when he wanted, a base for him to record whenever he felt the urge. There were many studios Jimi would use; none though would truly be his. Sadly, this would be his last visit to his new studio, shortly after these initial recordings Jimi boarded an Air India flight for London to perform at the Isle of Wight Festival; he died less than three weeks later.

Electric Lady Studios demonstrates just how resolute Jimi was to his craft, and his life in music. Especially considering this was way back in the 1960s. He invested in what was originally a bankrupt Manhattan nightclub and started the process of turning it into a studio. The studios are the other side of New York to Birdland and the Apollo Theatre, located at 2745 Broadway at 105th Street. As I passed through the area of Electric Lady Studios it felt noticeably different to the tourist district around Time Square, here you are nestled amongst the upmarket streets of Greenwich Village, an urban community bustling with performing arts with a cultural character of its own. An area befitting Jimi when he first planned his studio. To follow Jimi's career though, in the visual sense, you have to visit London; a city that was basking in the full glory of the 1960s, a place that put Jimi Hendrix into the mainstream.

I took the flight and planned a whistlestop tour of key venues and places around London, checking out the iconic clubs which were hosting some of the biggest acts of the day. These were places that were full of stars of music and stage, yet Jimi blew them all away, they had simply not witnessed anything like him. London proudly boasted some of the best guitarists of the era, despite Jimi's shyness and humble off stage manor, on stage he was simply on another level. Here was something very special.

Flying out of JFK, I got to thinking of Jimmy taking the same route, landing in England in late 1966. On that flight, somewhere over the Atlantic it is rumoured that the name change was first suggested, he took off in America as Jimmy but landed in England as Jimi. A spelling forever associated with his legendary status. There were many places to visit, this was a key City in the accession of Jimi Hendrix and his rise to stardom. A tour of London with Jimi in mind gives a glimpse into his time here, with many places attributed to him, a city to become immersed in Jimi Hendrix when his career truly took off. He may have had his grounding, and honed his early craft in America, but it was here in England that was pivotal in his career, it was where Jimi Hendrix was truly born.

The Bag O' Nails at 9 Kingley Street was a popular haunt for Jimi, and one of the first when he arrived in London. He not only played here but came to relax after performances and meet with other musicians like the Beatles and the Rolling Stones. It also stands as the venue that was his first official UK gig with his band - The Jimi Hendrix Experience. Many stars of the day came here, hearing of his talent.

Watching him perform at The Bag include John Lennon, Paul McCartney, Keven Ayers, Peter Townshend, and Mick Jagger - all of whom were blown away. Moving into Soho I arrived at Ronnie Scott's Jazz Club, located on 47 Frith Street, a venue that became synonymous for Jimi at the other end of his time in London. It was on the 16th of September 1970, that

Ronnie Scott's held a performance of Jimi alongside Eric Burdon, probably most famous for his time as the lead singer of The Animals, this time with his band. Incidentally it was reported that Burdon was the person Hendrix's girlfriend called when she found him overdosed, but that is for later.

This seemingly low-key event was a simple informal jam session; nobody present was aware however that this was to be Hendrix's last ever public performance; it's a sobering venue with this in mind. Rewinding back to another key setting was The Marquee Club, then situated a short walk away at 90 Wardour Street, was where Jimi truly launched his career with his performances in 1967. Here was where The Rolling Stones performed for the very first time on 12 July 1962, it also was a key venue for many famous bands during its tenure including, The Yardbirds, Queen, Led Zeppelin, The Who, David Bowie, Fleetwood mac, Elton John and The Clash to name a few. Jimi's first gig here broke all Marquee Club records; the place was rammed to the rafters; in this tiny venue over 1,400 people were crammed inside. Next stop in London is The Cromwellian situated at number 3 Cromwell Road. This three-story club, casino, and bar can proudly boast the first solo gig Hendrix ever played in London. It was here Jimmy played "Hey Joe!" while jamming with Brian Auger.

At this point London was in the grip of a cultural revolution – the baby-boomers were young adults, fashion and music was changing and evolving at a rapid pace, and 'Swinging London' was where it was 'at'. The clubs such as 'The Crom' were battling with each other for status, to be recognised as an 'in' club. Most of the clubs on this scene had some sort of underworld associated with them, a strong door policy was established as this was the era of the London Protection Gangs, The Krays and The Richardsons amongst them. Drawing the right clientele into these clubs was essential, the more A list arrived, the more they would attract. Gradually the reputation of The Cromwellian was established, and the 3-story club became a casino, bar and discotheque. It was soon the 'in' club and many pop stars, record producers, managers, agents and models would mingle away until the small hours. At the time the first floor was the casino. Two dice-tables were originally located on the ground floor until an infamous Molotov Cocktail was thrown through the window and scorched the surface of one of them. Dice tables were in short supply and gambling was ever more popular, so a more dedicated casino was established upstairs, and the vulnerable front windows of the building were protected with wrought iron security grills. But like many clubs that Jimi had previously played in over in the USA, it was down in the cellars that waves were made in the sixties music scene. The club made a policy of booking bands of respected musical ability, which attracted visiting stars to 'sit in'- Bands like Reg Dwight's 'Bluesology' aka Elton John, 'The Nightimers' and Brian Auger's

'Steampacket'. Basically, bands came to watch other bands, to check out the competition, this competition was of course tightly knitted, until Jimi came along.

Obviously, Jimi lived in London while he played these various clubs, and standing outside the flat that Jimi shared with his then girlfriend Kathy Etchingham on 23 Brook Street, gives a feel to the surroundings and culture he would have been exposed to during his time in 1968. He had a second flat that was even more intriguing located at 38 Montagu Square, this one has an impressive history; it was owned by Ringo Starr in the 1960s and was the first flat John Lennon and Yoko Ono lived in together, this is also the location where Paul McCartney wrote Eleanor Rigby. An incredible musical history for one flat in the wealthy area of Marylebone.

My final visiting place in London is the saddest one, Hotel Samarkand at 22 Lansdowne Crescent. It was here on September 17th/18th 1970, that Jimi Hendrix would spend his final night. Jimi's girlfriend Monika Dannemann was said to be the only person with him when he died – she was renting an apartment at the Samarkand. According to Monika, she brought Jimi back to her hotel at 3:00 am and they stayed up until 7:00 am before both falling asleep. Standing outside the Samarkand is a strange feeling, researching venues and locations in Nashville Tennessee, and iconic venues in New York and London gives a true feeling to the life of Jim Hendrix. Visiting the Samarkand is where it all came to an end. It was here that Monika Dannemann allegedly discovered Jimi around 11:00am to find him unconscious. He was rushed to the hospital but was declared dead at 12:45 pm, owing to the effects of an accidental overdose. There is however much speculation surrounding these final events, which we will come too later.

Visiting these places both in the USA and England gave way for this book to become a reality, a challenging one, but one that could not be ignored. Jimi Hendrix stands as one of the most iconic figures in popular music. To think his career lasted only a few years is quite staggering in relation to the musical and cultural impact he had. Even more astonishing is the relatively short periods he would spend in certain cities, only to be forever remembered wherever he went. His story is deep, with much to discover and uncover, but it's one that is worth researching and writing about: his life was short, but his story is a fascinating one, a unique one.

Artists who are no longer with us are often judged by the influence they have over those that follow. With Jimi Hendrix his influence is absolute and exclusive. To this day many try to replicate him, but no one can match the sheer scale of his genius on the electric guitar; the sound was unique, the presentation unique and the overall package was simply unlike anything that had come before, or after. Watching Monterey, Woodstock or any other recording of Hendrix Live is an experience like no other; in this respect he was and will always remain, incomparable.

Welcome to the Electric Church.

Acknowledgements

I would like to express my sincere gratitude to several individuals. The past few years have presented significant challenges that tested our family's resilience and required careful navigation. It is in such times that the strength of family and the loyalty of true friends become evident.

My sincere thanks go to my sisters, Beverly and Julie, and my brothers-in-law, Phil and Dean. I am also grateful to my nieces, Marisa, Pia, Gemma, and Megan, with a special acknowledgment to Sadie for her extraordinary assistance and kindness.

A big mention to Antony and Pete, my brothers, thank you for being there, and continuing to be. The very definition of friends.

To my sons, Charlie and Danny, I am immensely proud to be your Dad.

A big shout out to Molly, Liv, and Jack, thanks for your support; I hope you enjoy this!

Finally, to Katrina, My Beautiful, Thank you for everything....

This book is dedicated to my Parents:

Jim Court & Eileen Court

Missed forever.

With his blessings from above
Serve it generously with love
One man, one wife, one love through life
Sweet memories are made of this
Memories are made of this

Contents

Foreword	3
Acknowledgements	10
Chapter 1: A Little Indian brave	15
Chapter 2: House Burning Down	20
Chapter 3: Rainy Day, Dream Away	28
Chapter 4: Chitlin Blues	37
Chapter 5: Kiss the Sky	45
Chapter 6: A Train a 'Comin	51
Chapter 7: New York, A Slight Return	59
Chapter 8: Music is my Religion	67
Chapter 9. Road to Experience	77
Chapter 10. Butterflies and Zebras	85
Chapter 11. Way Down Where I Can Be Free	95
Chapter 12. Where You Gonna Run To Now?	103
Chapter 13. The Moon Turned a Fire Red	114
Chapter 14. Take Anything You Want From Me	123
Chapter 15. Killing Floor	132
Chapter 16. Light your Fire	143
Chapter 17. Gold and Rose	161
Chapter 18. The Magic Carpet Waits	172
Chapter 19. Gypsy Sun	189
Chapter 20. Fly On, My Sweet angel	200

- *Timelines* — 221
- *Discography* — 251
- *Posthumous Discography* — 252
- *Anthologies and Retrospective Albums* — 254
- *Dagger Discography* — 255
- *Jimi Hendrix Park* — 256
- *What Others Say* — 257
- *Electric Lady Studios* — 279
- *Funeral and Final Goodbye* — 281

About the Author — 284

Jimi Hendrix (C) Monica Dannerman

Chapter 1

A Little Indian Brave

"Imagination is the key to my lyrics. The rest is painted with a little science fiction."

In the history of popular music there are a handful of artists that simply need no introduction. A single name can envisage genius, originality and pure innovation. There is arguably one name above all others that defines this characteristic, a name that illustrates pure musicality and artistic performance. Rock and roll at its most electric. The humble guitar would never be the same again; the way it was heard, the way it was played and the way it was seen. Simply put there was a before, and there was an after. One name changed it forever. Hendrix.

He was a pioneer that took an instrument that was popular before and permanently changed the way it was perceived. It is impossible to get introduced to any guitar-based music without becoming familiarised with Jimi Hendrix. Once discovered, either musically, visually, or both, there is nothing higher; you have reached the summit. He *was* the Guitar, everyone after him was simply travelling in his wake. He is widely and accurately regarded as one of the most influential electric guitarists in the history of popular music, and one of the most celebrated musicians of the 20th century. The Rock and Roll Hall of Fame describes him as "*arguably the greatest instrumentalist in the history of rock music*". His guitar style revolutionised rock music in the 1960s, and he was an icon of the hippie counterculture that emerged so prominently later in the decade.

Jimi Hendrix had an impact that completely revolutionised popular music. During his short time there was a transformation, an altering of what was acceptable from a standard singer with a guitar. He was the first true musical prodigy, and with the electric guitar he singlehandedly reconditioned its impression in the minds of musicians and the public alike. On the guitar he was a pure musical genius, the likes of which no-one had ever seen before, or has ever seen since. He was the first true electric guitar hero. There was no one like him: he was unique, talented and without doubt the most influential guitarist of all time. He was one of the biggest forces in 20th century music and arguably *the* biggest. What's even more staggering is the fact that his mainstream career lasted for just 4 years. Jimi Hendrix stands as one of the greatest instrumentalists in the history of rock music.

Jimi Hendrix was born Johnny Allen Hendrix at 10:15am on November 27th, 1942, at King County Hospital in Seattle, which is now known as Harborview. He was the first of five children. His father was James Allen Hendrix, born in June 1919; although he was commonly known as Al. His mother was Lucille Jeter who was originally from Roslyn Washington, she was born in 1925. The future parents shared a keen interest in music and met at a concert in Seattle by jazz pianist Fats Waller. A concert gathering commonly known at the time as a rent party.

Fats Waller had a unique and innovative approach, specialising in a style known as Harlem stride, this would later go on to lay the groundwork for modern jazz piano. At this time Fats was a popular act and he toured internationally. He achieved critical and commercial success on both sides of the Atlantic, especially with compositions, "Ain't Misbehavin'" and "Honeysuckle Rose". These two would later be inducted into the Grammy Hall of Fame in 1984 and 1999 respectively.

It was in Harlem where this musical style was first created and developed - and where these rent parties originated. House rent parties stood as a popular social event in Harlem life even before the great depression, starting from the infamous Wall Street crash of 1929. The packed venues provided a release from everyday life, tenants could hire a musician or band to play and pass the hat to raise money to pay their rent. Not only would it be a source of valuable income, but parties also gave a much-needed excuse for black tenants to eat, dance, and get away from everyday hardship and discrimination. The rent party played a major role in the development of jazz and blues music, alongside other forms of swing dancing. Even the great Duke Ellington spoke about them at the time, "House rent parties were aimed at helping dwellers of Harlem's railroad flats meet their rents that skyrocketed monthly. Neighbors brought all kinds of food—fried chicken, baked ham, pig's feet, pork chops, gumbo, potato salad, and more—to which a supply of bootleg liquor was added. An admission was charged, and the *piano players supplied the entertainment.*"

The parties were more than casually thrown get-togethers: there was a complex set of home-grown industries built up around rent parties. Hosts would advertise them with rent party tickets printed from portable presses with snippets of poetry and bustling slogans one read *"You Don't Get Nothing for Being an Angel Child, So You Might as Well Get Real Busy and Real Wild."* Some events had more than one pianist, allowing them to musically battle with one another, attempting to outplay their competitors. It was a fitting venue for the introduction of the future parents of the greatest guitar player the world would ever see.

It is a common misconception that Jimi Hendrix only had a single brother, Leon Hendrix, but the truth is that after Jimi's parents met at the rent party, they would go on to have three more children besides Jimi and Leon: Joseph Allan Hendrix, Kathy Ira Hendrix, and Pamela Hendrix. The family tree was combined with a rich heritage, not dissimilar to others at the time. It was of African American and Irish descent and was littered with struggle and hardship. Jimi Hendrix's actual paternal lineage was intriguing.

Jimi's grandfather, Bertran Philander Ross Hendrix, was born from an extramarital affair, and his grandmother, Zenora "Nora" Rose Moore, was a vaudeville performer. They moved to Vancouver, where they had Al, Jimi's father. Tracing further back the Hendrix family's history is a rich tapestry of hardships and triumphs. From Jimi's grandparents' unique backgrounds to the trials faced by his siblings, each thread contributed to the fabric of his life and his music, it authenticated his future career.

Later when Jimi would start giving press interviews, he came across somewhat reluctant to discuss his life outside the rock and roll world he was engaged in. He was often cautious about giving too much family history away, and often for good reason, his pre-rockstar life therefore became somewhat of a mystery. It was a good strategy, even if it was one that was not calculated in any way, Jimi was a shy character, a modest personality, much different in conversation to his onstage wild persona. He was a musician looking forward, not back, a pioneer of new sounds and innovative experimentation. There was not much in Jimi's past that he viewed as relevant, and it's intriguing to discover that he would effectively become famous by leaving America behind, establishing himself in London after fleeing the Vietnam draft.

There was one aspect of Jimi's past however that he celebrated with affection, his Cherokee heritage. Jimi claimed that it was his grandmother, Nora Rose Moore, who told him of the family's Cherokee ancestry. It can't be clarified for sure that Moore was descended from the indigenous tribe, however as she existed in a time of great oppression of both First Nations and Black Americans, the chances of documentation confirming or denying the heritage is difficult to pin down.

Regardless to whether this was true or not, the young Jimmy took great pride in his Cherokee roots and stories told from his Grandmother throughout his life and career. He openly embraced its native imagery and fashion in his performances. He would even go so far as to occasionally speak about his indigenous roots in interviews. He was appreciative and seemed genuinely honoured with his heritage, in fact it seemed at times to be the only aspect of his past he was willing to share. There are explicit indigenous threads that run through each of the three studio albums that Jimi completed during his lifetime, extending to his historic performance at Woodstock. Throughout his recording career there are native themes and images intertwined that are core aspects of his music. There are many examples of connections to natural surroundings, especially of American indigenous culture. Themes of 'Water', 'Fire', 'Air/Wind', and 'Earth/Sand' songs. Within this, it is sand and water that stand as Jimi's two favorite metaphors. Jimi's compositions contain many distinctive lyrics, indigenous stories and symbology often associated with them. They are also characterised on an instrumental level by sonic adaptations and innovations aimed at capturing the most natural sound and tone possible.

Probably the most noticeable example of Jimi Hendrix honouring this cultural background is the incredible song 'Castles Made of Sand', released in 1967. Sitting on his second album, 'Axis: Bold as Love', and of course the title of this book, the song sees Jimi adopting a more delicate and mellow offering, it's an unconventional sound to this point, a striking departure from the psychedelic demeanor of tracks he was renowned for up to this point. 'Castles Made of Sand' is a reflective ode to one's past. Dealing with the inevitability of death and how a dream can be cut tragically short, the lyrics detail the stories of various characters, including one described as "a little Indian brave". The boy has ambitions of becoming a fierce warrior and chief, only to be suddenly snuffed out by a surprise attack in the middle of the night. Even more impressive is the fact that for the musical accompaniment, Jimi recorded the guitars and then played them in reverse, giving the song an eccentric and unconventional feel. The technique provides a psychedelic atmosphere, a signature sound over a deep and meaningful tale. Layered within is the sound of wind, which has raindrops reversed or echoed and phased, which captures and underlines the sound of the wind's actions. If you are looking for a Cherokee sound, if there is one, Jimi Hendrix put it all superbly within this track. The song isn't an autobiographical tale of Jimi Hendrix; it does however stand as an insight into his heritage. It's a celebration of Cherokee roots, especially within the context of the time the track was released.

Releasing this type of song, containing the subject of indigenous people within a rock composition, was a brave and important thing for Jimi Hendrix to do, as First Nations faced a great deal of oppression and attempted cultural erasure at the time. It could be argued that the wandering aspect of Cherokee decent captivated the young Jimmy to escape Seattle and seek adventure elsewhere, the gypsy spirits within him that had manifested through countless tales of generations from his childhood. It was this that undoubtedly carried him forward, to move on, to travel. Seattle would represent insecurity, indecision and self-doubt. *"I ran away from home a couple of times because I was so miserable"*, he would later reveal, *"My brother and I used to go to different homes because Dad and Mother used to break up all the time"*.

As Jimmy got older, and his love of music increased, he realised that his home city wasn't the place for blues. He was still very young, but he was becoming aware that the great blues master's he was interested in were from cities far away. Seattle just didn't seem the kind of city where blues and guitar-based music could flourish. Other cities in America had this well and truly in the bag. These big cities lay elsewhere, with origins nestled within the deep south of America, hubs that spread far and wide, cultivating new styles and becoming infamous for music; The Delta Blues, first recorded in the 1920s, was one of the earliest types of blues music and originated in Mississippi in the Delta. Tales of this resonated, and Jazz and Blues flourished in the years ahead in musical communities, dominant thriving cities emerged such as New Orleans, Louisiana, New York, Chicago and Kansas City. These were seen as the vibrant hubs of musical excellence, the special places where the greats came from and honed their talents. In comparison Seattle at this time was more famous for logging, it even had a red-light district named '*Down on the Sawdust'*. It didn't take much for the young Jimmy Hendrix to realise his ambitions where not in the place he called home.

Many factors, both in his ancestral past, and his ambitions going forward, drove him onwards. His aspiration for greater things was getting bigger and more prominent. He was unsure exactly what he wanted to do at this stage, but he did start to recognise early on that whatever he wanted to do in life lay elsewhere, and not in Seattle. Someone like Jimmy Hendrix was never going to settle for anything other than breaking away. His path was ahead of him.

Further on in his career Jimmy would also change his name, clearly searching for an identity of his own. This book will refer to Jimmy within these timelines, he would go from Johnny, to Jimmy, to Jimmy James and eventually on landing in England, to Jimi. The rest, as they say, is history.

As well as his Cherokee descent Jimmy was obviously African American, it is however the Cherokee that undoubtedly captivated him. It sculpted his identity, his sound. When he broke through it was one of the key aspects to his originality. It was a foundation that made him ever more individual, coupled obviously with his incredible talent.

As the Cherokee say: '*A Bird does not sing because it has an answer, it sings because it has a song...*'

Chapter 2

House Burning Down

"All I'm writing is just what I feel, that's all. I just keep it almost naked."

The resilience and talent of Jimi Hendrix, emerging from such a complex family backdrop, highlights his extraordinary journey from a troubled childhood to becoming one of the most revered musicians in history. To get to the heights he did, from the background he had, is nothing short of extraordinary.

About a year after Jimmy's future parents met at The Rent Party in Seattle, they got married. However, three days after the wedding, Al was drafted by the US Army to serve in World War II and left to begin his basic training, leaving his wife to face the early days of marriage alone. Jimmy's mother, Lucille, had ancestors who had been enslaved and faced various hardships throughout her life. Once married, she encountered immediate challenges, dealing with Al's departure for military service just a few days after their wedding was extremely difficult.

The birth of their first child, Johnny Allen Hendrix, the future Jimmy, then future Jimi, occurred while Al was stationed in Alabama, with the U.S. army in Camp Rucker, now known as Fort Rucker. He was still young himself, at just 22 years old. At the time there was a standard military furlough that allowed servicemen leave for impending childbirth however, this was denied to Al for fear he might go AWOL. "*I asked my commanding officer about going home*". '*No Chance*,' he said, '*You live too far away*'." Naturally Al was angry and argued his case to his superiors, noting his fury they had a feeling he may take matters in his own hands. As a result, he spent two months locked up without trial, and, while in the stockade, received a telegram announcing the birth of his son.

Lucille gave birth to Johnny when she was just 17. Naturally she struggled to raise the child alone during Al's absence, relying heavily on family and friends for support. Lucille was forced to work odd jobs to make ends meet, to help her she put young Johnny in the temporary care of a couple in California, who were friends of the family, among many other carers during his early years. Lucille did temporarily move in with a friend, Dorothy Harding, where she stayed during the pregnancy but after Johnny was born there simply wasn't enough room. Dorothy had two kids of her own in the tiny house already, so Lucille was forced to move out. From here she moved around various hotel rooms in downtown Seattle. To make matters worse there was a bureaucratic error with the army resulting in her receiving no money from Al for nearly a year, after he was drafted. Lucille was still a teenager at this time, she had gone quickly from enjoying her teenage years, partying around the bars, dance halls and nightclubs of Seattle to becoming a wife and mother. The responsibility was too great for her at just 17 years of age.

When Al did finally get back home, after he was eventually released from the army post World War II, he decided to take primary responsibility for raising Johnny, who was still being passed around frequently; he was living with Lucille's older sister at the time of Al's return. The family's life was constantly marked by instability and poverty. There was alcoholism and frequent arguments. They also frequently moved around and never settled anywhere too long. As a result, young Johnny's early years were fraught with turmoil, he didn't have any sort of paternal stability and witnessed domestic violence firsthand. He endured the persistent threat of fraternal separation. Lucille was a hard drinker and there were many occasions when those who were looking after Johnny would not hand him back to his young mother, unless she returned sober.

Despite the poverty and constant insecurity, the family carried on and expanded further. Leon Hendrix was born January 13, 1948, and at this time Al had begun receiving unemployment benefits thanks to the Servicemen's Readjustment Act, more commonly known as the G.I. Bill, which was much needed in the growing Hendrix family. Following on from Leon there was the arrival of Joseph, Kathy, and Pamela. Sadly, each child faced their own challenges. Joseph was born with physical disabilities and placed in foster care at age three. Kathy was born blind, and Pamela, facing minor health issues, was also raised in foster care. These circumstances deeply affected the early years of the young Johnny Allen Hendrix. It shaped his personality, one where he became withdrawn and introspective in nature.

In 1946 when Johnny was three years old the couple renamed him James Marshall Hendrix, which would be cropped to Jimmy, and then of course again to Jimi. Later in Jimmy's career, his then manager, Chas Chandler, is usually credited with switching this spelling, with some accounts suggesting the change was agreed during the transatlantic flight that brought Jimmy/Jimi to England to launch his career. There is, however, some speculation regarding the early intervention and initial name change. One theory is that the name was changed from Johnny to James Marshall Hendrix in honour of Al and his late brother Leon Marshall, who had died in 1932. Other rumours speculated that it was because Lucille engaged in a marital affair with a man of the same name, and therefore Al insisted that his sons name needed to be changed.

With Lucille's reputation for being unfaithful there was one man she was rumoured to have been involved with while Al was away in the US army, he was a black man named Johnny Williams, although it is thought that was not his real surname. He was originally from Kansas City and made his way to Seattle to work on the docks. Lucille went away with him for many months, travelling all over. He was described as a low life; Lucille's friend Dorothy Harding described him as 'Slime'. Dorothy claimed that one time they had to go and get Lucille back, he had beaten her, and Johnny was not in good health, contracting Pneumonia from the constant relocating from one temporary damp room to another.

It is not known whether the name change was because Johnny was thought to have been an illegitimate child, and Johnny Williams was actually his father, but either way Al thought it best to have the name changed, it was after all a name that he not been involved with and even if Johnny Williams was not Jimmy's real father, the name must have been annoying to Al, knowing of the affair while he was away. As a result, Johnny became James; and of course, later, Jimmy/Jimi. Whatever the reason on September 11th, 1946, Al changed his sons name from Johnny Allen Hendrix to James Marshall Hendrix. He was however often referred to as 'Jimmy'.

It was inevitable from the challenging circumstances that Al and Lucille faced that the marriage would end prematurely. They separated many times, and on one occasion were apart for quite a while. After this break up, they did try to get back together, they reunited shortly after the war, and even purchased a house together situated in Rainer View, Seattle, but the family ran into financial difficulties when Al found it hard to find steady employment. Both parents turned to alcohol to try and forget their problems, and the arguments and disruption continued. In 1951, they finally divorced.

Al was eventually granted custody of Jimmy and his younger brother Leon. The boys were raised in a strict environment, but although Al had custody, they were still often under the care of others, which included their paternal grandmother living in Vancouver. Lucille often visited but Al was unhappy with this, she would often turn up late at night, bottle in her hand with her latest boyfriend with her. Al had to be at work early and the boys in school, so it was another situation the boys had to frequently endure. She would also promise the boys things, things that they knew would never materialise, but they would go along with it just for the attention of their mother. She would then disappear for months at a time. This turbulent upbringing left an indelible mark on Jimmy, influencing his later life and music. There were also many times when he undoubtedly became the main carer for his younger brother, taking on the responsibility for him as his father was working, and his mother was away for weeks or even months successively.

Lucille had acquired a reputation as a socialite who enjoyed nightlife and frequenting various clubs and bars within the city centre and wider areas. Once Jimmy's parents divorced, there were numerous rumours of extramarital affairs and a series of relationships with different men during and after the marriage. However, this behaviour can be understood as typical for someone of her age, still just a teenager herself, she had been thrown into a huge amount of parental responsibility, she found it difficult to cope both physically and mentally. Her young life had transitioned swiftly from a carefree young soul enjoying life, to an individual grappling with responsibilities she did not recognise or could adequately handle, basically she needed help and was vulnerable. She was also independent-minded and resisted conforming to societal expectations of how a young married woman should behave, she sought excitement and valued her autonomy. Unfortunately, she also had the obligation of being a young mother, which she struggled to manage effectively. Her drinking appeared to be a coping mechanism to deal with the pressures of motherhood and marriage at such a young age.

When Jimmy moved back in with his father, he started missing school. Al did not insist that he attend, so this became a common practice. As a result of his truancy, Jimmy failed 9th grade and had to repeat the year. Jimmy's life was unstable; he was not attending school and falling behind, and another significant event was about to occur, something that would affect him deeply for the rest of his life. On February 2nd, 1958, Lucille died. Jimmy was 15 years old. Although some believed her death was due to excessive drinking, Lucille actually died from a ruptured spleen. When Lucille's sister and friend went to Harborview Hospital to visit, they found her lying in the hallway surrounded by doctors and nurses, who believed they could have saved her if they had known beforehand that she had a ruptured spleen. After informing Jimmy and Leon of their mother's death, Al did not allow them to attend the funeral. Instead, he gave them a shot of whiskey and stated that *"this is how men do it."*

Lucille died at just 33 years old. Jimmy was of course devasted by his mother's premature death, he rarely spoke about it, and kept his grief hidden away, a trait obviously passed down by his father, although he would sporadically speak about it in the years ahead. In 1967, at London's Saville Theatre, Jimi dedicated 'The Wind Cries Mary' to her and occasionally mentioned her in interviews. He once recalled, *"When I was four and wet my pants, I stayed in the rain for hours so my Mum wouldn't know. She knew though."*

A broken Al now worked even more hours, leaving Jimmy and Leon to basically fend for themselves. Lucille's death affected Jimmy most of all, who would often go to his aunts at this time, just for the additional company. Al noticed Jimmy's interest in the guitar. Al recounted: *"I asked him, 'Didn't you sweep up the floor?' and he'd respond, 'Oh yeah,' he did. But later, I discovered that he used to sit at the end of the bed and strum the broom as if it were a guitar. I used to have Jimmy clean up the bedroom while I was gone, and when I returned, I would find broom straws around the foot of the bed!".*

The image of a young man sitting at the foot of a bed with a broom, pretending it is a guitar, may appear comical. However, it represents a significant aspect of blues guitar history known as *'one strand on the wall.'* Children and indeed adults, who could not afford a guitar would use a wire from a broom handle and stretch it against a wall. A rock or another object would be used to tension the wire to achieve a specific tone, while one hand plucked the wire and the other slid a bottle along it to create sound. Notably, both B.B. King and Elmore James learned this technique during their early years. Consequently, a young Jimmy Hendrix using wires from a broom was consistent with the practices of past great blues guitarists of America.

Jimmy was now developing an early fascination with the guitar, and particularly the many blues guitarists of the day. During his time at Horace Mann Elementary School in Seattle during the mid-1950s, where he had to repeat his 9th grade due to falling behind, the teachers noticed he would carry a broom around the school constantly, notably a different one to the 'broom guitar' at home. The school's social worker noticed this and concluded he was using it as a kind of security blanket. At School Jimmy was an average student, ironically, he was graded poor at music, he did however do very well at art, which proved to be his best subject. *"I used to paint at school*, the teacher would say, *'Paint three scenes.' I'd do abstract stuff like a Martian sunset."*

Despite the issues and hardship, the young Jimmy had notable moments when he did bond with his father, mainly, and unsurprisingly, over music. He took a keen interest in his father's record collection, artists such as B.B. King, Muddy Waters and Howlin' Wolf. It was, however, the legendary Robert Johnson that peaked Jimmy's interest in the mid to late 1950s. Jimmy was fascinated with Robert Johnson's technique, which sounded as if he was playing two guitars at the same time. It's an interesting thought that Jimmy Hendrix would spend his childhood fascinated with a guitarist who had a similar fate to his own. Robert Johnson himself died young, before reaching his full potential and notoriety. It was rumored he had *'sold* his soul to the devil' and died by taking a shot of poisoned whisky. The notorious crossroads incident became the stuff of legend. Robert Johnson was 27 when he died, the same age as Jimi when he passed; they both therefore became part of the infamous '27 Club'.

Noticing his son's fascination with blues music, Al found him an old one-string ukulele, which he gave to Jimmy to play - a huge improvement over the broom. Jimmy played this constantly over the following months, placing his fingers where the other strings would potentially be. Jimmy discovered the nuances of tuning a single string to produce different pitches. This seemingly humble ukulele became the testing ground for the manipulation of sound which would later become a hallmark of his distinctive style.

By the summer of 1958, the one string ukulele was upgraded. Al purchased Jimmy a five-dollar second-hand acoustic guitar from one of his friends. Other reports however state that Jimmy was helping his father clear out the home of an elderly woman when he found the instrument in the garbage, and his father let him keep it. There were other theories too involving the first guitar owned by Jimi Hendrix. One common story was that his father let him keep it because he was sick and tired of returning from work to find straw all over the floor, where Jimmy had strummed the broom. Jimmy stated later that his father would beat him frequently because of this. Either way in 1958 Jimmy Hendrix had his first acoustic guitar. He instantly became obsessed with the instrument and played it constantly.

It was said that the first tune Jimmy learned to play was the television theme 'Peter Gunn', a show that ran from 1958-1961. A series about a James Bond type detective who loved cool Jazz. He learned quickly to play, replicating with ease any song that he heard; it was natural to him, effortless. From this point on, Jimmy and his guitar were inseparable, and music became his supreme passion, his one love. In addition to 'Peter Gunn' Jimmy also learned 'Louie Louie' by Richard Berry, released in 1957. He also learned by ear material by Billy Butler, Muddy Waters and Eddie Cochran, as well as singing many Elvis Presley songs, including 'Hound Dog' and 'Love Me Tender', which Leon says he used to sing to him when he went to sleep.

Jimmy was naturally left-handed, and Al tried in vain to get him to play right-handed, the so-called standard way. When Al was out of sight Jimmy switched the strings back around, but it caused the guitar to drop badly out of tune. Jimmy said later, *"I knew nothing about tuning a guitar, so I went down to a store and ran my fingers across the strings on a guitar they had there. After that I was able to tune my own."*

At this time Jimmy started jamming with a friend named Sammy Drain and his brother who played keyboards. He also met legendary blues guitarist Billy Davis in 1959, who was the lead guitarist in the band *Hank Ballard & the Midnighters* in Seattle. They wrote the original version of 'The Twist'. Jimmy had gone to see the concert and met the guitarist after the show. Jimmy was fascinated with the feedback that Davies created with his guitar, which was unusual at the time, and his wild stage antics. Jimmy was determined to meet him after the gig. Davies recalled the meeting. *"We were playing at the Eagle Auditorium in Washington and Jimmy came to the show. At the time Jimmy was 16 and I was 20. Pat* (one of the bandmates) *told me Jimmy had come to meet me, but I was so busy looking for girls that I rejected him about three times. I said, 'I don't have time to meet this guy, I'm trying to meet girls!' But finally, I met him and brought him backstage, and we hit it off so good. He was such a nice person. I spent a whole week with him teaching him what I knew about playing guitar and that's how we became friends. That was 1959 and our friendship lasted until he passed away"*. Davis later claimed that the signature Hendrix move of playing the guitar behind his head was his, as well as playing the guitar with his teeth.

Jimmy was now moving forward with ambitions of becoming a guitar player of sorts. His young childhood was fading behind him and he was pressing ahead, focusing on music. The death of his mother, however, cannot be underestimated as a devastating time in his young life. He occasionally referred to her, especially through the music he was now playing, opening up to thoughts and reflections, she was a major lyrical and artistic outpour. He often said that she came to him in dreams that he had, he wrote the ballad 'Angel' after one such dream. He recalled another during an interview in 1967 with journalist Meatball Fulton:

"My Mother was being carried away on this camel. And there was a big caravan, She she's sayin 'Well I'm gonna see you now', and she's going under these trees, and you can see the shade, you know, the leaf patterns on her face as she's going under…you know the sun shines through a tree and if you go under the shadow of a tree …Shadows go across your face…green and yellow… she's sayin 'Well, I won't be seeing you too much anymore, you know, I'll see you'. And about two years after that she dies, you know, and I said "Yeah, but where are you going, and all that, you know, I remember that. I never did forget. There are some dreams you never forget."

It was here that the guitar became integral to the life of Jimmy Hendrix, a young man becoming fully immersed in music, his path was opening before him. The acoustic guitar was played constantly, and he was fast mastering it. Noticing his son's talent, Al was persuaded to get Jimmy his first electric guitar. He took Jimmy to Myers Music Store based on 1st Avenue where he purchased a White Supro Ozark Guitar; he also bought himself a Saxophone so they could jam together. Father and son now had something in common, something to build upon, it was more than a hobby for Jimmy, he was as serious about music as Al was about his dancing. One purchase, however, from this trip was neglected: the amplifier. Without this, the electric guitar would not fully come to life. For the time being Jimmy was playing it as an acoustic, imagining the sounds he could make should he have the amp.

Jimmy didn't have to wait long, the resolution to this issue was just around the corner; he was given his opportunity to finally participate in something musically when he was invited to perform publicly for the first time, addressing the good people of Seattle.

Chapter 3

Rainy Day, Dream Away

"When things get too heavy, just call me helium, the lightest known gas to man."

Like many cities in the mid to late 1950s the best music clubs were to be found in the early hours of the morning, seedy smoky underground joints where those in the know mingled in the shadows, often until dawn. Venues such as the Palomar Theatre, The Rocking Chair and Esquire were just a few of the fashionable and prominent venues in Seattle at this time.

Long before grunge, which gave Seattle a musical identity from the mid 1980s, there was a vibrant music scene emerging within the city, it derived from the culture of the 1920s and was nurtured further by the wartime boom of the 1940s. Here the new musical traditions mingled with the old to produce a rich stew of jazz, swing, and rhythm and blues in nightclubs and dance halls along Jackson Street and in the Central Area.

Within this region Jimmy's mother Lucille had previously worked at a speakeasy known as The Bucket of Blood, today the venue is sporting some recently uncovered prohibition-era murals. Mainly in the United States, speakeasy bars date back to at least the 1880's. They came into wider prominence during the prohibition era, from 1920 through to 1933, but some lasted longer; a time when the sale, manufacture, and transportation of alcoholic beverages was illegal. The name came from the phrase, Speakeasies, known because they were *"the practice of speaking quietly about such a place in public, or when inside it, so as not to alert the police or neighbours"*.

Both Al and Lucille became regular fixtures on the scene, often leaving Jimmy and his brother Leon to fend for themselves. Speakeasies and the popular bars and clubs were a magnet for travelling musicians, it was here that up-and-coming stars would perform, names such as Quincy Jones, Ernestine Anderson, and Ray Charles. In 1948 Ray Charles was just 17 and living alone when he came to Seattle, he chose the city to get as far away from his native Florida as possible, without leaving the USA entirely. He stayed for just two years, but during that time he cut his first record 'Confession Blues'. He also met and formed what would become a lifetime friendship and collaboration with Quincy Jones. Charles performed regularly at the Black Elks Club on Jackson Street and at the blues-oriented Rocking Chair Club, on 14th just off Yesler. His 'Rockin' Chair Blues', recorded just before he moved on to Los Angeles, pays homage to these Seattle days.

The Washington Social Club was another venue where beloved blues acts such as Muddy Waters and B.B.King would play, drawing in Blues lovers from all over the city and beyond. That said even these types of acts tended to draw in a more mature crowd, certainly not many teenagers would engage in these live performances, even if they were popular on record players at the time. The demographic here was usually over 35 years of age. It was a musical legacy that was shaped by demographic changes that began in the early 1900s, these accelerated during the second world war when tens of thousands of African Americans migrated to the city, drawn by the prospect of jobs and greater opportunities. Within this migration to the Seattle area a rich musical heritage was founded, they brought with them jazz, blues, and jobbing musicians; this created many other styles of music that had originally developed in black communities in the South and Midwest.

The Jazz and Blues scene gave way to a sort of legal underground extortion, a culture of corruption and shadiness associated within such areas. Nightclub owners regularly paid off police and politicians in exchange to allow for a semi-official tolerance of prostitution, illegal alcohol or gambling. It was a soft agreement following the enactment of prohibition in Washington State in 1916, but it persisted even after the law was repealed in 1933, largely because of the state's reluctance to legalise the sale of hard liquor by the drink. Public establishments were not permitted to sell liquor in Seattle and Washington state until around 1949, and even then, they were subject to strict regulations. Politicians and police who willingly turned a blind eye to such practices would be well rewarded. The main area for most of this activity was the aforementioned Jackson Street, this came to be known as the Jackson Street Scene.

Although there were numerous illegal activities knocking around the various nightclubs situated throughout the city, gradually the action became concentrated along this one street. During its heyday, from 1937 to 1951, Jackson Street alone boasted a mouthwatering 34 nightclubs. These were places, one former patron recalled, where people "*did everything but go home*". This autonomous, self-sufficient atmosphere extended through to the music. These were talented musicians, a mix of locals and members of visiting bands that were passing through. They were fronted by the big names of the time, the likes of Lionel Hampton, Duke Ellington, Count Basie and others. They played for short periods, they came and went, learning from and teaching each other in jam sessions, that often lasted all night.

Segregation was still the norm during this time, especially within the music scene. For black musicians, the Jackson Street clubs were not only a proving ground for their various talents but also a major source of employment, in many cases it could be the only source of income available. Up until the 1950s, the music industry in Seattle was still formally segregated. White musicians, represented by Local 76, played for white audiences in uptown theatres, nightclubs, and ballrooms. Black musicians, represented by 'Negro' Local 493, found work primarily in small nightclubs and dancehalls in racially mixed neighbourhoods. The wages were lower on Jackson Street but, ironically, the tips were better.

Jimmy was absorbing the music wherever he could find it at this time, he immersed himself fully within it. Radio, records and anywhere he could listen for free. He would even pay a visit to the porch of old blues men who would just sit and strum for hours on end. Music was all consuming for Jimmy, whether it was in the bars, clubs, radio or elsewhere.

If 'The Jackson Street Scene' was notorious for the underground musical aspect of Seattle at this time, there was also a 'so-called' respectable selection of venues that were becoming available. These began to open towards the end of World War II, in response to population growth in the Central Area. Among these was the East Madison branch of the Young Men's Christian Association, established in 1936 in a small frame building at 23rd and E Olive (although not funded by the YMCA until 1942, when it became, in effect, a black servicemen's club). The Savoy Ballroom, later renamed Birdland in honour of legendary saxophonist Charlie "Bird" Parker, opened at 21st and E Madison Street in 1941. It was followed in 1944 by the Washington Social and Educational Club at 23rd and E Madison. These establishments provided alternatives to the 'joints' on Jackson Street. They also tended to draw wider audiences, a benefit of being located on the border between the predominantly white Madison Valley and the primarily black Central Area, as a result they became more integrated for this reason.

Al was now fully aware of his son's talent; they would jam together and occasionally swap instruments, but it was soon clear that Jimmy was a far better guitar player than a saxophonist. The guitar was becoming an extension of him, he lived it, breathed it, it was becoming an integral element of his personality, his soul. With the guitar he gained confidence, it took away the insecurities and rejections that had manifested during childhood. It gave him a purpose as well as self-esteem. It started to fully define who he was. Up until now, Jimmy had only played alone, or loosely jammed with his father, however he was now starting to tour the various clubs dotted around the city, consuming and absorbing anything he could. Jimmy mainly stuck to the black clubs that were situated in the Central district, Union Street, Madison Street and of course Jackson Street. One venue to note here is Spanish Castle which was further out of town on highway 99 not far from the airport, this was traditionally a big band jazz venue but would be forever associated with Jimmy from his second album, Axis: Bold as Love in 'Spanish Castle Magic'.

During the school holidays in the summer of 1959, Jimmy's circle of friends was becoming more musically minded. He gravitated towards those that could play. During this summer he was jamming with his friend James Thomas and his nephew, they soon discovered they weren't the only kids that were jamming though, they met Webb Loften and Walter Harris, who both played saxophone and Ulysses Heath Jr, who played guitar. Webb and Walter invited another friend to join them, James Woodberry who sang and played piano. The boys formed a friendship through music during this summer and started to play together in James's house situated on 21st Avenue. They searched for a drummer and soon found one, Lester Exkano. With this in place they decided it was time to officially form a band, it would be Jimmy's first exposure to a group scenario. The name was already in place, chosen before Jimmy and his friends joined, they were 'The Rocking Kings'. Predictably, Al wasn't keen on his son neglecting his schoolwork to form a band, he did, however, visit a full rehearsal and soon realised that maybe this was the way forward, Jimmy had found his vocation.

The Rocking Kings rehearsed and played continuously, James Thomas arranged their first couple of gigs, the first was at 21st Avenue followed by a dance which was situated at the nearby Polish Hall on 18th Street. Both these gigs were successful and the band started to get further bookings. While playing with the Rocking Kings, Jimmy continued with visits to the Central District, studying the various players and musicians that had already honed their craft over many years. Watching how they interacted with the audience, how they showboated and the way they would solo. He was particularly fascinated with the way they got the audience up on their feet, how they got them screaming at certain intervals and how they could whip them up to into a frenzy when they wanted too. He loved the horn sections and in particular the saxophonists, these were the guys that could showboat the most, while horn sections cut through the sound.

One thing the daily practice with The Rocking Kings brought Jimmy, was access to an amplifier, something he hadn't had to date. This allowed him to experiment more, to trade with different sounds, phrases and rhythms previously limited acoustically. Jimmy was now fast becoming a brilliant guitar player, a complete natural, a unique talent. He simply could not stop playing, even when he wasn't jamming on his own, or in a band he would be happy to show others how to play, to try and teach what he had learned himself.

Benorce Blackmon was a friend of Jimmy's brother Leon and recalled meeting Jimmy when he was trying to learn guitar. *"When I started to really play guitar, Leon used to tell me all the time 'My brother can beat you at playing'.... I remember seeing Jimmy around, but I didn't know who he was.... he was on his bicycle with all these fox tails and all the flashes and mirrors on it.... when I met him, he was dressed in black .... he was a funny cat.... Back in the those days he was always standoffish, you know, you could never get too close to him....I'm sitting on my mother's front porch and I said 'Hey man, show me that', and he'd just start to show me things...and I found out who he was and he was really nice, always showing you stuff... he was always showing everybody his stuff. Jimmy was always playing... my mother used to drive me away from the porch some time 'cos he would just pop up and come to play.... He'd just be standing on the porch wanting to play".*

From 1959 through to 1960, Jimmy continued playing local dance halls and events. The Rocking Kings even entered some competitions, notably coming second in the All-State Band of the Year Contest. From this came a residency for teenage dance nights located at Birdland three nights a week on Wednesdays, Thursdays and Sundays. Despite the residency, Jimmy wasn't satisfied with the band he was in; he would play with any band that needed a player and would regularly patrol the venues looking for another band to play with. There was a minor setback during this period when Jimmy's Supro Ozark guitar was stolen. He had left it backstage one night, and when he rushed back it was gone. For weeks, Jimmy was devastated, for him it was like losing an arm, a part of his identity, and as a result his father bought him his second electric guitar. Initially, Al flatly refused to buy another guitar, no doubt to teach his son a lesson for leaving his previous overnight, but seeing how depressed Jimmy had become, a friend took pity on him and took him to a local music store and bought him a new one. His father, being the proud man he was, was upset with the intervention and made Jimmy take it back. He then bought one for himself, this time a white Silvertone Danelectro; Jimmy painted it red. A very famous photo of the young James Hendrix was taken with this guitar on Yesler Street, Seattle, WA., circa August 1960, one of the earliest with the instrument.

It was while playing with the Rocking Kings that Jimmy Hendrix started to realise his true potential. He was finding night after night that he was able to make the guitar do things that simply no one else could do. His guitar playing was different, and it sounded different, and this wasn't just with his obvious talent for creating sounds from the guitar, but it also lay in the *way* he played it, which was utterly unique and not seen before. The sounds he was able to create were aided by the fact that he was left-handed: but because he couldn't afford to buy a left-handed guitar, and his father never sought one for him, he made use of second-hand standard right-handed guitars which he adapted. He made them work for him by swapping the position of the strings, but interestingly, and contrastively, he didn't swap the position of coils or pick-ups. This meant that the part of the coil designed to pick up the notes from the wider strings was now amplifying the vibrations from the thinner strings, and the thinner strings were amplifying the thicker ones. The result gave Hendrix a unique sound, which gave bright high notes mixed with delicate and softer low ones. It gave him a signature sound, in addition to his incredible talent. It also looked different, and he was starting to play with more flair and confidence. He was starting to be able to create any sound he wanted, and all in a completely new and 'never seen before' way.

This unique talent that was now emerging and playing alongside various downtown bands was not without its issues. The bands Jimmy was playing with had a certain standard way that guitarists should behave, to conform and integrate without too much fuss. This was simply too basic for Jimmy to cope with, the same routines, the same dance moves, he could do it in his sleep. Despite his obvious talent he was never egotistical or self-applauding, but this didn't stop bands and fellow musicians becoming annoyed with the way Jimmy would behave, particularly in the way he would branch out and solo, the attention therefore from the audience transferring over to him as an individual, as opposed to the band as a complete unit. Leon noticed this transition; he would often watch as Jimmy rehearsed with a new band: *"The bands were really starting to get on Jimmy's nerves, because he was getting freaky, he'd tie feathers to his guitar and the others would object, but everyone knew he was the best. People started to come down to see what was going on, sometimes Jimmy would be given a half bar lead solo and Jimmy would just take off. He would later apologise, 'Sorry I just had to do that'"*.

In 1960 James 'Tomcat' Thomas managed the Rocking Kings, despite the backlash towards Jimmy it was James who encouraged Jimmy to continue to be himself, to express his talent. The way Jimmy was playing was a direct influence from the records he was listening to, he was progressing into long solos founded at its core in blues. Later in 1967 he was interviewed and asked about his influences in his younger days, if he felt any heritage from the old bluesmen? *"No, cause, I can't even sing! When I first started playing guitar was way up in the Northwest, in Seattle, Washington. They don't have too many of the real blues singers up there. When I really learned to play was down South. Then I went into the Army for about nine months, but I found a way to get out of that. When I came out, I went down South and all the cats down there were playing blues, and this is when I really began to get interested in the scene".*

The first time Jimmy really got to extend his playing capabilities fully was at an event with The Rocking Kings, playing in front of their biggest crowd to date. It was an outdoor picnic event in front of over 2000 people. Here, Jimmy played behind his head, between his legs and performed other outlandish forms of showmanship for the first time. It went down brilliantly with the large crowd, many mesmerised by his skills and antics. This kind of showmanship was often criticised, especially when Jimmy first broke through to the many mixed-race crowds. Within the black club scene, where Jimmy first played, an element of showmanship was always required, the audience expected to be entertained. It wasn't showing off for showing offs sake, it was part of the performance. Jimmy was taking it to a new level, taking it out of the clubs and eventually into places that had not seen this kind of performance before, especially for a guitar player.

Eventually the Rocking Kings disbanded, they performed infrequently with gigs few and far between, the bands transportation a VW bus, which was borrowed, also decided it had had enough, this cut any tours and gigs further afield, and the band dismantled. It left just James Thomas, Webb Loften on Sax, the drummer Lester, and Jimmy. Undeterred, the band added a couple of replacements, Robert Green on bass and James Thomas's nephew Perry on piano. They were renamed Thomas and the Tomcats, and started where they left off playing gigs anywhere they could in Seattle and round Washington State.

It's an important pause at this point to remember that Jimmy Hendrix was still at school. He enrolled at Garfield High School situated at the time on 23rd Avenue, his main focus was again, art, which was by far his best subject. It was clear though, despite his artistic talents at school, that music, and the guitar in particular, was his main and only real focus. It didn't take much therefore, for Jimmy to have a change of heart after initially enrolling. At the end of October 1960, without taking any exams, Jimmy quit school. The reason officially for this was written as *'Work Referral Age'*, Jimmy claimed later though that he was kicked out for having a relationship with a white girl and holding her hand continuously in class. With Jimmy now not being at school he needed to find a job, the gigs he was getting were at best pocket money, nothing he was earning could be sustained as a regular salary. Al recalls this time, *"This was before the civil rights thing, and it was hard for Blacks to get jobs"*.

As far as drink and drugs were concerned Jimmy had to this point largely avoided any contact. Other members of bands Jimmy played with inevitably stayed behind after gigs to dabble in wine or other drinks, but Jimmy preferred to practice, to prepare for the next set, or the next gig across town. He didn't smoke either and was rarely interested in anything outside of performance or practice. The only real distraction he had was girls, who he had a keen interest in. They were of course the usual troublemakers around the various communities in Seattle at this point, Jimmy avoided them and for the most part stayed out of trouble. No doubt a reflection of his Fathers strict upbringing.

There were a couple of high-profile gangs in Seattle at this time, known as the Counts and the Cobras, but they respected Jimmy, he was low key in his personality and apart from his clothes, which were seen as a bit over the top, he wasn't bothered by them. He was noticed but left alone, he was an outsider, a bit of a non-conformist. Ultimately, he was kind of respected due to his talent. Things started to change somewhat though, when he eventually started to get into trouble.

Various misdemeanors eventually started to get Jimmy noticed, and for the wrong reasons. To this point he had only got into a few street fights, he was prepared to stick up for himself, but he was never going to be out in front, never a leader for any kind of unrest, never the instigator. He had admitted stealing, but these were petty items, bits of clothing etc. Nothing of major value and certainly nothing that was planned, anything he had stolen to date was small opportunist takings. Deep down, Jimmy wanted to get away from Seattle, it was a place that he had grown up in without knowing any kind of real joy. He had a tough childhood; he had been passed around and had experienced loss at an early age that affected him deeply. Music was his escape; he was always destined to branch out further afield to fulfil his ambitions. It wouldn't be music though that would give Jimmy his first big break to get away from the shackles of his home city.

During his troubled childhood Jimmy had stayed with many different relatives and families, some familiar, some not. He had been forced to move around from place to place, home to home, room to room. With Jimmy now forming friendships through music, he was fully aware of other places he could potentially travel to; the musical hubs of Jazz, Blues and Rock and Roll. He started to dream of getting away permanently and on his own terms, living life on the road with his guitar, to the places he had heard so much about, Florida, New Orleans, London or California. Although it was his home, Seattle was a place that at some point he knew he needed to escape from, he was searching for freedom, just somewhere to find himself, somewhere to escape to, but on his own terms.

He could not have anticipated, however, that his next location would present itself so quickly, and one that was absolutely not on his own terms. Additionally, Jimmy would not be pursuing a career as a musician; here he had no choice. Jimmy's next residence would be at Fort Ord in California, where he would join the 101st Airborne Division.

Chapter 4

Chitlin Blues

"Those times I burned my guitar it was like a sacrifice. We all burn things we love. I love my guitar"

Police records show that Jimmy was arrested for stealing a car, or *'Taking a Motor Vehicle without Permission'* on 2 May 1961. In the months prior to his arrest, he had become involved in petty crime which wasn't unsurprising given his dysfunctional background. He was mainly involved in small misdemeanors such as joyriding, he was also expelled from school. Three days after the first arrest for stealing a car, he was caught again riding inside another stolen vehicle. He claimed however that he did not know it was stolen and just got in for the ride. Either way, he spent time locked up at a youth center called Rainer Vista 4-H and subsequently presented to the Court.

Although Jimmy was looking for work before his arrest, there wasn't a great deal available to him, he was however considering joining the army as one of his options. His public defender at the time informed the prosecuting judge of this, it meant that he had a reprieve of sorts, and by volunteering to join the army, rather than being posted, meant he could choose where he went. He was given a simple choice by the authorities: serve in the army or go to jail. Jimmy had no choice, he joined the army and enlisted on May 31st, 1961; it also meant he had a way to branch out further than Seattle, even if it wasn't with his guitar. Given the circumstances, enlisting in the army at this time was a comparatively better decision than it had been for individuals of Jimmy's age who enlisted in earlier or later years.

Previously the Korean war had been fought between South Korea and North Korea, it began in 1950 and ended through armistice in 1953. It was a Japanese colony until the end of World War II and then divided between the Soviet Union and the United States. The United States entered the war led by President Harry S. Truman, and ended the war led by Dwight D. Eisenhower, who took over from Truman in January 1953. A few years later began the start of the Vietnam conflict, which was by all accounts a by proxy war between the USA and the then Soviet Union which began around 1955, with the United States involvement peaking around 1969.

Any young men therefore from the United States that were drafted would have been eligible to enter these two conflicts at the time. Fortunately for Jimmy he had started his basic training on May 31st, 1961, it was after the Korean War, but before Vietnam, therefore between the two conflicts.

Although Jimmy described himself as a patriot, he found the basic training tiresome and was constantly writing back to his relatives, in particular his father, asking for cash. Iconic photos exist of Jimmy dressed in his army clothes during this period, a stark contrast to the later Woodstock 'Star Spangled Banner' performance, often seen as anti-establishment. With his guitar in hand, he created a new visual and phonic accompaniment to the young men enlisted in war at the time, incorporating the guitar screeching sounds of dropping bombs, that would become legendary in the years ahead. A sonic distinction to the basic training he was now commencing.

It was in June 1961 that Jimmy located to Fort Ord in California. He was later transferred to Fort Campbell in Kentucky to begin training with the 101st Airborne division, a light infantry division of the United States Army, specialising in air assault operations. Despite his longing to escape Seattle, Jimmy was homesick and struggled being away. He wrote several letters at the time to his father, always signing them *'Love always your son, James'*. He would then draw a guitar under the signature.

The main issue Jimmy had was that the basic training was full-on physical training and little else. Jimmy did however feel the first real rush of a parachute jump; he spoke later in an interview for The New Musical Express on this first experience.

"The first jump was really outta sight- like you're in the plane and some cat had never been up in a plane before, some people were throwin' up. You had a big bucket, a big garbage can sitting in the middle. It was great. At the beginning the plane is going rrrrrrrrr- this 'roarin' and shakin'-you can see the rivets just jumping around. Talk about 'What am I doing here'. In a split second a thought through me like 'You must be crazy'. And it's almost like a blank, and like cryin' and laughin', in fact the sergeant said 'Who's this joker?' But all the time you're thinking, 'What am I doing here?' By that time, you're just there at the door and there's this rush and you're out like that and just-ooooh. It's the most alone feeling in the world and every time you jump, you're scared that this time it won't open. Then you feel that tug on your collar and there's that big beautiful white mushroom above you, and the airs going sssssshhhh past your ears. That's when you begin talking to yourself again. This jumping business is the most thrilling I ever did before, it's just as much fun as it looks, if you keep your eyes open."

Despite the thrill of the parachute jumps, Jimmy was yearning to have his guitar. On 17th January 1962 he wrote another letter to Al, this time pleading for him to send him his guitar. He ended the letter with a simple, *'I really need it now'*.

On receiving the letter, Jimmy's father obliged. Shortly after, a package arrived at camp, inside it was Jimmy's electric Danelectro guitar. He was so pleased he took it to bed with him, and slept with it every night. This practice, although a blues tradition, actually got Jimmy noticed for the wrong reasons, he was singled out by his Army colleagues and beaten for it. They even went so far as to take it, and hide it for days, humiliating Jimmy for having it, and making him 'beg' to have it back.

Despite the bullying for being slighlty different to the standard Army recruit, it wasnt long before Jimmy started to get noticed for the right reasons, that being, his god given talent. Inspired by his new surroundings, Jimmy began experimenting with innovative sounds. He created these through the guitar, emulating the *whoosh* and *Swoosh* sounds he previously described from parachute jumps, as well as sounds of planes, engines roaring, and the accompanying vibrations and shudders. He was able to project this through the guitar in a way that no one else could do. It was a world away from traditional playing, and a new skill that would obviously set him apart in the years ahead. He also discovered around this time that he wasn't the only musician on camp, when Jimmy met Private Billy Cox.

The story goes that Billy was running for cover with a group of other service personnel when he stopped outside service club number one to shelter. Inside there was a practice room, and Billy heard what he later described as a cross between 'Beethoven and John Lee Hooker'. He went in and watched Jimmy, who failed to notice Billy as he was playing. Billy said that he could see instantly that Jimmy was *'coming from a creative musical space'*. Jimmy looked up and Billy introduced himself. They talked, and Billy explained he could play bass, as well as upright bass, and that he had played in bands similar to Jimmy's back home, which for Billy was his home state of West Virgina. The pair became instant friends and naturally, it wasn't long before they decided to start their own group while on camp to entertain the troops. The duo expanded and brought in a drummer and a sax player, Gary Ferguson (drums) and Major Washington (sax), they managed to include some outside gigs, as well as the standard service clubs on site. This in turn took them to other camps that were based around North and South Carolina. They mainly performed in servicemen clubs on the base and at the Pink Poodle Club in Clarksville, TN.

With Jimmy back doing what he did best, it was inevitable that the army itself, and the routine that surrounded it, would soon lose its appeal. He began experiencing difficulties as he neglected his responsibilities in favour of playing his guitar. Consequently, as a form of discipline, the instrument he cherished was frequently taken from him. Nevertheless, he would go to great lengths to reclaim it. Whenever an opportunity arose to perform, Jimmy took it. He played at base clubs on weekends with other musicians in various informal groups. These groups were known by several names at the time, most notably the 'Casuals' or the 'King Kasuals'.

Despite not giving his all to the cause, Jimmy was promoted in January 1962 to Private First Class. He wrote proudly back to his father claiming, *'I made it, in eight months and eight days!'* Despite this, his ongoing obsession with his guitar began to infuriate his superiors, and they were at a loss with him, he seemed unable to concentrate and unable to conform to the standard regulations. He wrote back again to Al explaining how he had begun to feel resentment towards his superiors, and even his colleagues surrounding him. Jimmy was a free spirit, a free thinker, he summed up his feelings in one letter; *"Army people tell you what to do all the time, they tell you what you are interested in, and you don't have a choice. The Army is more for people who like to be told what to do"*. As a result, on July 2nd, 1962, James Hendrix left the army. The discharge report stated, *"He has no interest whatsoever in the Army ... It is my opinion that Private Hendrix will never come up to the standards required of a soldier. I feel that the military service will benefit if he is discharged as soon as possible"*.

There was also another note discovered regarding Jimmy's exclusion from service, it read that he was excluded because; *"While performing his duties, he is excessively thinking about his guitar"*. A perfect end to a military career. There were other reports on his discharge stating he was gay; however, it was a common practice at the time to give this as the reason for discharge from the army.

Once he left the army Jimmy relocated to Clarksville in Tennessee and settled into the local nightly music scene. He had previously agreed that he would wait here for Billy Cox to discharge, this was in September 1962. The pair eventually reunited and they began the pursuit of their ambitions, to tour together. They soon realised, however, that musically there wasn't the scene in town that they had hoped for. They decided to move on and made their way in a battered 1955 Plymouth to Indianapolis. To save money they slept in the car, but they soon discovered that Indianapolis was worse than Clarksville, so they headed back, determined to form a group together once again. On playing around Clarksville for a short period of time they managed to secure a run at 'Del Morrocco', at the time this was one of the best R&B clubs in Nashville.

Nashville was a fitting stop for Jimmy Hendrix, after escaping the trappings of his youth in Seattle, and then the authoritarian rules of the

Army. Nashville demonstrated a way forward, a future. Its history goes back as far as the 1870s with the Fisk Jubilee Singers, a vocal group that had emerged from Nashville's Fisk University composed entirely of freed black slaves, they had an operatic singing style popular at the time and would sing negro spirituals. They were wildly popular and not only toured the United States, but also Europe with their uniquely American sound. It signified freedom, emancipation, and paved the way for others to follow, an emerging musical legacy that also saw the growth of country.

At this time, around 1962, Nashville was still in a somewhat transition from a small country music scene to a larger hub that would be on a par with the already established musical centers of LA or New York. From 1958 to 1962, many international hits were recorded by country artists in Nashville, such as the Everly Brothers, Johnny Cash, and Patsy Cline. However, the market for pure country music was diminishing, with only about 80 radio stations playing it by 1961. The Country Music Association set criteria for country radio, leading producers to choose between country or pop records. Artists like Roger Miller and Glen Campbell managed to succeed in both markets, but Brenda Lee and Roy Orbison largely saw their pop hits ignored by country radio.

Jimmy and Billy arrived at 'Del Morrocco' in October 1962 and met the manager. He arranged for some accommodation for them both, but money was thin, and Jimmy spent many nights under the stars, naturally with his guitar next to him. The band was very fluid but initially consisted of James Marshall Hendrix, Billy Cox, Gary Ferguson (drums) and Major Washington (sax) with a later addition of singer Johnny Jones. Jimmy was notoriously lazy, however, the band had to frequently fetch him for rehearsals and gigs, and when he did perform if he saw a girl he liked, he would be off stage, asking others to fill in for him as he took her away to a side room or somewhere else nice and quiet. Apart from his guitar, the ladies were his only real distraction. Despite Jimmy's natural talent it's quite well known that at this time he was somewhat underrated as a guitarist, he wasn't playing on the main circuits so remained undiscovered. Others, therefore, were rated above Jimmy, notably Johnny Jones who was the lead guitarist with The Imperials. It wouldn't be long though before Jimmy would begin to earn a reputation of his own and outshine everyone.

Over the next few months Jimmy played in several venues around Nashville's Jefferson Street, where they were now located. Hendrix and Cox moved into an apartment above a beauty store, located on Jefferson Street itself. This was the traditional heart of the city's black community; it had a thriving music scene and was home to rhythm and blues music and many live venues, clubs and bars. He later claimed this was the place he really learned to play the guitar. To gain extra income, Jimmy and Billy would rent their services to other acts around the central hub of Nashville. The artists at the time were R&B singer Nappy Brown, Carla Thomas, known as The Queen of Memphis Soul, and electric Blues Keyboardist Ironing Board Sam. Jimmy also had a brief tour with Curtis Mayfield, although at the time Curtis didn't want any wild guitarists with him on stage. As a result, when Curtis came on stage, Jimmy had to exit. That said, Curtis was a good influence on Jimmy in these early days of his career. He was especially swayed with the melodic side of Curtis Mayfield, something Jimmy took onboard and was motivated by.

Although Nashville at this time was fast emerging as a musical hub, it wasn't a place for any kind of Blues. This was more akin with Memphis, and Jimmys natural tendency on guitar was leaning ever more in this direction. It's important to reflect on the area where Jimmy was playing at this time, today this area is unrecognisable from what it was back then, especially the area around Jefferson Street. It would be later in the 1960s, when the construction of Interstate 40 carved a destructive path through Jefferson Street, that the area changed completely, taking many of its best music rooms with it.

This was where Jimmy was set up, within the epicentre of black music, lively and bristling with bars and nightclubs - in fact there were around twenty in this one area alone, it was a real focal point for any R&B performers. *"You really had to play, cause those people were really hard to please."* Jimmy recalled in a 1967 interview with the Los Angeles Free Press. ...*"That's where I learned to play, really, in Nashville."*

In 1965, at 22 years old, Jimmy was captured for the first time playing guitar on video. He made his television debut backing up soul duo Buddy & Stacey on the show 'Night Train'. Produced at Nashville's WLAC-TV studios, Night Train predated 'Soul Train' by five years and was the first television programme to feature an all-black cast. On the footage, you can clearly identify a young Jimmy Hendrix looking freaky and sliding his hand over the front of his guitar's neck. This was one of the early issues bands and singers had with Jimmy, even as a standard back up guitarist, he stood out.

Despite the obvious country routes, the R&B scene became hugely significant and grew steadily throughout the 1960s. The list of stars here was significant, they included Etta James, who in 1963, played for over two nights at Nashville's New Era Club, here the singer recorded her live album 'Etta James Rocks the House'. Little Richard was at the outset of his career, the rock and roll pioneer would stay in Nashville for long, lucrative stretches, performing at the New Era Club and Club Revillot. *"I packed the house. You couldn't get in."* he told The Tennessean in 2009. In addition

Ray Charles would have his biggest crossover hit yet with 'What'd I Say' in 1959 with Charles and his band thrilling the crowd at *Maceo's*, on Jefferson Street. Aretha Franklin herself had successfully transitioned from gospel to secular music in 1960, Franklin's earliest years as an R&B singer included a four-night run at The New Era Club. Soul Singer Robert Knight recorded the pop hit 'Everlasting Love'. Another notable hit came from Nashville native Bobby Hebb who wrote and recorded the classic 'Sunny', which reached No. 2 on the pop chart in 1966. This led to him opening for the Beatles on their final tour. Nashville was becoming known as a musical hub in its own right during this period, transitioning from country to R&B, its reputation increased so much in fact, it started to now be known as Music City.

The Del Morocco itself, where Jimmy had his own residency with The King Kasuals, was located at 2417 Jefferson St. It was owned by Theodore 'Uncle Teddy' Acklen and was seen as an upmarket place that was also a dinner club venue, with a capacity of around two hundred. The King Kasuals were initially given a one-year residency here. Jimmy of course, had free reign to play with others if he wasn't playing with his own group. The band had a slightly evolved line up for the residency, which changed again frequently throughout the period. This line-up started as Jimmy on lead guitar, his good friend Billy Cox on bass guitar, Harry Batchelor on vocals, Alphonso 'Baby Boo' Young on guitar and Buford Majors, who played saxophone. The drummer remains largely unknown but on occasions it was Raymond Belt, who was also the club's MC. The King Kasuals would play the Del Morocco at weekends for their residency and spend the rest of the week touring the so called chitlin' circuit anywhere within a two-hour travel time from Nashville. These clubs were all affiliated with the *Theatre Owners' Booking Association,* which was the vaudeville circuit for African American performers in the 1920s; incidentally the theatres within the association had mostly white owners.

The chitlin circuit was a somewhat insulting name, especially for extremely talented musicians. Chitlins were pig intestines and were a mainstay in black communities' diets. It was the cheapest meat available at the time, hence why the name was often seen, understandably, as derogatory. The chitlin circuit successfully sustained black musicians and dancers during the era of racial segregation in the United States from the 1930s through to the 1960s. Crucially though, this circuit provided black artists with an ongoing income and a building fan base. America at the time, still did not embrace black performers on TV and radio, so this 'circuit' provided a live fan base for artists to perform, the likes of James Brown, Sam Cooke and Jacki Wilson being some of the key names at the time. It wasn't just male performers on the circuit. Many female dancers and high-profile singers toured frequently, including the aforementioned Etta James, standing as one of the most prominent black superstars who performed in Nashville's famed R&B clubs. These acts made the city a top destination in the 1940s, 50s, and 60s. This eventually brought about the birth of rock 'n' roll in the 1950s as well as the Civil Rights Movement, which rose into prominence. Things have changed since then, but the pioneering efforts of the chitlin' circuit's great performers and business people, who operated in a time when just being black was dangerous enough, would and should always be admired and respected.

To this point. Jimmy had been a stage performer, his wings had yet to fully open to the electric pioneer that he would become famous for, and of course this was restricted. He had had very little studio time, engineers found him too experimental. As a result, Jimmy had found it hard settling to be a backup musician, it was difficult for him making any extra money as a studio musician. He was also frustrated with the circuit he was in; the ever-revolving clubs were never going to be somewhere he could accept as an end goal. He was bigger than that, and he knew his talent was. It would only be a matter of time before Jimmy could finally get to a studio, and work with people who would embrace, not restrict, his genius. His overflowing pent-up creativity would soon be well and truly 'experienced'.

Chapter 5

Kiss the Sky

"I wish they'd had electric guitars in cotton fields back in the good old days. A whole lot of things would've been straightened out."

Around the end of 1963, Jimmy decided to take a break from his weekly residency and the ever-revolving circuit of black artists and made his way north, interestingly by-passing Seattle. He visited his grandmother in Vancouver. Naturally, it wasn't just family visits that occupied Jimmy's time, he again joined various bands for a short tour. He visited the many clubs around downtown Vancouver and the wider area, always keen to see what bands were playing. He visited one such club called 'Dantes Inferno' where a band were playing called 'The Vancouvers'. It was fronted by the club owners, Bobby Taylor and Tommy Chong, who were motown inspired musicians. Guitarist Tommy Chong would later find fame as the hippie duo Cheech and Chong. Around this period Jimmy also referred to himself as "Jimmy James" as an alternative stage name.

After staying with his grandmother in Vancouver, and playing for a little while with Dantes Inferno, Jimmy decided it was time to head back south to Nashville, reacquainting himself with the King Kasuals and playing with any group that would require his services. By now he had a good selection of friends in Nashville, and he was looking forward to heading back, meeting up again with his close friends Billy Cox and Larry Nashville who had a mutual interest in music. Jimmy also had lots of girls around, who would come and go, a pastime that Jimmy was always interested in, and very successful in.

It was here though, that artistically and musically Jimmy was starting to move away, to outgrow. Although he was in several bands, someone like Jimmy Hendrix was never going to be sidelined, never going to be content with the standard circuit of bands and bars. His ambition and creativity was too strong, it was becoming obvious to him that his path was different, and he was moving on quickly. Jimmy simply wasn't set up to be in a band, to be sidelined on stage out of sight on the left or to the right, settling for the odd minute of showmanship here and there. Increasingly, when he was given a solo, he would go on too long, extending out of context, playing as an individual and doing his own thing. It often looked like he was never going to stop.

The issue with Jimmy at this juncture was that he needed freedom in his playing, he was searching for it, night after night. To break out of the restriction that a song or melody had. He couldn't fit in the box. His playing was often described at this point, by those in the know, as 'disjointed' as he searched for a direction, for flexibility and unrestraint in his playing. His phrasing seemed somewhat disconnected in parts, he was seeking for a direction, his own bearing in what he was doing. He was often not even the lead guitarist of a band but would be regularly praised for his stage presence and skills, including the Chuck Berry 'duck walk', and the fact that he could play with his teeth and behind his head, skills he replicated previously from watching a local guitarist with The Sharps named Raleigh 'Butch' Snipes. Jimmy's position in the bands he was appearing with started to break down as he began to get carried away with his playing, frequently moving away in his own direction, using excessive amounts of feedback and going off on individual jams in the middle of songs. Despite this so-called disconnection, his onstage natural ability was increasing his reputation, for those on the circuit he was becoming talked about, an immense talent, his notoriety amongst these circles was fast growing.

It wasn't long after Jimmy was back in Nashville that he went on the road again, this time as George Odell's guitarist. "Gorgeous" George Odell, was searching for a new guitar player at the same time that Jimmy wanted out of his contract with the Club Del Morocco, searching onwards for a fresh start. If it was money that motivated Jimmy, however, this tour was going to be disappointing. George opened up to Jimmy and told him in confidence that although he wanted him on tour, he couldn't actually pay him, he simply didn't have the funds. Jimmy though, had become somewhat acclimatised for living a life on little to no means. He agreed to the arrangement, asking only to be fed and allotted the opportunity to play live.

Unfortunately, Jimmy would run into the same issue as he had many times before, that of restriction and being told what to do, as a result the tour was relatively short lived. Jimmy and the bands he was playing with were often given around twenty minutes or so as a set, meaning that he was forced to stay on track, to not solo too much and to maintain the discipline of what was expected at the time. It was incredibly frustrating for him. That said, he spent the next two years on the circuit, travelling around playing for various artists and groups. One of these tours, without pay of course, was helping George valet for Hank Ballard and the Midnighters. The main act on this tour was Little Richard, and one night after the main show there was an after show, an opportunity for Jimmy and others to let loose, without too much restriction. Jimmy sat in with 'The Upsetters' and was quickly noticed. The Upsetters assistant tour manager was Henry Nash, he recalled one night at a local nightclub in Greenville South Carilina, when Jimmy was on stage. '*He possessed what other guitarists didn't. He did what other musicians didn't, or couldn't, he had good ears."*

After travelling around with various bands and outfits, Jimmy had again gained a solid reputation that was growing within the circuit, someone to watch, a potential star in the making. He kept himself to himself, even on the boring bus trips between gigs, he rarely opened himself up, always remaining a little aloof, keeping himself away from the main crowd. While others were boozing, or smoking weed, Jimmy preferred to discuss music, to practice, remaining somewhat shy and private, always a little distant and not engaging in anything too deep with others. No one knew him too much. Before they could, he'd move on. These crucial tours gave Jimmy a valuable lesson in what audiences needed, the constant playing with different bands who had players with real genuine on the road experience. They all had played multiple live performances, and sometimes with decades of playing experience.

This was an interesting time, a somewhat transitional period in the life of Jimmy Hendrix. Despite his obvious talent, Jimmy was increasingly getting disheartened. From a musical perspective, he had little or no choice in what he was able to do, he was harbouring his dissatisfaction within these various 'musical restrictions'. That said, his grounding to this point had served him well. Clubs such as the residency at The Club Del Morocco had moulded Jimmy into a full-time musician but lacked the repetitive nature of life on the road. With these tours he was gaining the extra travelling aspects of gig life, as a jobbing musician moving from state to state. Previously, the aspects of the military had trained Jimmy for a life of preparedness and routine, but this was boring to Jimmy, conformist in attitude and left him uninspired and disconnected from his work. In a small club rocking out with an after show, where little or no one attended, Jimmy had the freedom to play as he pleased, when he pleased, and how he pleased. With the Midnighters and others for example he was told what to play, when to play it, and how to play. It was never going to last for someone with such incredible talent.

Jimmy returned to Nashville once more after again travelling around the US, to reconnect with his friends and to relax a little. One evening while Jimmy was playing with Memphis born guitarist Larry Lee, he met a promoter from New York, and the pair got chatting. Incredibly impressed with Jimmy, he offered to promote him in New York, convinced he could make Jimmy a star. Although the promotor said what a thousand promotors normally say in these situations, Jimmy was taken in. The fact here though is Jimmy took little persuading and agreed to go or at least give it a try. It was, after all, New York.

Jimmy was ambitious, on stage a larger-than-life character, and most of all he had no real responsibilities. In essence he was a free spirit. Larry recalled this moment when Jimmy decided to head to New York; *"He was kind of in a rut, he wasn't going nowhere. He had big dreams, he always had big dreams...and he always said he was gonna be famous and have a thousand guitars laying around in the house, and he always said he had some songs, but he never brought them up... he said... 'I got these songs man', but nobody would be paying attention. It was cold... he didn't have a coat, so I told him to take one of mine".*

The promotors' promise to make Jimmy a star was slightly ambitious. Jimmy, with his borrowed coat arrived in Harlem, and the plan led to nothing. Not dissimilar to his father when he arrived in Seattle looking for work, Jimmy in New York, was starting over. In January 1964 Jimmy Hendrix moved into the Hotel Theresa located at 2082-96 Adam Clayton Powell Jr. Boulevard.

Occupying a large part of northern Manhattan. Harlem as a neighbourhood has no real fixed boundaries; but in general, it lies between 155th Street on the north, the East and Harlem rivers on the east, 96th Street, 110th Street and Cathedral Parkway on the south, and Amsterdam Avenue on the west. Harlem had a rich heritage, especially amongst the black communities, as it does to this day, which is one of the reasons why the boundary is fluid it; over the years it had expanded in all directions. Black communities continued to pour into Harlem from points in lower Manhattan, the American south and as far wide as the Caribbean. With the onset of the First World War in 1915, many foreign immigrants set sail for their homelands, leaving employment opportunities available in the war industries in the north. Black populations migrated in record numbers from the south to northern cities in search of opportunities and increased wages. This gave areas such as Harlem a unique outlook, one that although segregated, was in a way full of opportunity. It was during the 1920s, that Harlem flourished with cultural and artistic expression. This period was christened the 'Harlem Renaissance'. It was popularised by figures such as Langston Hughes, Aaron Douglas, Alain Locke and others who felt that they would use their artistic creativity to show America and the world that people of colour are intellectual, artistic and humane, and should be treated as such. Ridiculously obvious to claim now, but part of a consistent undercurrent of affirmations having to be declared at the time, igniting the various civil rights movements that were to come.

The Great Depression of 1929 rocked the whole of the USA, naturally this weighed heaviest on the poorest of society, as these things usually do, as a result it devastated black communities such as Harlem. An increase in rents followed, coupled with high unemployment and racist practices, this culminated in the Harlem riots in 1935 and 1943. The Second World War offered people of colour few opportunities for advancement, leading to them becoming mobilised against the war industry, demanding fair practices. Militant activities during the 1940s set the stage for the 1960s. Harlem was both stage and player during the turbulent period of the Civil Rights Movement. Religious and political leaders articulated the sentiments of the masses from street corners and pulpits throughout the community. It was a hot bed of activity as civil unrest and a refusal to comply with the ongoing laws grew, these were seen as oppressing the black communities.

When Jimmy arrived during the start of 1964, figures like Malcolm X, Adam Clayton Powell Jr., Queen Mother Moore and Preston Wilcox used Harlem as a launch pad for political, social, and economic empowerment activities. These social problems caused a decrease in Harlem's population during the late 1960s going into the 1970s, leaving behind in its wake a high concentration of underprivileged residents and a fast-decaying housing stock.

It wasn't long before Jimmy met a stylish and streetwise woman named Lithofayne Pridgon, she would be better known as Faye. She had settled her way successfully around the music scene and was involved with many of the movers and shakers in Harlem; she was a lover of the nightlife; and was known to have a somewhat soft spot for musicians. For Jimmy, she became a muse, and a confidant. She was a free spirit through the 1950s and '60s music scene, intersecting again and again with the careers of Sam Cooke, James Brown, Jackie Wilson, Etta James and - of course -Jimmy Hendrix, whom she first connected with when the soon-to-be-insanely-famous guitarist, was rising in his own right. For Faye, Jimmy was exactly her kind of guy.

Another infamous rumour, and one she herself has repeated, was that her initial meeting with Jimmy Hendrix was actually at a 1962 orgy held in the Harlem apartment of her friend and patron "Fat Jack" Taylor, a local drug kingpin, restaurateur and aspiring music mogul. Her attraction to Jimmy, a then 19-year-old budding musician two years her junior and newly discharged from military service, was immediate. "He was skinny, he was raw-boned, he was my type." she said.

The areas around Harlem were significant to the backbone and culture of the black community in New York. Something Jimmy was not a stranger to. On his arrival in the city, he was heading into a magical time in music, coupled with an underground culture that would soon erupt into the mainstream. Various pockets were coming to life within New York, and one that was more evident than most was in the Manhattan bohemian enclave of Greenwich Village. It was already known as the nexus of a folk music revival that was yielding not only stars, but soon-to-be legends like Bob Dylan, Peter, Paul & Mary and Simon & Garfunkel.

Many believe that Jimmy became the legendry groundbreaking artist we now know today after he landed in England a year or so later. It was true that as far as the mainstream goes this was correct, the culture and bands in London at that time were honed perfectly for Jimmy to break through with and essentially rise above. It is also true though, that during his soon to be brief but critical time in Greenwich Village, and other areas of New York, was where he evolved, propelling into the artist and personality that would become a musical and cultural icon in the years ahead.

While absorbing himself into New York life, Faye had already introduced Jimmy to many musicians around the various clubs in the city's key areas. Jimmy had tried hard to find his feet, but getting on stage regularly was difficult. He was constantly knocked back in these early weeks in New York. On many occasions he walked off stage, disheartened with his treatment. It would take a while for him to eventually get settled in the twisty back streets of New York night life. But it was coming, someone like Jimmy Hendrix was never going to be in the sidelines for too long. His time was coming.

To this point one aspect of a musical performance had not presented itself to Jimmy. That of being in an actual recording studio. Despite his past touring and incredible skills, Jimmy had not yet had the opportunity to enter a studio or been invited to record in any way. In December 1963, at 21 years of age, this would change: It would be a recording that, in the history of recorded sound, would be significant. These short sessions would become the first ever studio recordings featuring Jimi Hendrix

Chapter 6

A Train A' Comin

"Are you experienced? Have you ever been experienced?"

In New York, Jimmy set his sights on getting a gig with Sam Cooke, with an aim to work with him and to be his sideman. Faye was a former lover of Cooke and arranged for the two to meet. At this point in time Jimmy and Faye were often described as inseparable. Not only did she provide Jimmy with a place to sleep, but she also gave him that key element of entrée into the Harlem and wider music scene.

Even though Jimmy was still shy and retiring, which sometimes came as a barrier when trying to meet new people, he was equally ambitious and driven when it came to any opportunity that would allow him to perform and play. Faye helped him bridge this awkwardness, especially when meeting new people. He considered on many occasions, that himself and Faye were a normal couple, faithful to each and rarely apart, and Jimmy loved her dearly. Although 'Foxy Lady' would always be attributed to Faye, Jimmy's perception that she was a regular girlfriend, was somewhat masked by her networking. She was certainly not the type to be settling down, and refused to give up her other relationships, preferring to move around within the various musical circles. This made Jimmy extremely jealous on many occasions, but he reluctantly had learned to accept the fact that his Foxy Lady would never be exclusively his. Although this was painful for Jimmy to accept, it did have its plus side. The fact that she had so many connections, acquired through various scenarios; a full ongoing roster of associates and acquaintances within the area's music scene: she was extremely well connected, including of course to Sam Cooke. Because of these connections she was able to introduce Jimmy to many opportunities within the circuit, and one of these was with Cooke himself.

Towards the end of 1963, Jimmy stopped over in Philadelphia and was hired to record some sessions with Saxophonist Lonnie Younglood. Obviously, Lonnie could not have known at the time the significance of these sessions, or the magnitude of the future legend that was hired to simply back him up while he was recording. These sessions and recordings were later hashed together and released in various forms on illicit compilation albums. One such album was released in 1986 as 'Jimi Hendrix and Lonnie Youngblood -Two Great Experiences -Together'. Later in 1986, after a court case in New York, it was deemed that some of the recordings had been faked, not featuring Jimmy at all. The full track listing on the album was listed as:

Jimi Hendrix And Lonnie Youngblood – Two Great Experiences – Together

- Wipe The Sweat (Vocal)
- Sweat Segway II
- Sweat Segway III
- Two In One Goes
- Goodbye (Bessie Mae)
- All I Want
- Under The Table
- Table II
- Table III
- Psycho

Lonnie Youngblood recalls; *"These companies started to put the shit out and didn't even put my name on it. They would say it was Jimi Hendrix singing, without my name on it - so many lies, man. The stuff that came out on that album called Two Great Experiences Together! - what happened with that, one company took that and tried to doctor it up to make it have more Hendrix activity. See Hendrix is more or less just backing me up. The companies wanted to say they had a little more activity by Hendrix, so they found some Hendrix wannabees and they put them on the tracks. And what they really did was they messed the tracks up with the overdubs."* Hidden amongst this spurious release, however, were some genuine recordings featuring Jimmy. As a result, the tracks *'Under the Table'* and *'Wipe the Sweat'* became attributed to his earliest genuine recorded songs. Jimmy's guitar playing on the sessions is incredible, for someone of such a young age. His influences of B.B.King and Robert Johnson are evident. Jimmy sounded like an old master, his phrasing and subtlety were sublime, it's hard to imagine this was a young man encountering his first ever recording experience.

Faye eventually got Jimmy to meet Sam Cooke backstage one night at The Apollo in Harlem. The venue was significant for any notable acts during this period. It opened in 1914 and was infamous for its amateur night contests, something Jimmy was interested in attending. If you won one of these it was a great piece of kudos for any budding artist. The theatre itself served as key player in the development and emergence of jazz, swing, bebop, R&B, gospel, blues, and soul - all quintessentially American music genres.

Countless key acts had emerged over the years while playing there, ranging from Ella Fitzgerald, Sarah Vaughan, Billie Holiday, Sammy Davis Jr., James Brown, Gladys Knight and even more modern acts like Luther Vandross, D'Angelo and Lauryn Hill to name just a few. It was designed by George Keister and first owned by Sidney Cohen. Later in 1914, Benjamin Hurtig and Harry Seamon obtained a thirty-year lease on the newly constructed theatre, calling it Hurtig and Seamon's New Burlesque Theater. Like many American theatres during this time, African Americans were not allowed to attend as patrons or even allowed to perform. In 1933, Fiorello La Guardia, who would later become New York City's Mayor, began a campaign against burlesque, and Hurtig & Seamon's was one of many theatres that would be forced to eventually close down. Sidney Cohen reopened the building as the 125th Street Apollo Theatre in 1934 with his partner, Morris Sussman, serving as manager. Cohen and Sussman then changed the format of the shows, moving away from burlesque to include more variety and music. They redirected their marketing attention to the growing African American community in Harlem. Later, in 1935 Frank Schiffman and Leo Brecher took over The Apollo, from here the Schiffman and Brecher families would operate the theatre right up until the late 1970s.

The amateur nights had attracted huge attention around The Apollo and the wider community, giving acts an opportunity to show their stuff. It was in essence, a talent contest. The audience, however, had the last say, often if an act was dying, they would hurl obscenities from the crowd, get booed off stage or in many cases have objects thrown at them until they quit. It was a regular occurrence and not one for the faint hearted. The amateur night sat at 11pm every Wednesday evening, they were so popular that there was over a three-month waiting period at this time, however Jimmy got in immediately, thanks to Faye's connections at the theatre. Jimmy sat off stage and waited nervously for his cue to enter the stage in front of the audience, an audience ready as ever to get rid of any act not cutting the mustard.

Jimmy walked nervously on stage when it was his turn to play, he performed his full set and returned unscathed. At the end of the night, it was customary for all acts to be brought back on stage to announce the winner, this was usually settled by the length of the applause, and the noise given for each act. It was Jimmy's night, he won, and more importantly, got the prize, a handsome $25.00. Jimmy wasn't the only winner of Amateur night at The Apollo that would go onto to achieve notoriety. Other past winners included Gladys Night, Sarah Vaughn and James Brown.

Jimmy settled into the Harlem music scene and played with various bands. Despite his illustrious win on amateur night it didn't give him the bank of work he had hoped for. He was back again working for other bands, he even played alongside the local house band dutifully performing without any fuss or conviction, despite gaining a further reputation for his skills. These credentials, alongside Jimmy's thriving notoriety soon caught the attention of Tony Rice, an associate and friend connected to The Isley Brothers. This led to an audition and an opportunity to become the guitarist with their back-up band, known as the I.B. Specials. Jimmy saw it as a great opportunity, and a move forward.

The Isley brothers began performing gospel music with their Mother in and around their native Cincinnati. Later Kelly, Rudolph, and Ronald Isley gained pop recognition in 1959 when they wrote and released their song 'Shout', the track also became a hit for Lulu in the UK In 1964. They also had huge success in 1962 with a version of the Top Notes' 'Twist and Shout' which remained on Billboard's pop chart for 11 weeks, the song was covered again in 1964 by The Beatles and featured on their album 'Please Please Me'. It has gone on to be covered many more times through the decades. The brothers were on the lookout for a new guitarist, they had to this point moved around many different labels frequently and were ever evolving. They started with RCA in 1959 before moving to Atlantic in 1960 and then Wand in 1962. United Artists followed before they signed with Teaneck. They then formed their own T-Neck label with the distribution through Atlantic. An exhausting amount of record labels in a few short years. Tony told them that Jimmy was the best guitarist he had ever seen. On hearing this, the brothers were skeptical. Tony had also told the brothers he thought Jimmy was about fifteen years old, Ronnie Isley reportedly listed his top guitarists of the day, notably Curtis Mayfield and Bobby Womack, Tony insisted Jimmy was better than all of them. Intrigued by the bold claim Ronnie decided to go and see Jimmy for himself.

Jimmy wasn't playing with anyone at this time, he was banned from playing with the house band due to his habit of excessive solos and distortion that he was inclined to improvise with. Another issue was that Jimmy rarely had a full set of strings, and when he did break one, which was frequent, he didn't have the cash to replace it. On meeting Jimmy, The Isley Brothers leant him some spare strings, and Jimmy started to tune his guitar up. They watched in amazement as Jimmy blasted through what he considered to be a tune up. He was hired there and then.

The next day, Jimmy was invited to a rehearsal at Sally Isley's house in Englewood. When he said he had no way of getting there, and also nowhere to stay, Kelly arranged for him to live in his mother's back room.

"*He was quiet.*" Ernie Isley says of Jimmy. "*He minded his own business. He just practiced that guitar all the time. I really didn't understand that because he was already so good. It was like his guitar didn't have any wrong notes on it. He'd be rehearsing a lot of things in the house without an amp. We'd see him going behind his back or through his legs or playing guitar while drinking a glass of orange juice at the same time.*"

Mrs Isley was very fond of Jimmy, so much so that the brothers and other band members became quite envious of the attention he was getting. Once rehearsals had finished the other musicians would be getting ready to leave the house to get something to eat, Jimmy would be sitting down at the dinner table for one of Mrs Isley's home-cooked meals. "*They hated him for it,*" Ernie recalls. "*The house smelled like a restaurant - you know, Cornish hens, dressing, green beans and some sort of pie or cake.*"

With Jimmy onboard, The Isley brothers' first step was to get to the studio and record with their new guitarist. It would be their first single on their own label. The track 'Testify' was recorded with Jimmy on guitar. Released in June 1964 the track has Jimmy Hendrix uncredited, although he plays lead...

"*We made a deal with Atlantic Records to distribute our label, T-Neck*", Ronnie recollected, "*I think we were one of the very few groups who had their own label at the time. Jimi walked into the studio - he'd never been in one before - and said, 'Oh, is this how you make records?' We cut Testify on four tracks. The band was on two, Rudy and Kelly were on one and I was one. The rest of the stuff we cut, though, was on eight tracks. Atlantic had one of the few eight-track studios at the time, so for the rest of the material on this album, Jimi had his own track. We've remixed it so Jimi is more up front.*"

After the release of the single The Isley Brothers went on tour, with Jimmy as their new guitarist. It was a good tour for Jimmy, he loved the packed-out venues that the Isley Brothers played at, a world of difference to the small clubs he had become used to thus far. Another important aspect of this tour was that the brothers let Jimmy perform as he wanted to, for now. He was able to showboat, and to dress slightly differently. Nothing too out there, but the odd scarf hanging down or his hair pulled up in a wild way. This is an important point. Many acts of the day were reluctant to let their band members stand out too much, they never wanted anyone but them to get the limelight. The Isley Brothers, however, embraced Jimmy, they knew he was bankable, he pulled in crowds and he put on a brilliant show, and crucially at the end of the day it was their concert, their names. In short, he made them more money. They even went so far on many occasions to let Jimmy go out alone and play as the warmup act, a time for him to shine with the usual tricks of playing with his teeth and behind his head.

Ronnie recalled the first few gigs with great affection. *"First gig he played with us was in Canada. He was crazy about places he'd never been to before. It was on that gig that - well, we'd have so much fun playing with him - I'd sing like his guitar and then he'd play it back at me! Then we went to Bermuda. We played in a baseball stadium. We'd been advertised for months, so the place was filled and those who couldn't get seats were standing on hills overlooking the stadium. It was us and local talent. Our band backed the other acts. We were in the dressing room when we heard what sounded like a riot going on and we figured one of the local acts must have made a big hit. But this guy came into the dressing room and said, 'Who is that out there?' so we all peeked and there was Jimi, down on his knees, biting the guitar, and the crowd was just going crazy. Jimi was people. He never sat in a corner and cried about his problems or money or anything like that. He met people as people, and they took him the same way. He didn't have any hang-ups personally. He didn't have any money hang-ups neither."*

One key observation the brothers noticed with Jimmy was that he never stopped playing, even in his free time he never put his guitar down. It was as if it was a part of him. He even rarely spoke about anything else other than music and his guitar, only then would he come alive, and sound generally interested. Outside of this he was quiet and reserved, somewhat introverted. Another key element was that as incredibly talented Jimmy was, and he knew he was, he never took it for granted, he practiced all the time, breaking down key phrases and tones, working through different sounds and expressions. He was consistently perfecting his craft, above and beyond anything that the other members of the band had ever seen.

At this point in time, in mid-1964, music was flowing through Jimmy constantly. He was becoming acutely aware of his talent but had not yet come to terms with it completely. Often overpowered by it on stage, his genius would channel itself within his performances, he was frequently taken over. He would absorb what his fellow musicians were doing and take it to another level, far beyond where everyone else was. At times he was as baffled by his talents as those around him. One fellow musician was Chicago based blues player Tommy Tucker. Jimmy performed with him during this period and Tommy was as amazed as everyone else observing him when he played. Tommy asked Jimmy where he got the sounds from, puzzled by how he did it, he was expecting some kind of response where a secret would maybe come out, something he could try and understand, so others could learn it; Jimmy responded, *"I don't know man, I just don't know".*

Jimmy eventually outgrew The Isley Brothers, it was obvious looking back that he was bigger than the role he was playing, and in hindsight everyone else recognised this too. Also, he was reprimanded several times for his dress code, the small embellishments he was making to his appearance started to get to a point where the brothers had to reign him back in, he was becoming a little too extravagant and flamboyant for their liking. If, for example his shoelaces were different colours he would be fined. It started to become very restrictive, and he soon became tired of the tour.

"Later on we went to Motown," Ronnie reflected, *"But just before that we were doing a gig at the Apollo. Murray K had one of his British shows going on at another theatre, The Animals and Tom Jones were there. Well, Jimi was just like everybody else, he wanted to see what those fellows looked like. So he'd get backstage and say hello and then he'd spot a guitar in the corner, maybe a 12-string, and right away he'd be playing it. The English guys would go nuts. They'd say, 'You've got to come to England. Why don't you come with us?' Jimi was dying to go to England. So that was where we split up. We went to Detroit and he went to England."*

Before this, Jimmy headed back to Nashville, he arrived in October 1964. He knew his old friends and musical acquaintances would still be around, and he also knew it was probably his best place to get work and to continue to play in the short term. It was shortly afterwards however that Jimmy got the call from Sam Cooke, and after several more auditions he agreed to go on tour. This was scheduled from October through to December. Unfortunately for Jimmy he missed the transfer, and the tour left without him to Kansas. A shocking turn of events, however, prevented him from being able to follow on as planned.

It was on 11th December 1964 that Sam Cooke was shot dead at the Hacienda Motel in Los Angelas. Local Police arrived on the scene to find the musician dead on the office floor, he had been shot three times in the chest by the motel's manager, Bertha Franklin. The authorities ruled Cooke's death a case of justifiable homicide, based on the testimony of Ms. Franklin, who claimed that Cooke had threatened her life after attempting to rape a young woman with whom he had earlier checked in with. Even as the lurid details of the case were becoming common knowledge, some 200,000 fans turned out in the streets of Los Angeles and Chicago to mourn the passing of Cooke, a man whose legacy seemed able to transcend the scandal surrounding his death. That legacy was built during a brief but spectacular run as a singer, songwriter, producer and music publisher in the 1950s and early 1960s. Cookes death however, like many before and after, Jimmy included, became the subject of widespread theories and suspicion.

In these early years of Jimmy's career, he often called himself different names, most famously of course, soon changing his spelling from Jimmy to Jimi, which would forever be his calling. When he arrived back in Nashville towards the latter end of 1964, he was calling himself Maurice James and sought out Gorgeous George hoping he would find him some more work. He arrived in Atlanta, the home of George, to find further work. It was here that Jimmy, or Maurice, would land another key association. This time playing with the self-proclaimed King of rock 'n' roll himself.

Chapter 7

New York 'A Slight Return'

"I try all night to play a pretty note."

While in Atlanta, Jimmy was brought to the attention of a certain Richard Wayne Penniman, better known of course as Little Richard. At this period, Little Richard was spending many weeks in and around Nashville, touring the circuit with his lavish shows. Jimmy was invited to join his touring band 'The Upsetters'. Little Richard told his biographer Charles White of when he first met Jimmy.

"*I first met Jimi Hendrix in Atlanta, where he was stranded with no money. He had been working as a guitarist with a fella named Gorgeous George. My bus was parked in Auburn Avenue and Jimi was staying in this small hotel. And so he came by to see us. He had watched me work and just loved the way I wore these headbands around my hair and how wild I dressed.... So he came with me. He wasn't playing my kind of music though. He was playing like B.B.King Blues. He started rocking though and he was a good guy. He started to dress like me and even grew a little moustache like mine.*"

Little Richards touring band, The Upsetters should not be confused with the Jamaican reggae musicians, of the same name. The Upsetters in question here, were an already established, and very much respected, American rhythm section. Sadly, despite them being a key element in the evolution of blues, rock, and R&B, they remain largely unappreciated for their talents and musical contributions. Originating in the mid-1950s, the group consisted of Wilburt 'Lee Diamond' Smith on saxophone, Nathaniel 'Buster' Douglas on electric guitar, Charles 'Chuck' Connor on drums, and Olsie 'Bassy' Robinson on bass guitar. They became notorious for their talents with a short but critical burst from 1956 to 1957, when they collaborated with many prominent musicians.

During this period, Little Richard had several touring bands, he wasn't anyone that would be overshadowed by them in any way, which is obviously why someone like Jimmy wouldn't be around for too long. The Upsetters were not his primary band, they did, however, work very closely with him. They even appeared in several of his films, including The Girl Can't Help It (1956), which also featured Jayne Mansfield. This was the main film that helped Little Richard move into the mainstream, it solidified his reputation as a true rock and roll icon and in turn showcased the talents of his supporting musicians.

In the late 1950s, tracks such as 'Keep A-Knocking' and 'Ooh! My Soul' became popular hits, embedding themselves within the cultural dynamics of the time and reflecting the era's dynamic energy. Drummer World noted the impactful performance of The Upsetters' drummer, Connor, stating: *"The lethal pummelling that The Upsetters drummer, Connor, administered to his drums must have left a lasting impact on all future rock 'n' rollers, because 15 years later John Bonham practically reproduced that intro note for note in his opening to Led Zeppelin's 'Rock 'n' Roll'."* A notable aspect of The Upsetters' career was their collaboration with Otis Redding in the early 1960s, where they supported him during some of his live performances. This partnership added another dimension to their musical legacy, as Redding was on the verge of becoming one of soul music's most significant figures. The contributions of The Upsetters to music during this period were substantial, they played a crucial role in shaping the sound of rock and roll. Their work with Little Richard and other prominent artists left a significant mark on the music industry, and they impacted many musicians who followed. The Upsetters were one of the most important backing bands in American music history and their influence is evident in some of the most iconic tracks of the 1950s and 1960s. Their collaborations with legendary artists like Little Richard and Otis Redding exemplify their versatility and talent. Despite their relative obscurity, the band contributed significantly to the development of rock, blues, and R&B, and their legacy continues to have an enduring impact today. Although the backing band possessed such pedigree, joining Little Richard was not without its issues. Richard was the star, the band were literally that, a band, and that included Maurice James aka Jimmy Hendrix, who was just a guitarist. He was definitely not one to be overshadowed in any way.

Later in a 1973 documentary about Jimi, Little Richard talked about him, saying:

"He was a star. When I got him, he was a star. Jimi Hendrix could play that Rock and Roll, I used to be singing, rocking away 'Uh Uh Uh' and he had that thing just romping, at times he made my big toe shoot up in my boot, he did it so good. Jimi Hendrix's perseverance to go on... he didn't mind looking freaky like I don't mind it, because I was doing it before he was and I knew when he saw me it gave him confidence and great recompense of reward. I had something to tell him, and I never did, so now I have to talk about it and let him know that I knew he was gonna make it."

That said, he did have to reprimand Jimmy when he hit the stage with him. Not dissimilar to others that Jimmy played with, he would often get carried away and do his own thing, never to be contained for too long. In an interview with Music Radar back in 2012, Graham Nash recalled when he was still a member of The Hollies and saw Little Richard and Jimi Hendrix fighting after a performance.

"*I first met Jimi in '65. He was in Little Richard's band at the time. This was at the Paramount Theatre in New York City, the Soupy Sales Easter Show. I'll give you a story from my book: When we came to America for the very first time, we went to the Paramount Theatre where the gig was, and we thought we were going to do our set – 45 minutes of dynamite. 'Which two songs are you doing?' we were asked. We were like, 'What? Two songs?' But there were 12 other acts on the bill, five shows a day – two songs. So that was a shock. Little Richard closed the show, and we would watch him from the side of the stage. One night I heard this argument before they went on: 'Don't you ever fucking do that again! I'm Little Richard, the king of rock 'n' roll, you fucking guy! Stop playing your fucking guitar behind your fucking head!' And he was yelling at Jimi. It was this argument as they got in the elevator to go up. The volume decreased as they went, but you could still hear them arguing. I can hear it now. So that was Jimi. It was obvious he was a talented guy.*"

Although Little Richard had to reprimand Jimmy, or Maurice as he was now calling himself, Jimmy did have respect for him at the time. He loved the fact that Richard didn't compromise on his looks, or his flamboyant personality. He was a true original. Jimmy would have recognised he was a pioneer of Rock 'n' Roll; he had something special, he was a unique talent and worked the circuit brilliantly. What James Brown was with funk, Richard was with Rock 'n' Roll. Many replicated or were influenced by him in the years ahead, notably The Beatles, Michael Jackson, Prince and others, but Richard was the first to bring this style of Rock 'n' Roll to the masses and his contribution is immense. Correctly described as the Architect of Rock 'n' Roll, Jimmy recognised this.

Musicians like Richard were true pioneers, they were musicians who resisted conformity. He was among the first true crossover artists to integrate various cultures and backgrounds into his music and live performances. This was particularly significant during a period when racial segregation was prevalent and often endorsed in the United States. Although their collaboration was brief, Richard's narrative and his approach to celebrating music likely influenced Jimmy's perspective. He promoted an ethos of freedom and inclusion, without constraints or filters in both music and performance. Richard himself had a tough upbringing, he was born in Macon Georgia, he was a black man from the redneck south, who was openly gay and had been since his teenage years. His father had disowned him, and having a troubled childhood he eventually ran away from home. His father was later involved in a fight and was shot dead.

Although this admiration was there for Richard, Jimmy was given strict instructions, much like the rest of the band. They were there to play, to wear uniforms and to stay in the background. Little Richard was the star, and that was how it was. Eventually after several nights of performing with Richard, Jimmy had had enough. He failed to turn up when the band reached Los Angeles, he decided it was time to move on.

Jimmy became acquainted with a musician named Arthur Lee, who was searching for a guitarist. He had heard about Jimmy, especially because he could play in the style of Curtis Mayfield, which was what Arthur was looking for. They recorded a song called 'My Diary', it was released in May 1965 on Revis Records, a 1960s R&B and soul label from Los Angeles, owned by Billy Revis. The track was credited, this time to include Jimmy:

- Lead Guitar – Jimi Hendrix
- Producer – B. Revis
- Technician – Doc Siegel

Although Little Richard had been touring constantly, he was desperate for a hit record. Despite Jimmy not performing with him he did agree to go in the studio to record a song, again stylistically in the Curtis Mayfield approach. In February 1965, Jimmy recorded his one and only single with Little Richard, the track *'I Don't Know What You Got (But It's Got Me)'* was released on Vee-Jay Records and became a minor hit. Richard's popularity was in decline at the time and the record failed to have the impact he had hoped for. The record was released in October 1965, it reached number 12 on the R&B chart but disappointedly failed to make any impact on the Billboard chart.

In July 1965, Jimmy made his first television appearance on Nashville's Channel 5 Night Train. Richard himself did not appear, remaining back at his hotel, giving the spotlight to Buddy Travis and Stacey Johnson to perform a cover of Junior Walker & the All-Stars' recent hit 'Shotgun'. Jimmy is immediately apparent in the background, looking larger than life. He can be seen handling his upside-down Fender with the ease, swagger and assurance that would soon make him famous. The video recording of the show marks the earliest known footage of Jimmy performing. Richard tried in vain to control Jimmy, even going so far as to have the lights dimmed to try and hide him away. Understandably, for Little Richard, he was the guy out front and that was it; he famously said, *"I was the only one allowed to be pretty"*. Jimmy also stated later that he didn't get paid for nearly six weeks.

In late July, despite Jimmy already making plans to move on, Richard's brother Robert officially fired him. Despite this, Richard spoke fondly of Jimmy in the years ahead. He even stated he tried to go and see him when he eventually made it through on his own terms, only to be refused access to the star. Reflecting later on Jimi, Richard said he was, *"The greatest guitar player I ever had. Not one of my men ever came close to him."*

Around this time, Jimmy played briefly with Ike and Tina Turner, however Ike was not impressed with the guitarist who should have been tucked nicely away at the back. His awe for his ability soon turned to resentment as he found himself being upstaged by Jimmy's flashy style and performing theatrics. During the performances women in the crowd were captivated by him, and he performed for them. The audience would scream, and Ike would realise it wasn't for him, it was for Jimmy: he was playing guitar with his teeth, or above his head. There were also rumours that Ike was uncomfortable with the charm Jimmy could bring for the female singers in the band, and with Tina herself.

Jimmy was now back in New York after his time with Little Richard ended. It felt like he had gone full circle, back where he started. But he now desperately wanted to record for himself, and on his own terms. To have his own band and to push on as an independent artist. He made the decision to visit record companies in New York, taking his own material with him, desperate for some kind of deal.

At this moment he was highly influenced by Bob Dylan, as were many young aspiring musicians in New York and beyond. It would be a few years later when he would take Dylans 'All along the watchtower' and make it his own, but during this period, Jimmy played Dylans records constantly. Reports from those who visited Jimmy's hotel room at this time note that Dylans albums were so overplayed, you could hold the vinyl to the window and see light coming through them.

It's difficult to pin down the precise date that Dylan arrived in New York. The best guess, and most commonly agreed, is 24 January 1961, this was during the coldest winter New York had seen in 28 years. He'd dropped out of the University of Minnesota and spent the last twenty-four hours driving east with Fred Underhill and two others. Just a few hours after slamming the car door shut, Dylan was walking into Café Wha? at 115 MacDougal Street. Fred Neil, the club's MC, found out that he was a musician, and asked him to play something. It was his New York City debut.

Dylan had been in New York for some time when Jimmy started to discover his music. He had already had his first professional gig, on April

11, 1961, supporting blues great John Lee Hooker. The city gave him his first major break, most notably when his performance was reviewed in the New York Times. Dylan was one of many who had arrived in New York looking for stardom and recognition, he would have easily blended in amongst the many James Dean lookalikes in the winter of 1961, all congregating on the vibrant creative hub in and around Greenwich Village. He was unknown, and just another teen impersonator, but things changed, and Dylan quickly became 'the' singular creative folk singer very quickly. He soon separated himself from others around him and set himself apart, changing the face of popular music in the years ahead. Jimmy recognised this and was fascinated with Dylans lyrical prowess. With just a guitar, harmonica and a voice - albeit not the traditional singing one - he arrived in New York with a unique outlook and an artistic ambition to succeed. Most crucially, Dylan had a vast library of his own songs, American Folk songs that up-and-coming artists like Jimmy found inspirational.

What Dylan managed to demonstrate was an ability to write music as he experienced life, much like the blues that Jimmy was influenced by. Folk has its lyrical content in real life dealings, something Jimmy related to, the difference was that Jimmy also spoke through his guitar, as well as lyrics. He was able to tell stories through it and wasn't reliant on just vocals for storytelling. Producer John Hammond would reflect on Dylan in New York and wrote in the liner notes of his debut album one year later, *"The young man from the provinces began to make friends very quickly in New York, all the while continuing, as he has since he was ten, to assimilate musical ideas from everyone he met, every record he heard."*

Dylan's rise in New York is well documented, and one venue that was significant was his first appearance at Gerde's Folk City in 1961. This is also where he first played 'Blowin' in the Wind,' and met Joan Baez. She was quickly rising in popularity at the time, becoming known as the 'Queen of Folk,' and he was apparently eager to impress her. She would help launch his career, inviting him to play with her on stage, never holding back if anyone were to criticise Dylans voice. Surrounded by such acts, of such quality, and witnessing that they had stamped their authority in and around the New York circuit, made Jimmy even more determined to get some kind of deal.

During his search, Jimmy came across New York-based R&B singer Curtis Knight. Originally from Fort Scott in Kansas, Knight was in New York performing with his own band The Squires. They met in the hotel lobby where they both happened to be staying. During a later interview Curtis recalls their first meeting, *"I remember the first time I saw Jimmy, we were on 47th street New York, at a place called Hotel America, which is now a parking lot. In the lobby of the hotel they had a recording studio, I* *stopped by there one day, I had some music business to attend to, standing by the elevator I saw the most incredible looking guy, that I had ever seen in my life. This guy had hair out to here";* Curtis stretches his arms out above his head to make the point; *"Now this was 1964/65, and I had seen some strange things, but I thought to myself this must be a very special person. I walked up to him and said 'Hi I'm Curtis Knight, what your name? What do you do?' He said 'My name is Jimmy Hendrix, and I play guitar, but I don't have one cause I just come off tour and I had to pawn one, and if they catch me in the lobby they'll put the key in my room and I won't be able to get back in', I told him I had a guitar in the back of my car and an amplifier, a fender Strat, I told him go back to your room so you don't get locked out, I went and got the guitar and amplifier and took it up to his room. He picked up the guitar, turned it upside down because he's left-handed, and what I heard almost blew me out the door like an atomic blast. I had never in my life heard anyone articulate, play chords, and lead at the same time. I was totally blown away. I had a group called The Squires, we were playing clubs at the time under the 59th street bridge where all the British rockers came, people like The Animals, The Rolling Stones, The Beatles. It was the Rolling Stones that brought Chas Chandlers attention to Jimmy. From then on, I gave Jimmy a guitar and amplifier, and we played all the rock clubs in New York."*

The influence of Dylan, and the folk scene that followed, inspired Knight to write his own version of 'Like a Rolling Stone' renamed 'How Does it Feel'. With this, he booked himself in to record a session at Studio 76 located on the corner of 51st Street and Broadway and took Jimmy with him. The Studio was run by record executive and producer Ed Chaplin. Chaplin had met Knight previously and signed him for record production and management.

As soon as Jimmy started playing in the studio, Chaplin moved in. He obviously saw the talent and quickly drafted a single piece of paper for Jimmy to sign. Jimmy knew nothing of the record industry, and certainly nothing of contractual obligations. On this day in the recording studio, 15th October 1965, Jimmy signed with Chaplin's company PPX Enterprises. Whether Jimmy was aware, or simply didn't care too much at the time is up for debate; either way the contract he signed was for three years. It was with PPX Enterprises giving them total exclusivity, this was on anything Jimmy would play or sing, including all producing. The contract gave Jimmy the bare minimum, and absolutely no control on future releases.

In retrospect, it is evident that Jimmy's actions can be seen as naive. However, it was a different era, and contracts and negotiations, particularly for emerging artists yet to establish themselves, were not familiar territory for young musicians. Regrettably, this single document, now bearing his signature, would have adverse consequences in the years to come.

Chapter 8

Jimi, Up From the Skies

"If the mountains fell in the sea, let it be, it ain't me.

Towards the end of 1965, shortly after Jimmy signed his first recording contract, he formed his own band for a residency. He soon attracted other musicians and settled on the name Jimmy James and the Blue Flames, although he would later sometimes refer to the band with alternative names such as The Rain Flowers, The Blue Flames, and the Blue Flame. Apparently, Jimmy chose the name because it rhymed with his own and he thought it sounded catchy. It was also a nod towards Blues singer and harmonica player Junior Parker, who named his own band The Blue Flames, formed in 1951.

While playing further gigs, either with Curtis Knight and The Squires or any other bands, Jimmy's reputation was now high level. He was becoming recognised as one of the finest blues guitarists anywhere. He was unmatched and word was spreading fast. Even in London, word of his talent was becoming widespread, many bands had travelled through New York and witnessed him outright, flying back to London and spreading the word. On one gig with The Squires, they played at George Club 20 in Hackensack New Jersey. The club was the main hang out of saxophonist King Curtis, a session musician of the highest order, he also had hits in the bank, notably playing on 'Yakety Yak' by The Coasters in 1958. He also played on Soul Serenade in 1964 and would later feature on Respect by Aretha Franklin, along with many others. Jimmy took a brief audition for Knight, who was looking for a second guitarist, he got the gig.

Guitarist Cornell Dupree remembered Jimmy from this time, *"At the time Jimmy joined the band, Curtis was trying to expand it. There was one particular gig I remember where Jimmy and Billy Preston were on a gig together, which was really something...We played opposite and behind Chuck Berry... upstate in one of the colleges. Jimmy just stole the show...when he felt the spirit I mean he would go out and perform. It was just those magic moments, I guess... when he felt like it and he did it, because he didn't do it all the time-it wasn't planned. But he stole a few shows."*

Although this band was by far the best Jimmy had performed and jammed with to this point, he was still to some degree sidelined. He genuinely struggled with not being able to launch into long solos, where he could freeform at will. This was his home; this was his uniqueness. Staying within a standard structure of a song, within boundaries was always a conflict of style for him. Unsurprisingly Jimmy was becoming frustrated again, he wanted to leave The Squires, but at this point his only guitar was borrowed from Curtis. There was also the standard issue of money, with Jimmy being paid the bare minimum - or not at all. At the time one of Jimmy's girlfriends was Carol Shiroky, better known as Kim. She had moved in with him at his hotel, she recalled: *"He was having lots of problems with Curtis, he was unhappy, having fights about not being paid, or being paid a pittance. You know, just enough to keep him fed."* These ongoing frustrations spurred Jimmy on even further to go it alone, or with his own bands. With this, he could perform on his own terms and perform what and how he wanted. He'd played the club circuit long enough by this point to know where to be, to suit him best. He concentrated on Greenwich Village.

Although Jimmy was deeply unhappy, he still carried on playing for Curtis Knight, despite the differences. Kim couldn't understand this but later discovered it was simply because of the guitar; Jimmy still didn't have one of his own, which meant leaving Curtis meant no guitar. Once she found out the reason, she bought Jimmy, a brand-new white Fender Stratocaster. Jimmy would spend hours restructuring it, filing down the frets so he could reverse the strings just the way he needed them. Once his own guitar was ready, Jimmy played his last gig for Curtis, reportedly unplugging himself at the end of the night with the words *"That's the last time I play this shit"*. Jimmy walked off stage and began the next phase of his career; the time had come for him to have his own band, and for him to be front and centre.

Initially, the band he set up started as just a three-piece consisting of Jimmy, bassist Randy Palmer and drummer Dan Casey. The band, however, like many of the bands Jimmy had been involved with to this point, flowed freely with various incarnations. It wasn't long before a secondary guitarist was added in, Randy Wolfe, who Jimmy had met at Manny's Music store on 48th street when he was trying out a new guitar. Suitably impressed, Jimmy invited him for an audition, this time at Café Wha?. Randy was just 15 years old at the time and had run away from home. To avoid confusion by now having two Randy's in the band, Jimmy called Wolfe 'Randy California' and Palmer 'Randy Texas' after their home states. Jimmy taught the young Randy his songs while in the boiler room at Café Wha?.

They had a short residency at the club, it was a good venue in respect to the crowd, who were more patient than other venues, allowing Jimmy to fully perform. He was finding his way in a new type of performance, that of a front man and bandleader. Jimmy was reported to earn around $50 to $60 per night during the residency, which lasted around three months. Jimmy made sure he split all earnings equally between all the band members, determined not to treat his band the way he had been treated previously.

One of the first songs the new band performed was *'Wild Thing'*, at the time a Top 40 radio hit by the Troggs, one of many covers Jimmy would make his own. Another was *'Hey Joe'* although this was usually a lot slower. There were other songs the band played which were popular at the time, including Dylan's *'Like a Rolling Stone'*, *'Hang on Sloopy'*, and *'House of the Rising Sun'*. Jimmy was finding his own style and moving away from the Harlem R&B scene, where he felt he was scrutinised too much because of his ever evolving and expanding guitar style. He was developing a kaleidoscope of styles, more undefined in approach, he did not fit easily in to any one genre, and in any one performance he covered virtually everything, expanding further into his own higher world. He also started to produce his own compositions, keen to not be noted as just another cover band in a Manhattan Club.

Songs people remembered him playing at this time were raw early versions of 'Red House', 'Third Stone from the Sun' and 'The Wind Cries Mary', although the latter must have been a very early version as it was confirmed to have been finished lyrically in London.

Jimmy James and the Blue Flames often played five sets a night, six days a week, earning very little, and surviving on tips from the crowd. It wasn't long, however, with the amazing performances he was giving night after night, before he became noticed by prominent individuals within the music business. He was now becoming continually scouted. Model Linda Keith had been watching Jimmy for weeks and was astonished no one had taken him under their wing; she had met him backstage after one of his performances and the two became good friends. At the time she was the girlfriend of Stones guitarist Keith Richards. Linda was surprised when they first met by the difference between Jimmy onstage and offstage - it was striking. The confident, brilliant, flamboyant musician was quiet, polite, shy and lacking in confidence. She also noted that he was also in need of a good meal.

Jimmy was also joined at this time by guitarist Randy California, who would later go on to form the band, Spirit. He recalled playing with Jimmy James and The Blue Flames over these few months: *"When Ed Cassidy became my stepfather in 1966, he moved the whole family to New York City* where he had a jazz gig. It was there at the age of 15 that I played in a band called Jimmy James & The Blue Flames. Jimmy James of course was Jimi Hendrix. Hendrix gave me the name California to distinguish me from the Texan born Randy who played bass in the band, This magical event in guitar history took place one year before 'Are You Experienced?' and two years before the first Spirit LP. As far as I can remember, the group lasted three months." Randy recalled how he first met Jimmy during this period; "My family and I lived out on Long Island, and we would take the subway into town. I took a ride in for the day... and I guess my parents were trusting enough that I could take care of myself. In those days it wasn't quite as dangerous for a young kid to be wandering around the streets of New York. I met Jimi in Manny's Music store. He was in the back of the store playing a Strat. Our eyes caught each other, and I asked him If I could show him some things I learned on the guitar. He then gave me the Strat and I played him slide guitar. He really liked it and invited me down that night, which I believe was his first night of this gig at the Cafe Wha? I don't think he played anything solo before then. I'll never forget that moment our eyes met and froze on each other. Some type of real spiritual affinity or connection happened between us. It was like we knew each other. Not the first night, but as time went on, he was able to acquire a Fender deluxe reverb. I remember I was playing through a Sears Silvertone amp which had a lot of power, we used to switch amps quite a bit. When he got this Fender amp he would start sticking the guitar in front of it. This would create a feedback noise. He was always really moving on stage, as far as being a sexy kind of performer... He wasn't burning his guitar or anything. He had a real knack for moving the whole band with him when he was on stage. He would do this by his presence and the way he moved to the rhythm of the song. On a lot of the songs, he would teach us as we're going along. We really didn't have time to rehearse."

During these months Randy also recalled Jimi working in other clubs as well; "What happened was guitarist John Hammond came down and saw us. He had a gig down the street at the Cafe Au Go Go. John liked Jimmy so much that he asked him to back his band up. I was there too, although I didn't think they needed another guitar player. I remember running in between sets in the rain from the Cafe Wha? to the Cafe Au Go Go then back to the Cafe Wha? John Hammond Jr. was only doing two sets a night and we were doing five so this was a luxury kind of a gig. There was some good money involved too. I think we made about twenty bucks each on the nights that we worked with John. On the other nights when we just worked at the Cafe Wha?, I think it was only seven or eight bucks. I remember Jimmy getting the money from this guy, I think his name was Manny, and *sharing the money with all the band members, even though he was the leader, the person out front. Well, I really can't say 'out front' because it was a really small stage (laughs). So that was the connection, we would sit in with John Hammond. He had a proper blues gig down at the Cafe Au Go Go."*

As the nights and performances went on, Jimmy was now being watched by the best of British, as well as the key players within New York City and those who were passing through. During this short period, word had got around so much that anyone in the know was talking of him, and they all seemed to have travelled to wherever he was playing to witness what everyone was talking about, intrigued by the rumours of the wild black man with a Fender Stratocaster; once seen however, they never forgot.

The sounds he was producing each night were astonishing, he also looked different, no one had ever seen or heard anything like him. He was getting every sound possible through the room, with just a Stratocaster, a Fender Twin amplifier, and a Maestro fuzz box. The element of performance was also unlike other acts, it wasn't just the dexterity of his playing, where he could jump effortlessly from melodic rhythm to blistering solos, it was also the theatrics, the guitar behind his back, playing with his teeth; and imitations of guided missiles flying. Many also discovered, when they watched him for a second and third time, just how wonderfully melodic his playing was, and that behind the virtuoso guitar genius, there was also lyricism and an astute songwriting prowess. He had simmered his skills into a perfect blend. Linda Keith invited various musical managers and promoters down to Cafe Wha? determined to get her new friend a break.

This was a pivotal moment in the accession of the future Jimi Hendrix. Linda Keith would play a key role and a crucial element in getting Jimmy discovered. At this time, she was a 20-year-old British vogue model, and she loved the blues. Back in London, Linda enjoyed listening to blues master's on BBC radio. She had also seen live American Piedmont blues and folk musician Sonny Terry and also harmonica player and blues singer Sonny Boy Williamson, when they played in London, or at various folk festivals. She even lent Jimmy a white Fender Stratocaster, his own was now at the pawn shop, claiming later that this gesture did not go down too well with her then boyfriend of three years, Keith Richards. The Stones at the time were on their 1966 tour of the US. Keith and Brian Jones, who would become a good friend of Jimmy and incidentally would sadly become part of the infamous 27 Club, reportedly wrote 'Ruby Tuesday' about Linda Keith.

The borrowed guitar sadly didn't last long, Linda recalled during an interview with the Observer, "*It was the night he smashed up a white guitar,*

I was beside myself. I'd lent him a guitar belonging to my boyfriend and there he was smashing one up on stage! I was absolutely livid with Jimi because to me that's the most un-cool thing to do". Despite this Linda was absolutely determined to get Jimmy his break, she recalled the first time she saw him play in New York at The Cheetah club. *"It was so clear to me. I couldn't believe nobody had picked up on him before because he'd obviously been around. He was astonishing - the moods he could bring to music, his charisma, his skill and stage presence. Yet nobody was leaping about with excitement. I couldn't believe it."*

Linda's best friend was Sheila Klein, at this time she was dating Andrew Oldham, who became the Rolling Stones' manager. Although she was primarily a fan of blues music, her frequent travels with her best friend during The Rolling Stones' tours inevitably led to her becoming part of the band's inner circle at that time. *"I'd seen them in clubs. They were interesting but it wasn't anything that really grabbed me."*

During The Stones tour, Linda based herself in New York. It was the band's fifth tour in just three years, and it was here that she saw Jimmy for the first time. *"My initial thought, of course, was Keith must see this,"* she says. But word soon reached Richards that his girlfriend was hanging out with Jimmy. *"I was determined that he should be notified, get a record deal and blow everybody's mind. I knew it was all there, so I went for it."* With her connections she eventually started to get key people down to watch him, but some were still yet to be convinced. *"Some of his movements were great but he was also a trickster - playing the guitar over his head or with his teeth. He didn't really need any of that."* Linda says. *The songs that would become 'Are You Experienced?' were already in their elemental state and he was yet to do the psychedelic militaria that became his trademark.* *"Oh, his fashion sense was absolutely dreadful. He wore dreadful clothes - big Copacabana shirts with too-short bell-bottoms and shoes with holes in them. He had processed hair that had spent the night in curlers so when he took the curlers out it remained in exactly the same form. It wasn't a good look!"*

Absolutely determined to get Jimmy his break, Linda was convinced beyond anything that those watching Jimmy were deluded, ignorant, or both, if they didn't offer him some kind of deal. To her it was bordering ridiculous, the best of British at the time had seen him and yet this incredible talent was playing 'undiscovered and unappreciated' night after night in a club in New York. Eventually, Linda's persistence was rewarded. She invited the Animals' guitarist-turned-manager Chas Chandler down to see Jimmy play his regular mid-afternoon set at Cafe Wha?. It would be the perfect moment, *"You'd come out the bright sun into this cave of a room. Then the stage lights would come up and Jimmy playing the opening chords* of *'Hey Joe'*. Well, it was quite mind blowing and I'm not surprised he blew Chas's mind with the first chord. It even blew my mind - and I knew it was coming!". Hey Joe, would become a staple for Jimmy going forward, and of course one of his most memorable songs.

The track has a rich history and had been covered many times. When Chas Chandler discovered Jimmy performing it, the song was already a well-known standard for live bands, but Jimmy popularised it into the mainstream. The 'Second-hand Songs' database lists over 435 versions of the track since its release, not including live performances. The song's origins are debated, with some attributing it to Billy Roberts, others to Dino Valenti, and some even considering it public domain. The most widespread story of 'Hey Joe' has William Moses Roberts Jr (aka Billy Roberts) coming up with 'Hey Joe'... possibly in an Edinburgh folk club way back in 1956. Scottish folk singer Len Partridge claims that he added some bits, but many don't agree, and either way Patridge acknowledges that it was really Billy's song. *"We played quite a lot together, and one of the things that came out of that period was 'Hey Joe'."* Len told The Independent. *"Don't even ask me now which bits were added by me. I can't claim credit for it - that really has to go to Bill."* This relates to Jimmy and the Blues based music he was exposed too. Within these circles countless jamming sessions would occur, after-hours music that would be played in various clubs through to the early hours. The folk and blues musicians would take songs of the distant or not-so-distant past, and riff on them constantly, with different players reworking the same basic chords, changing things ever so slightly here and there. They had ideas and lyrics and would put their own twist on them. By this rationale 'Hey Joe' wasn't a million miles away from a ton of other folk and blues songs, and Roberts hasn't always given the same story of how he came up with it. There are also claims that it was taken from Niela Miller's song Baby Please Don't Go to Town. Miller stated that Roberts, her boyfriend in the late fifties, used her melody and altered the lyrics. Despite it being copyrighted, she was advised against suing due to Dino Valenti's involvement. Miller said she wrote the song between 1954 and 1955, and Roberts learned it when they dated in 1956. Folk icon Pete Seeger supported her story.

Dino Valenti, born Chester William Powers, Jr., allegedly learned 'Hey Joe' from Roberts and copyrighted it in Los Angeles. There are also claims by Tim Rose, who said he learned the song from Vince Martin in 1960, calling his version 'Blue Steel .44'. The Leaves, an American garage rock band, popularised the song with their 1966 hit, however they credited it as Traditional/Public Domain. As a result of the above, the song had been bouncing around for quite a few years on the live circuit before being covered by The Leaves. It became popular, especially on the Los Angeles scene - with Dino Valenti and David Crosby's versions, later of Crosby, Stills & Nash fame, picking up a lot of attention. It was said that The Leaves first heard the song watching Crosby's Byrds play at Ciro's in Los Angeles and set to work. They recorded three versions of the songs between 1965 and 1966. It was released initially by The Leaves in either November or December 1965 but was a flop. It was the third version, produced by Nik Venet and released in May or June 1966, that hit the charts, eventually peaking at number 31 on the Billboard Hot 100. Around the time of The Leaves releases, The Standells, The Surfaris, Love, The Music Machine, and The Byrds all released their own versions of the song. Some people claim that The Surfari's version - released on the B-side of their 'So Get Out' single - dates from 1965, but it seems much more likely that The Leaves got the jump on them.

The story of the track is drawn from many others of a similar ilk, traditional 20th century ballad 'Little Sadie' (also known as 'Bad Lee Brown', 'Cocaine Blues', 'Transfusion Blues', 'East St. Louis Blues', 'Late One Night', 'Penitentiary Blues' and other titles) tells the story of a man on the run after shooting his wife, but the earliest record of the song dates as far back as 1922. John Dilleshaw & The String Marvel recorded an unissued version of 'Bad Lee Brown' in 1929, while Clarence Ashley put 'Little Sadie' on vinyl the same year. A country song of the same name written by Boudleaux Bryant was released in 1953 by Carl Smith. There were also a few tweaks and twiddles made to the song, musically and lyrically, before Jimmy got his hands on it.

The Byrds' recorded versions of the song have slightly different lyrics... "gun in your hand" was re written as "money in your hand". The Byrds' take was called 'Hey Joe (Where You Gonna Go)' and was included on their album Fifth Dimension, released in July 1966. It's claimed that lead singer David Crosby wanted to record the song as far back as 1964, but his bandmates vetoed it. The reason Crosby sang lead on 'Hey Joe' was because it was his song, the bands Roger McGuinn said in the liner notes for the album in 1966. "*He didn't write it but he was responsible for finding it. He'd wanted to do it for years but we would never let him. Then both Love and The Leaves had a minor hit with it and David got so angry that we had to let him do it.*" Crosby's version didn't really match the power of the Love and Leaves version it inspired, and he later said that recording it was "a mistake", though they did continue to play it live, including at the Monterey Pop Festival in 1967 (where Hendrix also played the song). Despite the rich history surrounding the song the liner notes for Are You Experienced call 'Hey Joe' "A blues arrangement of an old cowboy song that's about 100 years old".

Jimmy's version at this time was more moderate and gradual than the others previously released, and more blues based. Randy recalled Jimmy showing him the song; *" I kind of remember we went back to the dressing room - the boiler room, and this is where Jimmy taught me 'Hey Joe' 'Wild Thing' 'Shot Gun', and some standard blues things. I know he showed me the chords to 'Hey Joe' because I had never heard that before"*. Watching him perform such a track for the first time in Café Wha? would have been an incredible moment, especially for Chas Chandler. Chas had a reaction very similar to Linda, one of amazement that Jimmy had not been signed by anyone. Chas wanted to make Jimmy an offer, but his time in New York was limited, he had to complete a tour with The Animals before the band disbanded. The fact was though, Jimmy had already signed a deal.

Whether Jimmy took it seriously or not, he had signed the contract with PPX. He had also signed a piece of paper with Juggy Murray of Sue Records, famous for signing and launching the careers of Ike and Tina Turner. Jimmy reportedly failed to mention this to Ed Chaplin. Chas offered Jimmy the chance to play in England, he would be able to have his own band and to record. In response Jimmy didn't give too much away, and was calm and conversational, he asked about the equipment used in England and about various musicians, especially Eric Clapton who also had a reputation at the time.

Randy California recalled the moment Jimmy was offered the chance to go to England; *"It's not really that simple. There was a bunch of guys from England that showed up. I remember Keith Richards running down the street and girls following him. There was a series of meetings at a little bar across the street. We were talking about concepts and what Jimmy would do if he went to England. He was playing more Delta-type of blues material then. Jimmy asked me to go with him to England, but I was a bit too young to make that journey. I think he wanted to have another musical influence with him. I also remember Chas was courting Jimmy for a while and then Keith Richards girlfriend, Linda, bought Jimmy his own Strat. Jimmy was always borrowing guitars and having a hard time because there weren't any left-handed guitars."*

In truth, when Chas left to complete his tour with The Animals, Jimmy thought he wouldn't see him again, not paying too much attention to the offer of going to England. To Jimmy's surprise a few days later Chas returned, it was rumoured it took him around a week to locate Jimmy, and it was here that Jimmy started to realise that this could be a reality. Chas had brought along The Animals manager Mike Jeffery with him to discuss things further. Chas was full of enthusiasm, he simply said to Jimmy, *"Let's Go"*.

Randy reflected on his time with Jimmy; *"Jimi was a very spiritually attuned person. He was always searching for the truth - the reality of life! The answers to some of his questions appeared in some of his songs via his imagination, his hopes and his dreams for humanity. I love the quote on the back of the 'Cry Of Love' album – 'Hello My Friend...' - it's kind of like an exit statement in a way. It's so intense, so beautiful, so spiritual. He had so much compassion for what was going on. Even though I was at a very young age when I worked with him, I could tell he was a very loving, caring and open person.*

Interestingly, up to this point, Jimmy had written to his father Al on most things that he was doing or involved with. On this decision, however, he wrote to no one. It was as if he was there one minute and gone the next. No one in his family back in Seattle, or any of the musicians around New York that had played with him, knew anything about Jimmy confirming the trip to England. Many didn't even realise he was gone: one minute he was Jimmy James and the Blue Flames gigging around New York, and the next he appeared as a superstar in England; and when they did catch up with him, he was renamed. He was Jimi Hendrix.

Chapter 9

Music Is My Religion.

"When things get too heavy, just call me helium, the lightest known gas to man."

Whether Jimmy strenuously considered the trip to England or simply nonchalantly agreed is up for debate. Either way the offer he was given was accepted and plans were put in place. The trip would transform Jimmy into a star, and ultimately a legend, simply put London would not know what hit it. His initial thought was to take Randy California along for the trip, but he was persuaded against this due to Randy's young age, there was also the fact that he was a second guitarist, something that Chas was against. The only person within the musical inner circle that Jimmy contacted about the trip was his old friend Billy Cox.

It was on Saturday 24th September 1966 that Jimmy landed in London. He travelled first class and hit the tarmac at London Airport at 9am, it would change its name to Heathrow the same year. All he travelled with was a single change of clothes, some cream to wash his face, a set of hair curlers, $40 (which he'd borrowed) and a Fender Stratocaster.

Getting into the UK proved difficult for Jimmy, he didn't have a work permit, it was The Animals roadie Terry McVay that carried Jimmy's guitar through immigration, Jimmy walked through with virtually nothing, and of course the way he looked would have flagged attention at the border in 1966 London. Initially, because there was no permit, Jimmy was denied access, his visa was stamped as cancelled. It was Chas Chandler that reportedly convinced immigration that he was someone special, a gifted songwriter that was visiting the UK just for a short period to collect some royalties that were owed. The story worked; Jimmy was granted a two-week non-work visa, it later emerged that his passport was actually forged, it needed to be signed by someone who knew Jimmy for many years, the only people that could verify were in Seattle, and Chas couldn't travel that far. Getting into England was a battle, but Jimmy eventually entered the country and travelled on to London.

Once through the airport, Chas decided to take him to number 11 Gunterstone Road, West Kensington, the home of British musician Zoot Money. Zoot was a major figure on the Soho music scene at the time, his house was on route to central London from the airport and became a sort of stop off point for musicians travelling to the capital. Whilst at the house, Jimmy, now Jimi, took part in jamming sessions with Zoot's friend, Andy Summers - who would later go on to play with The Police. At the time Andy was living in the basement part of the house, he later recalled this initial meeting, and subsequent jamming sessions; he described Jimi as being *"from another planet"* and recalled an impromptu jam with the guitar icon, during a recent chat with Rick Beato. Summers was establishing himself within London's blues scene when Jimmy arrived and *"blew everyone out of the water"*. Walking into one of his first UK shows at London's Cromwellian Club, he very quickly understood what all the fuss was about. Says Summers: *"I walked into this club to see this guy, and there he was with an afro this wide, wearing all-white buckskin with the fringes and he had a white Strat in his mouth. It was an incredible vision to walk into. It was a mindfuck. His was like a being from outer space,"* he continues. *"There were all these wannabe blues players in London, and then there was Jimi, who was from another planet. It had a lot of shock value. A lot of famous players were blown out of the water completely."* Soon, Summers said the scene "somehow" moved over to LA. There, he was invited to meet up with Jimi at A&M Studios. Little did he know, this would lead to an impromptu jam with the blues icon. *"I walked into the studio and there was Jimi wailing away. He had the hat on with the feather and he was just going for it; classic Hendrix. He was a very shy guy. He was an introvert; it was all in the guitar playing. So he gave us a wave, put the guitar down and we talked a little bit. Then Jimi starts talking with Eddie Kramer, the engineer, so I go into the other room where Mitch was. There was a Les Paul and it was right-handed, I don't know why it was there,"* he expands. *"And it was probably outrageous that I even dared to do it, but I picked it up and I started jamming with Mitch. It's all going great, then Jimi comes up, picks up the bass and starts playing with us. We played for about 10 minutes and then Jimi turned round and said, 'Hey man, mind if I play the guitar for a while?' So I picked up the bass and we played for about half an hour. That was a good moment; that was probably the last time I saw him"*.

Zoot had his own band, heavily influenced by James Brown, Ray Charles and Jimmy Smith. Jimi enjoyed jamming at the house, this was during the day time when all the equipment was stored, in the evenings it was packed up for various gigs. Zoot recalled the first guitar Jimi played when he arrived at his house; sitting proudly with the guitar on his lap he explained *"I bought it some fifty years ago, it was known as a Teenager blue jean model, also known as Italian fetish guitars. I got it because I needed something to play on stage, I had it in my house for many years. However, when I first got it, I had a visitation from Chas Chandler and Jimi Hendrix* when they got off the plane, they needed a guitar to play that night, so I said you can use this if you like and he had a little tinker on it. This is the first guitar Jimi Hendrix played in this country."

Zoot was amazed with Jimmy's skill and ingenuity, as was everyone who witnessed his talent. His wife Ronnie was also awestruck by what she was witnessing, this exotic American guy playing in her living room. She wasn't the only female in the house, sharing the top floor flat was 19-year-old Kathy Etchingham.

Kathy became an integral part in Jimmy's life, she recalled to the BBC some of her memories of him at that time; *"Jimmy Hendrix hit the London scene like a bomb, every band, every guitarist wanted to see him. We went down to the Scotch, and everyone was standing perfectly still, listening to this guy, I'd never seen anyone quite like him. But he'd called me over to sit next to him, and he said, 'I think you're beautiful', I thought that's corny, but it worked."* She also remembered Jimmy adjusting to England, *"He'd never crossed a road in England before, he'd only arrived that morning and I looked to see if there was a taxi coming, and Jimmy looked in the opposite direction coming from America, stepped out and nearly got ran over. I grabbed him by the back of his jacket just in time, pulled him back, otherwise there wouldn't have been any Jimi Hendrix, he would have been squashed there and then. That night at the hotel we talked all night, he was just a very gentle sort of person, we suddenly became boyfriend and girlfriend. It stayed like that for two and a half years. It wasn't exactly glamourous in those early days, we stayed in a lot, we played games, we played monopoly, we played risk."*

London at this point was truly swinging, a cosmopolitan cultural hub, bristling with rock stars, models and wannabees. The Scotch was located at Masons Yard near to The Houses of Parliament and St James Square. It would hit the headlines later through its then owners Louis Brown and John Bloom, relating to its finances and a washing machine business that collapsed. The Scotch officially opened its doors on 14th July 1965, for the first time. At the time it stood as just another club opening on the London circuit, but it quickly became a popular and trendy place to be seen. This small after-hours nightclub would become one of the epicenters of the swinging sixties. Attending the launch were three members of the Beatles, all the Rolling Stones - except for Charlie - and members of The Who, The Kinks, The Animals and The Hollies. Obviously with The Animals, Chas had experience of the club, hence why Jimi was quickly booked in for this night. It was a great location to get Jimi seen for the first time, just about every known face from the 1960s music scene could have been spotted at some point, making their way through cobble-paved Mason's Yard to enter The Scotch of St. James, through its heavy wooden doors. Nearby clubs such as the Ad-Lib in Leicester Square and Blaises in Kensington were all pretty much in sync for attracting the 'in' people of the time, fashion designers, rock/ pop stars and various socialites.

As Kathy remembered, the crowd stood motionless as Jimmy performed, he wasn't on that long, a strategy by Chas to give just enough to have people talk about him. Another reason perhaps was the work permit issue, limiting his time. During the next few weeks Jimmy and Kathy were inseparable, she took him all over London and showed him the sites, it would become the longest relationship in his life. Chas honoured his promise for Jimi to meet Clapton and arranged for Jimi to attend the Polytechnic on 1st October 1966. At this point Cream were just becoming established to the wider public but were highly regarded within the music world. Clapton in particular already had the reputation as the greatest guitarist in England, for now. Upon meeting Clapton and engaging in a brief jam session, it was agreed that Jimi would join the band that evening, despite Ginger Baker's apparent displeasure with the arrangement. They decided that Jimmy could perform as long as Clapton was not on stage. The British audience, accustomed to a more reserved musical style, was left astonished by Jimmy's daring musical talent. He introduced a wave of vibrant, psychedelic genius to the scene. Clapton, as the nation's undisputed guitar virtuoso, was front and centre of this amazement. Clapton immediately acknowledged the new formidable music contender, willingly relinquishing the spotlight. It stood as a testament to the respect and camaraderie that would develop between them. At that time, Clapton and his band, Cream, were at the forefront of London's music scene and had already made significant strides in the emerging psychedelic rock genre. Chas Chandler had previously considered adding a keyboardist, but he and Jimmy ultimately decided to emulate Cream's three-piece setup. This move signalled a direct challenge and indicated an impending transformation in the musical landscape.

Jimmy took to the stage for a rendition of the Howlin' Wolf classic, 'Killing Floor'. Clapton said in later interviews that this was a song he always struggled with, after watching Jimmy for a few minutes however he walked off to the side, stood and watched. Reminiscing in 1989, he said of the performance, *"He played just about every style you could think of, and not in a flashy way. I mean he did a few of his tricks, like playing with his teeth and behind his back, but it wasn't in an upstaging sense at all, and that was it ... he walked off, and my life was never the same again"*.

At this time Keith Altham was a rock journalist working for The Guardian newspaper; he recalls the meeting between Clapton and Hendrix; *"Chas Chandler going backstage after Clapton left in the middle of the song 'which he had yet to master himself'; Clapton was furiously puffing* on a cigarette and telling Chas: *'You never told me he was that fucking good.'* Chandler had clearly discovered not just a talented artist, but also a genuine contender for a position of power". What happened to Clapton repeated with other guitar greats of the time, Pete Townshend and Jeff Beck had similar encounters. The best in town were no longer, Jimi scared them all.

In 2019, Townshend recounted to Rolling Stone magazine about the first time he witnessed Hendrix's greatness, a moment which is seemingly a clear memory that has become engrained in his mind. *"Well, that was a cosmic experience,"* he shared. *"It was at Blazes, the nightclub in London. He was pretty amazing. Now I think you have to have seen Jimi Hendrix to understand what he was really about. He was a wonderful player,"* Townshend uncharacteristically noted with humility. *"He wasn't a great singer but he had a beautiful voice. A smokey voice, a really sexy voice… When you saw him in the live arena he was like a shaman. It's the only word I can use. I don't know if it's the right term. Light seemed to come out of him. He would walk onstage and suddenly he would explode into light. He was very graceful."*

There are many accounts of Jimi's impact on the London Rock scene when he first arrived. One fan wrote a summary that was later released in 1973; *"Hendrix had unbelievable impact with amazingly powerful psychedelic blues, the heaviest rock ever heard at that time, a supremely cool vocal drawl, dope-and-Dylan-orientated lyrics, the acid dandyism of his clothes, and the stirring element of black sexual fantasy. Evidently, it was not only his guitar playing that impressed!"*

In an interview back in 2016, Jeff Beck recalled the power of experiencing Jimmy for the first time: *"It was probably one of the first shows he did (in London). It was in a tiny downstairs club. It was a fashion club - mostly girls, 18 to 25, all dolled up, hats and all. Jimi wasn't known then. He came on, and I went, 'Oh, my God.' He had the military outfit on and hair that stuck out all over the place. They kicked off with (Bob Dylan's) Like a Rolling Stone, and I thought, 'Well, I used to be a guitarist."* During the same interview he was asked if he had the chance to know him well, to which he replied: *"As well as you could in the fleeting moments. When the Jeff Beck Group played the scene (in New York in 1968), he was there most nights. What an education, having him come in with his guitar. One night he played mine. He didn't have his guitar. I ended up playing bass. There's a photo. Jimi's in the shot; Ron Wood is in the background. You don't even see me in the picture."*

Jeff Beck released his first solo album "Truth" in 1968 when Jimmy was still alive. The record had Ronnie Wood as the bassist, who would obviously later become The Faces and The Rolling Stones guitarist. Eric Clapton was with Jeff Beck at that show as Beck recalled in an interview with Classic Rock in 2021, saying *it was 'quite devastating' to see Hendrix do all his tricks with the guitar: "When I saw Jimi we knew he was going to be trouble, and by 'we' I mean me and Eric, because Jimmy Page wasn't in the frame at that point. I saw him at one of his earliest performances in Britain. It was quite devastating. He did all the dirty tricks - setting fire to his guitar, doing swoops up and down his neck. All the great showmanship to put the final nail in our coffin. I had the same temperament as Hendrix in terms of 'I'll kill you'. But he did it in such a good package with beautiful songs."*

Additionally in an interview back in the 80's, Jeff Beck talked about meeting Jimmy. He recalled that the first person who said Hendrix's name to him was some girlfriend who called him in the morning and said *"You gotta hear this guy Jimmy Hendrix. I was at a club last night, it's unbelievable"*. Jeff Beck then went to see Hendrix and was so impressed by his talent that he kept an eye on what he was playing and what he was doing: *"I followed him around a bit. He'd heard of me, which I couldn't believe, you know"*. When the two finally met face to face, Jeff Beck recalled that Hendrix even asked him about his music: *"What is that lick you play in 'Happening Ten Years Time Ago' (from the Yardbirds)"*, Jimmy asked and then continued saying *"I swiped that on this"*. Jeff Beck then said he thought at that moment: *"This is really incredible; this is kind of like we could talk music now, instead of he is an 'immovable force'. I can actually get some inspiration, and he was a great source of inspiration. The fact that he was doing things so upfront and so wild."*

Jimmy was now highly sought after, not just musically on stage, but as someone to be around, to hang with, to be seen with, he was becoming talked about within inner circles. He was someone who the elite liked, because he wasn't in the mainstream just yet. It was obvious that he would be soon, but at this moment he was more an underground artist, someone to boast about if you actually knew him or had seen him. It kind of elevated your own status if you knew or were friends with Jimmy Hendrix. The cinema was a popular place for Jimmy; he loved to go and just watch what was on. Musicians were looking for him on evenings, trying to find out where he was so they could sit with him, talk to him or simply be around him. Paul McCartney, Mick Jagger, Brian Jones, John Lennon, Eric Clapton, all became encircled around Jimi, the genius guitar man that had come to London looking for fame and fortune. There was a feeling of pride in this, that Jimi was actually trawling the same small clubs which many of the stars of the day were performing at, they felt a protection towards him, as Mick Jagger famously said, *"He was ours"*.

It's important to add here, that although Jimmy's reputation was becoming plauded from all the inner circles of the music fraternity, outside of this it was still challenging in certain areas of public life for a young black man in England at the time. It wasn't all adoration and admiration, off stage Jimmy felt it, as he did in areas of the USA. In England in the 1960s it was not too far from the end of World War two, the country was still on a rebuild, structurally, economically and socially. The 1970s in England were particularly difficult, with much unemployment and social issues, and this wasn't too far ahead. The present was infamous for being the swinging 60s, a time of freedom of expression and the rise of some of the most iconic musical influences and archetypical fashion statements the world had seen, it was always reflected upon as a golden time in the cultural landscape of music.

Behind the glamour though, England was in the midst of the now infamous *'Windrush Generation'*, named after the ship HMT Empire Windrush that arrived in 1948 from the Caribbean. Windrush represented the thousands of people who migrated to the UK between 1948 and 1971. They were invited to help rebuild the country after the devastation of World War II and address labour shortages in key sectors. The Windrush immigrants made valuable contributions to British society, these included areas such as healthcare, transportation, manufacturing and public services. They were an integral part of the post-war reconstruction efforts and added significantly to the economic and cultural fabric of the UK. Despite this they encountered initial discrimination and prejudice.

Even though they had been invited by the British government, who at the time were desperate for workers, the Windrush generation faced pervasive discrimination and prejudice from the moment they arrived. It was a stark contrast to the initial welcoming promises they had received. Many found themselves confronted with a hostile environment, experiencing racism in various aspects of daily life. In housing, it was not unusual, astonishing though it may seem to us today, for rental listings to include signs that read *'No Blacks, No Irish, No Dogs'*. Not only was this demoralising and degrading for the newly arrived immigrants, but it also made it very difficult for black people and their families to secure accommodation. Housing discrimination exacerbated racial segregation, contributing to the isolation of black communities. To help to try and counter this, the government set up a legal framework to assist in discrimination. The reason that black people were powerless to protect themselves at that time was because during the 1950s and 1960s, the UK lacked specific anti-discrimination legislation, which allowed systemic racism to persist. Discriminatory practices and policies were deeply entrenched in various areas, including employment, public services and housing. For example, in employment, black workers faced wage disparities, receiving lower pay for the same work as their white counterparts. They also encountered barriers to career progression and faced discrimination when seeking employment opportunities. They could be overlooked for jobs or promotions just because of the colour of their skin. Because of the system that was set up, there was no recourse for them to take.

This was also widely evident in the music industry, especially in the USA, where music was divided between white and black artists. Emerging black artists like Jimmy, as he was then, faced these challenges, notably on the chitlin' circuit and within the segregation of black charts from the mainstream billboard charts. It wasn't until the early 1980s, with the rise of MTV, that black artists like Whitney Houston, Prince, Lionel Richie, and Michael Jackson gained equal exposure.

Despite these inequalities, Jimmy pushed on regardless, he continued to stun London audiences wherever he performed with his musical talent. Chas began the search for a band for Jimmy to perform with, a stable one that would allow him to become established, a simple three piece that would allow Jimmy to be front and centre. To this point Jimmy had been in many bands, and even his own collaborations on stage were subject to change. Now, he needed an identity to move forward with, and one with a name. In his short time in London, he had already blown the best of the best out of the water. It was time for Jimmy to become Jimi, and time for him to get truly experienced.

Chapter 10.

Butterflies and Zebras

"In order to change the world, you have to get your head together first".

Although Jimmy had been performing regularly, and gaining adoration wherever he went, there was still to this point a tentative feeling from those around him regarding his work status, they were still unsure if he would be officially allowed to stay. It was on September 28th that Jimi eventually got his work permit, which had been granted until the end of the year. It was a relief, especially in respect to his issues in getting into England in the first place. He was now free to push forward.

The Harold Davidson agency was a key driver for various auditions in London in the 1960s. It was Harold Davison himself that introduced Frank Sinatra to European audiences and was acknowledged for being instrumental in launching British rock to America. London based, he was a key talent agent, manager, producer and executive during his illustrious career that began at the end of the Second World War. He was renowned for becoming the first to book concerts in the UK and continental Europe by Sinatra, Ella Fitzgerald, Judy Garland and Bing Crosby. During the forthcoming Rock 'n' Roll era, Davison was a strategist for the British invasion, launching the Rolling Stones and the Dave Clark Five on the American scene. He would later go on to play a key role in the merger of EMI and Capitol Records.

Around the same time as Jimmy was granted his work permit, there were some rumours circulating that the Howard Davidson Agency were possibly holding auditions for a guitarist. These rumours were picked up by a guitarist named Noel Redding. Noel was out of work at the time and on the brink of quitting music altogether. Previously, he had toured clubs in Scotland and Germany alongside Neil Landon and the Burnette's who were formed in late 1962. He also toured briefly with the Loving Kind who formed in November 1965. He had also played with various bands supporting bigger ones, such as The Beatles and The Hollies, but he hadn't worked since. He entered the offices at Harold Davidson enquiring about auditions for Eric Burdon's New Animals, Noel was approaching his 21st birthday and saw it as a kind of last chance in his ambitions of becoming a permanent musician.

Disillusioned with the whole music industry, he had come to the conclusion that if this opportunity didn't work out, he was going to become a milkman back in his hometown of Folkestone, Kent. During an interview in 2000 he spoke about these early years. *"I first began playing music when I was about 9 and when I was about 12, I got an acoustic guitar and started playing. When I was about 15, I got my own little group together, called The Lonely Ones. At grammar School I was asked if I should become a commercial artist or a musician, I choose musician. I should have chosen commercial artist; I would have earned more; I went professional when I was about 17. I was disillusioned because there was a lot of guitar players about, but I realised there were no drummers in Kent, so I suddenly thought I'd take the train to London and take my guitar and amp, swap it, and get a drum kit. On the way to London, I'd read in The Melody Maker or one of the musical papers that Eric Burden was auditioning for the new Animals."*

Noel was told to head for an audition with Chas, who was putting together a band with Eric Burdon. He asked to join The Animals but there was no position for this, it was recently filled, Noel was too late. Chas informed Noel though, that there could be something alongside a guy from America, it would have to be bass though. Noel agreed. Reflecting on this he recalled, *"I attempted to blag my way in, which I did, but they'd got a guitar player by then, at which point Mr. Chas Chandler, the late bass player for The Animals and our producer and manager, God bless him, came up to me and said, 'can I play bass?', and I said 'No, but I'll give it a go'. We played three tunes with this American gentleman, myself, a keyboard player and a drummer. This American gentleman said, 'Would you like to go down the pub?', which is what most musicians say, 'Of Course', and we went down to this little pub, and he had a pint of bitter, which he was just getting used to, and we got talking about music. He was asking me about the English music scene and I was asking him about the American music scene, I'd never been there at that point, and he said, 'Would I like to join his group?'. And that was it, that was Mr. James Hendrix."*

Although Noel had no direct experience on bass, Jimmy did. He'd been playing bass for quite a while sitting here and there with various bands. He knew exactly what he wanted from a bass player. In addition, Jimmy could give instructions and mold Noel into the style he wanted, he would have no preconceptions and would be shown a style by Jimmy that best suited him as a frontman. Jimmy also liked the way Noel looked, a huge tight brown afro that shouted out non-conformist. Jimmy had his bass player; it was now onto drums.

Mitch Mitchell was a seasoned London drummer, he was self-taught and had been around the circuit for quite some time, most notably with

Georgie Fame and the Blue Flames, but had also gained a wealth of musical experience via stints with several early sixties' bands including the Tornados, the Coronets and the Riot Squad. He was born John Graham 'Mitch' Michell in Ealing, West London and had his first taste of show business as a child actor, appearing in BBC television's Jennings at School. Whilst still at school, Mitch worked at Marshall drum shop in Hanwell, run by Jim Marshall in North West London. Previously, he had auditioned alongside several others for The Who, only to be trumped by Keith Moon. Georgie Flame and the Blue Flames split on October 1, 1966. Just 5 days later, on October 6, he attended his first rehearsal with Jimmy's band. Mitch provided the perfect accompaniment for Jimmy's music, embellishing it with his lavish style. He could play anything for the band, straight punchy rock songs, blues, R&B or jazz. He matched Jimmy all the way, even pushing and inspiring him at the same time. Like Noel, Mitch had not heard of Jimmy prior to rehearsal. The new trio jammed together for around four hours.

Drummers are unique to any band, but in a three piece they are transformed and elevated, they become more than the standard guy at the back keeping time. They can ad lib, solo and express themselves more freely, especially with someone like Jimmy Hendrix up front. They are the strong bedrock from which the magic arises, often hidden at the back and unfairly eclipsed by their outfield teammates. To make themselves heard, rock drummers must be thunderous, a musical refusal to be sidelined, examples like John Bonham and Keith Moon, or if not thunderous in approach, then unconventionally dynamic like Ginger Baker. Mitch Mitchell fell into the latter and would go on to compliment Jimmy perfectly. In Mitch's head Jimmy was his guitarist, a mindset that all the best drummers have, in reality of course, it was Jimmy that was very much the figurehead of his band. Still, it is quite remarkable, or musical fate, that he would form a band with the Hendrix of the drumming world. Mitch was interviewed in 1998; he remembered jamming with Jimmy in an audition session of sorts. He said at the time that the trio, sculpted by Chandler, reminded him of Cream; Eric Clapton, Jack Bruce and Ginger Baker; *"I came out with some facetious comment like, 'So, you want me to try to play like Ginger Baker or something?' Jimi just goes, 'Oh, yeah, whatever you want, man.'"*

The set up was something different for the three members of the new band, it gave them an incredible amount of musical flexibility, something they would not have in a standard band, something they weren't used to. *"It was like a feeling of freedom,"* he reflected. *"I don't know if it's a spiritual awakening. It was just a situation where I'd gone, 'Hey, you've never worked in a three-piece band in your life, ever, and there is something with this player that is very, very special.'"* Mitch Mitchell wasn't the only drummer that was auditioned, Chas and Jimmy had received applications from several other London-based drummers. *"London's not that large a place, and in those days, there weren't that many drummers about,"* he added. *"A lot of my peers, colleagues - call them what you will - they'd gone for the job. Aynsley Dunbar and Mickey Waller had gone and knew about this guy, and they wanted the job, basically. That's what surprised me because I didn't hear about it."* Despite being impressed with Mitch, Jimmy and Chas were initially undecided on which drummer to take, they whittled it down to two, between Mitch and Aynsley Dunbar. It was Mitch who got the job, rumoured to be decided after a coin toss.

As with Noels audition, a keyboard player was present in a four-piece set-up; they even switched Noel onto rhythm guitar at one stage to see if it would work, it didn't, there was only one guitarist needed. It was on the second audition, that the soon to be power trio gelled for the first time; and in the third, Mitchell received his official offer. *"I think I actually asked Chas, the manager, 'What's on offer? What's the deal here?'"* Mitchell recalled. *"Well, look. We've got nothing apart from a chance,"* Chandler replied. It was a chance, and one of course that was to be an immortal success. At the time, Mitch was just 19 years old. Chandler offered him just two weeks' work to begin with, and since he was impressed with Jimmy's guitar ability, he said he'd give it a crack. *"We had no songs when we first started."* he recalled.

It is widely believed that Jimmy became Jimi during conversations on the flight across the Atlantic from America to England. This is highly plausible considering the planning that would have been in place to launch Jimmy in London. It was now though, with the band in place that the conversation turned more seriously to agree a name. The fact was though, that despite Noel and Mitch being talented musicians in their own right, they were there initially to simply back up Jimmy. They were paid musicians, simply to showcase Jimmy Hendrix, who was the focus, the star in the making. When Chas first saw Jimmy James performing 'Hey Joe' underground in New York, that is exactly what he saw, Jimmy James, nothing else.

Changing the spelling of Jimmy to Jimi was a simple way to get him recognised and to stand out more. The backing band name of *'Experience'* was suggested in discussion. Initially this was to be 'Jimi Hendrix and the Experience'. Chas decided that the *'and the'* should be dropped. This puts the focus on Jimi, by making it *The Jimi Hendrix Experience*. If the 'and the' stayed in place it would put the backing band as an identity in their own right; You would have 'Jimi Hendrix', and you would have 'The Experience', its two separate things. The Jimi Hendrix Experience makes it all about him, if it didn't work out, the bass player and drummer could be replaced, who would care? Who would notice? Most musical minded people could easily name the members of Cream as a trio, because they were 'all' Cream. With 'The Jimi Hendrix Experience' it was all about Jimi. Unfortunately for Noel Redding and Mitch Mitchell, despite their talent, they were simply a backing band, Jimi was just too much of a phenomenon, and the name change reflected this. He was now Jimi Hendrix.

In the background to all these decisions was manager Michael Jeffery, who many described as being an untrustworthy character with links to organised crime, which proved to be the case as time went on. It was alleged that while he managed The Animals, all cash went into an offshore account for tax purposes, and this would be the same company that all of Jimi's money would later be filtered through, Yamata. For now, he was managing things behind the scenes, with Chas being more hands on, but later Michael Jeffery would become an integral part of Jimi's career, especially in the last days of his life. While Jimi was a child and learning his trade in Seattle, Michael Jeffery was in the British Army, there were even rumours that he was in the secret service, with connections to SAS and MI5, but this could have been fabricated and just hearsay. He was also reported to have worked undercover in Egypt working for the Intelligence Corps. He could speak Russian and was reputed to have been dropped into Russia at the heart of the cold war. He joked that all his accounts should be in Russian. Many of Michael Jeffery's early nightclubs had burned down, and with the insurance money, new and larger venues soon emerged - it was jokingly circulated that he had his own fire engine. It was safe to say Michael Jeffery was not your typical management profile. Later, Jimi would find this out to his own cost.

The music industry was cutthroat, both figuratively and literally, and most bands during the 50s and 60s earned their dues in clubs, seedy dark places, often until the early hours of the morning. The Chitlin circuit in the USA where Jimi honed his craft was notorious for it, the mainly black acts controlled and managed by white business men. These acts often just received a wage, there was no telling what was made. Contracts were also signed without much scrutiny, a common issue for any act that became famous, even the likes of Elvis Presley, with Colonel Tom Parker, had major issues with contracts and agreements signed. Jimi would be no different.

Many of the high-profile acts started to have high profile managers, individuals who wanted to be just as important as the actual act themselves, flamboyant characters who wanted to build empires, to gain control. Robert Stigwood was one of the key players, he managed Cream at this time and went on to manage Andy Gibb and the Bee Gees. He moved into theatrical productions with Hair and Jesus Christ Superstar, and film productions including Grease and Saturday Night Fever. He became one of the most powerful individuals in the entertainment industry: He was a true mogul owning the record label that issued the artists' albums and film soundtracks, and he also controlled publishing rights. Andrew Oldham for the Rolling Stones was also massively ambitious, there was Kit Lambert controlling The Who and of course Brian Epstein with The Beatles. They all wanted to be respected in their own right, and some even craved the limelight more than the actual bands they represented.

Jimi was surrounded by these key bands, and of course must have observed the managers around them, it was the norm for bands to have high profile management looking after their affairs, which is why many were vulnerable to the sharp businessmen who looked after their finances. Jimi was listening to all music at this point and often compared what England was doing in comparison to America, especially with the British invasion taking place; on The Beatles he once said, *"They're one group that you can't really put down because they're just too much. And it's so embarrassing, man, when America is sending over the Monkees - oh, God, that kills me!"* Jimi's comments here on The Monkees would be something that would come to haunt him later on, especially while under the management of Mike Jeffery.

Mike was a different character to these other managers, he was in the background, almost in the shadows it seemed. He owned clubs in Newcastle, England and regularly had issues with rival gangs trying to put him out of business, he would go toe to toe with these types if needed and was notorious in these circles as an individual who, behind the big smile, was not to be messed with. Previously, he had managed the girl group Goldie and the Gingerbreads as well as, of course, The Animals.

Chas was convinced that Mike had taken cash from the Animals, they had the adoration, they were front and centre with the fame, but it was Mike Jeffery who amassed the fortune. The Animals had broken up, and although Chas had his suspicions of Mike, and with good reason, he was also quite savvy himself. Going into agreement with him on Jimi was a good move, he knew Mike was smart and he stayed close to him. The keyboardist for The Animals, Alan Price had set up his own band after The Animals had split, 'The Alan Price Set', Chas had agreed with Mike to have an equal stake for both The Alan Price Set and Jimi.

It seemed quite common for managers of rock stars in the 50s and 60s to be underhand in some way, the very fact that they handled their affairs was easy to manipulate, especially if managers had other forms of business, such as nightclubs. Here, monies could be put through these places, or even in offshore accounts, which was the way Mike Jeffery liked to operate. In the US, it was the Mafia that were interested in the wider entertainment industry, they had a grip on a variety of different businesses that would turn a profit, and the music industry at the time was one of the most lucrative out there. When the first British invasion occurred, and then the second, with the likes of Led Zeppelin and others, the Mafia took a particular shine towards music. They saw it as a great place to operate. One of the main reasons for this was that many of the transactions that took place in music were made in cash. This was more in the live aspect of music, through performances in clubs etc, the actual sales of records through the industry was a little trickier to manipulate. The drinks bought at nightclubs, deals for performances, attendance at events and spending going into jukeboxes were all cash purchases. It was where the continual cash flow happened within the industry, so this was where the interest was.

On the business side, a significant portion of the capital generated by organised crime at the time came from selling publishing rights for various songs, which provided a profitable revenue stream. It was also straightforward for these groups to expand into other business ventures, often interconnected through the music industry. For example, by purchasing bars and venues, they could conduct multiple business activities simultaneously in one night. Due to the extensive involvement of organised crime in the music industry, it was relatively common for musicians to encounter risky situations while touring. At that time, bands were often composed of individuals who differed from the typical person; they were dreamers, dropouts, or creatives not suited for conventional jobs. Although they sometimes presented a tough exterior, they did not operate on the same level as experienced organised crime members. Consequently, they required managers who could secure favourable recording contracts and tours, as well as handle potential issues that may occur when touring. For instance, when The Yardbirds were on tour, they faced a serious situation when a group entered their tour bus and brandished firearms after the band arrived late to a performance. Their manager, Peter Grant, who had connections with organised crime, was able to manage the situation and smooth things over. If bands wanted to make it big in music, it was a given that they would encounter some dodgy characters at some point. So, often, it was left to the band managers to be in a position to step in if things were ever going badly. If bands didn't have a good muscle manager, they were almost guaranteed to get screwed over. This was one area where someone like Mike Jeffery was capable, he had a reputation for being a solid businessman, and someone who should not be crossed.

Jimi did contact his father at this point after arriving in England. Later he recalled the conversation, he was clearly in a reflective mood as his fame was rising, *"I just called my dad once when I came to England to let him know I'd reached something. He asked me who I had robbed to get the money to go to England, actually, I'm scared to go home. My father is a very strict man. He would straight away grab hold of me, tear my clothes off and cut my hair!"*

Mike Jeffery arranged for a short promotional outing for Jimi, just four dates alongside Johnny Hallyday, the man widely credited for bringing Rock 'n' Roll to France, he was sometimes known as the 'Elvis of France'. Johnny remembered his time with Jimi during an interview in 1993: *"My favorite musicians are American. In the early '60s, Eddie Cochran and Gene Vincent. After that, Creedence Clearwater Revival, and after that, Rick James a little bit. And Jimi Hendrix. You know, he was my opening act for a while. I discovered him in London at a club one night. I was with Otis Redding, and we were eating at the restaurant of the club, and we heard about this incredible guitar. We went to see who was playing, and it was Jimi. I was about to start a tour in Europe, and I needed an opening act and said, 'Do you want to do it?' And he said, 'Yeah.' So he toured with me for six months, and we became friends. After he did Hey Joe, he said, 'I have a version I'm not using. Do you want it?' I said, 'Yeah.' I went to London and recorded Hey Joe in French, with Jimi Hendrix playing acoustic behind. It became a No. 1 hit for two months"*.

There were many others during this period that were witnessing Jimi for the first time, and everyone who did remembered it vividly, Jimi was something very special and witnessing him play for the first time was a moment nobody forgot. Mick Jones was one such musician. Mick would go onto to be the guitarist with Foreigner and later become inducted into the Rock 'n' Roll Hall of fame, at this time he was the in the backing band with Johnny Hallyday and recalled seeing Jimi for the first time and watching him play during the short tour. Mick recalled: *"Johnny Hallyday was doing a tour and we needed musicians to back him up, so we were out one night at a club in London, The Cromwellian, where [British jazz/rock star] Brian Auger was playing. Jimi got up to jam with him and he just tore the place apart. He was extraordinary. He had this charisma about him before he even picked up his guitar. And when he played the blues, it was unbelievable. I'd never heard or seen anything like it and nor had anybody else. So that evening, they did the deal in the club to take The Jimi Hendrix Experience to France for a month's tour, opening for Johnny."* As Mick remembered it, Johnny Hallyday's fans were completely bemused by Hendrix's performances. *"Those people didn't know what hit them!"* he laughed. *"They were sitting there aghast. I'd watch Jimi every night from the side of the stage, and I was amazed. You had Eric Clapton and Jeff Beck and all these great guitar players, but Jimi blew everybody's socks off!" Mick also recalled how different Hendrix was offstage. *"He was beautiful,"* Mick said. *"Kind of shy offstage, very mellow and warm. He was on his own little planet, but we had a lot of fun together."*

Jimi and his new band mates performed well on the first night of the tour, it was the second performance however that seemed to light the touchpaper, this was in Paris at the 14,500-seater L'Olympia. It was from here with The Experience, that Jimi truly started the redefining of rock music. Alongside him, Noel Redding on bass and Mitch Mitchell on drums formed the revolving core of the Jimi Hendrix Experience. This trio was a cohesive unit, with Redding and Mitchell providing a dynamic backdrop that ranged from intense rhythms to spontaneous bursts of energy, perfectly complementing Jimi's. 'Hey Joe', was played at all the venues Jimi performed at, and this was now sighted as the first single to release. To all purposes however, Jimi Hendrix was a live act, it was here that he would consistently showcase an innovative and pioneering approach, creating an unforgettable impact on the world of music. It was a musical force, unlike anything seen before on stage, unleashing a storm that defied mere musicianship

The Jimi Hendrix Experience was a unique band, with the guitar virtuoso now front and center. Jimi wielded his guitar as a sonic paintbrush, conjuring both whispers and screams from the strings, telling tales that transcended mere riffs. The trio worked seamlessly together. Noel became a bedrock of rumbling thunder, his basslines anchoring the chaos with earthy grooves that pulsed through the stage. At the back, but by no means out of sight was Mitch, a rhythmic maelstrom, his drums a whirlwind of precision and controlled fury, shattering the boundaries of timekeeping.

It was reported that Noel and Mitch were paid £15 per week for their talents, Jimi's salary slightly more, but not that much. It did however, allow him to move in with Kathy. On December 6th they moved into a flat on Montagu Square, formerly owned by Ringo Starr. She had quit her job and was now with Jimi as much as possible. They worked well together, he helped her, guided her and in turn she introduced him to key people in London, helping him navigate the city and the people within it.

It was now time to head to the studio for Jimi to record his first release. On 23rd October 1966 he was booked into De Lane Studio in Kingsway scheduled to record two versions of 'Hey Joe' and 'Stone Free'. Today, the studio is covered by a modern office block and a chemist, but 129 Kingsway was once home to a branch of Midland bank, and the basement of the building harbored a recording studio. It was originally established by advertising firm, SH Benson as a workshop for capturing voice overs and catchy jingles. The studio was acquired in the 1960s by Major Jacques De

Lane Lea; a French intelligence attaché who ran a side-line dubbing English films into French. In 1965 De Lane Lea expanded his facilities considerably, installing a top-of-the-range sound desk which soon began to attract some of the greatest names in music. During Jimi's sessions at the studio, he completed *'Hey Joe'* and *'Stone Free'* as planned. There were some tensions during the sessions, mainly because the studio was not geared for high volumes, that said it was perfect for Jimi's vocals, and the tracks were eventually completed without issue.

Jimi was now settled into London life. He was happy at this time, his band was in place, and he'd moved in with his girlfriend Kathy, the pair becoming inseparable. Jimi enjoyed London and spent many hours when he wasn't rehearsing and gigging, recording or partying, exploring London's streets. He described it as a "storybook", and took particular inspiration from the city's parks, statues, churches and stained-glass windows. *"One of the things I liked most about London was seeing window boxes filled with pretty little flowers,"* he once said. *"I really enjoyed being alone and getting in touch with my imagination, my actual thoughts. Music can be such a night-time thing, and the way I grew up, I was used to being part of nature."*

Now, armed with actual recordings, Jimi needed a record contract to push forward with. Having performed in many places since arriving in London, during that short time he had gained a reputation as the greatest guitar player that anyone had witnessed, he was a true sensation when he performed live. What he didn't have yet though, was any sort of chart success. The Stones had started out with covers, but record companies now wanted originality, and songwriters were needed. Jimi had his own songs, and he was writing continuously, it was now key for Jimi to get into the charts to gain that mass appeal. Chas started the search to get Jimi his first record deal.

Chapter 11

Way Down Where I Can Be Free

"The story of life is quicker than the blink of an eye, the story of love is hello, goodbye"

Chas was adamant that Jimi had created a hit record, so confident of this he headed straight to Decca records. At this point, the band had little to no money coming in and what they did have had been loaned to them in some way, it was imperative Chas got a record contract signed quickly. In all honesty, he didn't think this would be an issue, considering Jimi's reputation. Decca was seen as one of the key labels at the time; it had been growing in stature for many years and was perceived as one of the main labels for any up-and-coming band or artist. The label had proved itself around the mid 1950s, when music shifted. Decca successfully and strategically moved with the times and remained relevant as rock 'n' roll became the in thing. It boasted a catalogue of breakaway labels that specialised in pop music, including London, RCA, Brunswick, and Coral.

It was the Brunswick label that successfully scored the smash hit of 1954 with 'Rock Around the Clock' by Bill Haley & His Comets. The arrival of rock 'n' roll changed the record industry forever, the demographic quickly changed and sales of records to a teenaged audience rocket over the coming decades. Decca Records quickly snapped up Tommy Steele, Britain's top rock 'n' roll guy at the time, who went to No.1 with his version of 'Singing the Blues,' and then Lonnie Donegan, whose 'Rock Island Line' was a Top 10 hit in 1956. Donegan was a jazz musician who spearheaded the skiffle craze that was sweeping Britain. Skiffle combined elements of jazz and blues but could be played on homemade instruments, such as tea-chest bass and washboard, a style the young Jimmy Hendrix would have no doubt excelled in. The skiffle craze saw hundreds of new bands spring up around Britain - the long-term effect of which would come to the fore with the explosion of British beat groups in 1963-64, almost all of whom got their first experience of playing in a group thanks to skiffle. But, while many of these youngsters loved to play skiffle, their real passion was rock'n'roll. And through homegrown acts like Tommy Steele and Billy Fury, they were offered a chance to see the stars in the flesh. It was always to America that British teenagers looked, there was something a little different with American acts, and of course with the rise of Little Richard and Elvis, it peaked the imagination. Decca's London /American label had the cream of the crop with affiliated licensed labels, it introduced Britain's future stars to Chuck Berry, Johnny Cash, Eddie Cochran, Buddy Holly, Jerry Lee Lewis, and Bo Diddley. Decca, however, like many labels didn't always get it right.

It was on New Year's Day 1962, that a former skiffle group from Liverpool famously auditioned for Decca. They were previously called The Quarrymen and had added new members; they were now renamed The Beatles. Decca turned them down. This decision has gone down in pop folklore, but they weren't alone. Pretty much every record company in the UK - including EMI, where they would ultimately find fame - did likewise. Decca had a choice between The Beatles and Brian Poole and The Tremeloes; they choose the latter.

At this time labels were leaning towards songwriters rather than cover bands, who were becoming more common, and although The Beatles had the progressive techniques of Brian Epstein, on the 15-track demo that they presented, there were only three songs that were Lennon-McCartney originals. Because of this, Decca failed to capture the magnificence of the group. In addition, their location was another element, Brian Poole and The Tremeloes came from London, and therefore making life easier all round, after all no one would want to listen to a band from Liverpool, of all places. During that period, the industrial north of England was largely regarded as a cultural desert. Consequently, Decca's A&R representative, Dick Rowe, did not go against prevailing attitudes by deciding not to sign the pre-Ringo Beatles.

As the 1960s began, the pop music market was undergoing significant changes. With the decline of rock and roll, forecasting trends in the music industry became increasingly complex. The British beat boom, emerging from Britain's skiffle craze, soon impacted the US and global markets significantly. This movement was greatly influenced by the signing of The Rolling Stones. Alongside Decca Records, EMI emerged as one of the most prominent record companies in the United Kingdom. With the eventual signing of The Beatles and subsequent Merseybeat acts such as Cilla Black and Gerry And The Pacemakers, EMI appeared poised to dominate the pop music market. If a Merseybeat act was not at the top of the charts, then EMI's other major artist, Cliff Richard and The Shadows, was achieving significant success.

Ironically, it was due to The Beatles that Decca Records made a strong comeback, following George Harrison's recommendation to Decca's Mike Smith to sign a local band, which turned out to be The Rolling Stones. Additionally, The Rolling Stones received an early boost on the charts when

John Lennon and Paul McCartney donated the song "I Wanna Be Your Man" to Keith and Mick. This track reached No. 12 in the UK charts, kickstarting The Rolling Stones' career. While British bands were preparing for their invasion, Decca's London/American imprint continued to supply the UK with hits from the United States, including tracks produced by Phil Spector, often referred to as "the American Joe Meek." Notable examples include 'Be My Baby' by The Ronettes and 'Da Doo Ron Ron' by The Crystals.

The story of Decca - and, indeed, the record industry as a whole - in the 60s was of a transatlantic competitiveness that enriched the music (and coffers) of all involved. Managers who were trawling the clubs looking for acts and bands to represent, like Chas, knew that if they could penetrate past the offices of these labels and get an act signed, they could forge a lucrative career on the back of it, this is one of the reasons it attracted many unsavoury characters, night club owners and dodgy individuals who leaned towards industries where cash could be moved and manipulated. Brunswick launched The Who and Decca the Small Faces. In return, their licensing business scored great success with The Righteous Brothers and The Birds, before latching onto the American R&B market with acts like Otis Redding and James Brown.

Decca was also looking forward, although rock 'n' roll was still in its infancy, it was still trying to be at the cutting edge, striving to predict where things were heading. It launched its progressive Deram label in 1966 to showcase pop recordings made using 'Deramic Sound' (Decca Panoramic Sound), this gave engineers more scope to use technology to create a more dynamic stereo field, placing individual instruments in their own space within the stereo picture. Acts broken by the label include David Bowie (Decca released his debut album), Cat Stevens, The Move, and Procol Harum. The Moody Blues, Amen Corner, and The Flowerpot Men enjoyed success on the label, but by the mid-70s, Deram was used less and less.

Jimi's sound was nothing like anyone had really heard, he was creating music, especially live, that was unique. His mix of blues & rock, blended with a trippy psychedelic acid mix was in short, ahead of its time. Chas approached Dick Rowe, but despite the success of Decca, and the confidence of Chas Chandler proudly representing Jimi with the demo, it was a residing no from the label. They couldn't hear a hit with 'Hey Joe' and didn't hear anything special. This was not part of the plan. Looking back, this label not only turned down The Beatles but also Jimi Hendrix, which is quite astonishing in hindsight.

Jimi was still without any kind of deal, but it was a connection with The Who that finally got things moving in the right direction. Jimi was performing one night at the Scotch of St James's, in the audience were Kit

Lambert and Chris Stamp, who just happened to be the management of The Who at the time. Impressed with what they saw, they were immediately interested in him. They initially wanted to produce him, but on hearing that he already had management they couldn't do this, what they could do though, was offer him a record deal that fitted in with their own ambitions.

They were in the process at the time of trying to set up their own label, they had hustled their way around to various people and places to try and get this set up. Previously, they had approached Polydor for backing, this was in a negotiation stage when they witnessed Jimi Hendrix. Although they had success with The Who, Kit and Chris were convinced that Jimi's sound was the way forward, not the clean rock 'n' roll sound that the Who were bringing to the table, but a more acid rock and blues that Jimi was producing. It was this sound that they pushed for as a new direction going into 1967, for them Jimi was where it was heading; the psychedelic kaleidoscope that he brought was utterly unique, they were convinced this was where they needed to be and pushed hard for Jimi to be their first signing on the new label.

Eventually they got the backing they wanted and founded Track records in 1966, which became one of the first British owned independent record labels. The negotiation however was very much touch and go, it stemmed basically on 'Hey Joe' becoming a hit, and if it did, Polydor would finance Track Records. The team also promised that they would get Jimi on to the show Ready Steady Go, or RSG, which was massive in the 1960s for any band coming through.

For any teenager in Britain in the 1960s, this was the only show to watch, any band or singer featured on it would have an instant impact. It was broadcast early on Friday evenings, and this 30-minute program completely dominated. RSG made a simple statement, it promised, *"The weekend starts here"*. The first show aired at 7 pm on Friday 9 August 1963 and was presented by Keith Fordyce and David Gell, with 200 kids in the studio. The line-up for the debut show featured Pat Boone, Chris Barber, Billy Fury, Brian Poole and The Tremeloes, and Joyce Blair. Originally, to begin with, it was only broadcast in the London area, but due to massive popularity over the next three years, Ready, Steady, Go! proved to be quite simply the best television pop show ever, combining its unique atmosphere and vitality with the best sounds around. There may have been the grumblings of parents in the background, but kids loved it. By Autumn 1963, the program had been extended to 45 minutes and moved to a slightly earlier slot. From the opening title music - originally The Surfers 'Wipe Out' but replaced in January 1964 by Manfred Mann's countdown-like 5-4-3-2-1 - the show oozed vitality, and the studio discotheque set allowed the general public onto the studio floor for dancing and mingling with the appearing stars. This wasn't a format that had ever been done before and was seen at the time as cutting edge, the camera on the dance floor moving around, giving the feeling you were actually there. Broadcast live to air from Associated-Rediffusion's home at Television House in London's Kingsway, the show featured both new releases, existing hits and off-the-cuff interviews with the artists. The program's look slowly changed, drawing on the world of pop art to dress the studio walls with giant paintings, collages and Mod symbols like arrows and targets. The Rolling Stones, The Moody Blues, The Animals and the kinks all had their TV debuts on the show.

In 1964 there was a spin-off series featuring the RSG! team in a talent competition show called Ready, Steady - Win!, searching for new pop talent. The panel of judges changed constantly but included Brian Epstein, Bill Haley, Lulu, Mick Jagger, Helen Shapiro and Brian Matthew. Each week, six groups participated in a contest to find the best new beat combo, with £1,000 of musical equipment on offer as the top prize, followed by a second prize of a £750 van and £250 of clothes for third place. The ultimate winner was The Bo Street Runners from Harrow. Despite securing a Decca recording contract and enjoying the exposure the programme provided, they failed to register a chart hit. In May 1965, the show's theme tune changed to 'Anyway, Anyhow, Anywhere' by RSG! favourites, The Who. Also in 1965, a spin-off programme - entitled The Sound of Motown and hosted by Dusty Springfield - featured an array of Motown talent, fresh from their recent British tour. The programme gave tremendous exposure to the Motown sound and the show's stars - including Stevie Wonder, The Temptations and Smokey Robinson & the Miracles - who were all hit-less at this time in the UK.

A year later, in March 1965, the programme abandoned miming in favour of live studio performances. This meant the show's weekly budget had to rise by 50% to cover the cost of backing singers, musicians and arrangers, and a five-figure sum was spent on acquiring the latest equipment to guarantee high-quality sound reproduction. To publicise the change, the show's name was temporarily altered to Ready Steady Goes Live! Although the original title returned after nine weeks, with briefly-seen co-host David Goldsmith stepping aside and Cathy McGowan now fronting the show alone. The miming ban coincided with a move to a new studio at Associated-Rediffusion's Wembley Studios, which offered more space and better facilities. While efforts were made to recreate the intimacy of the original set, artists were now not so tightly hemmed in by fans and probing cameras, and dancers - up to 250 per programme - were given more room to show off their latest moves. The final episode of Ready, Steady, Go! -

titled Ready, Steady, Goes! - aired on 23rd December 1966, a victim of more progressive fashions and rising production costs. When Jimi was looking at appearing on the show it was coming to the end of its amazing run.

A short tour of Europe was now in place, one of the reasons for this was some venues around the UK were unwilling to book a band that was unheard of, despite the obvious pedigree. Chas and others simply had to rely on phone calls to book The Jimi Hendrix Experience in. Of course, the fact that they were saying how amazing Jimi was, was something clubs and venues had heard a thousand times before. Without venues to travel around to in the UK ,the second option was Europe, and here it was easier to book venues. The tour took in Germany, France and Scandinavia.

The tour wasn't without issues, drummer Mitch had started to have problems turning up and went missing and on many occasions there were discussions at this time from the management that he should be fired, as he was proving unreliable. Because of this, they took along a stand in drummer, John Banks from The Merseybeat's, who filled when Mitch didn't turn up. The tour was quickly set up and a roadie put in place, mainly because he had a van; the roadie in question was Gerry Stickells who would go on to be a legend in touring over the years ahead for many different high-profile bands and performers. He was a school friend of Noel Redding who asked him to assist in helping get Jimi's equipment through customs at Heathrow Airport. The deal was that if he succeeded, he would be rewarded by being able to join the tour as a roadie. The deal paid off because after Jimi, Gerry would become the go to man for touring bands. From 1977, Gerry would ensure that complex tours for Elton John, Queen, Rod Stewart, Fleetwood Mac, Michael Jackson, ABBA, Paul McCartney and Madonna, among many others, would go as smoothly as possible.

The tour was an incredible success, especially in Germany. They loved the theatrics of Jimi, and in particular the way he would smash up his guitar after shows, and sometimes even the whole set. Despite the incredible reception Jimi was getting for his on-stage performances, the fact remained he still hadn't had any impact. 'Hey Joe' was now in motion and it was time to get the promotional activity in place for the release. A lot was at stake for the first single, it needed to be a hit.

Back in London, Chas had worked hard to gain attention for the new single. He set up a press launch for the band, hoping to gain momentum. As the journalists gathered, Jimi came on and performed his small set. The fact was though, he was a little too good for the small club he was in. Everyone knew they were watching something phenomenal; it was loud and it was brash, but somehow a little lost on the journalists watching. It was, however, when he played 'Wild Thing' that things changed. This was a relatively simple number, one that an untrained ear could understand, the way that Jimi manipulated this song, the way he branched out away from it, while simultaneously keeping the basic structure in place was incredible.

After the performance, the Record Mirror headlined with *'Mr Phenomenon'*. They would go on to give Jimi his first interview. Jimi spoke about his life in these early interviews and spoke about home and his career to this point, when asked about his influences he explained; *"Well, I don't have any right now. I used to like Elmore James and early Muddy Waters and stuff like that. Robert Johnson and all those old cats. When I first started playing guitar is was way up in the Northwest, in Seattle, Washington. They don't have too many of the real blues singers up there. When I really learned to play was down South. Then I went into the Army for about nine months, but I found a way to get out of that. When I came out, I went down South and all the cats down there were playing blues, and this is when I really began to get interested in the scene. I haven't been on the West Coast for a long time. But when I was on the East Coast the scene was pretty groovy. I'd just lay around and play for about two dollars a night, and then I'd try and find a place to stay at night after I finished playing. You had to chat somebody up real quick before you had a place to stay. I like very different jazz, not all this regular stuff. Most of it is blowing blues, and that's why I like free-form jazz, the groovy stuff instead of the old-time hits like they get up there and play 'How High Is the Moon' for hours and hours. It gets to be a drag. I get a kick out of playing. It's the best part of this whole thing and recording too. I wrote a song called 'I Don't Live Today,' and we got the music together in the studio. It's a freak-out tune. I might as well say that cause everyone else is going to anyway. Do you want to know the real meaning of that? Now, alright, I'll tell you this, don't think anything bad, okay? This is what they used to say in California ages ago: Guess what I seen in a car down on Sunset Strip. I seen Gladys with Pete, and they were freakin' out. That's what it means - sexual perverting. Now they get freakin' off and out in all these songs, so it's got nothing at all to do with sex now, I guess. Anyway, that's what it used to mean, perversion, like you might see a beautiful girl and say she's a beautiful 'freak,' you know. I'm being frank that's all, so I guess I'll get deported soon."*

A month prior to the release of 'Hey Joe' Jimi celebrated his twenty fourth birthday on November 27th. He had come a long way in the year that had passed. It wasn't too long ago he was still jobbing around the circuit in the USA with Curtis Knight and others, now he was poised to hopefully enter the charts and gain his first hit record. He had amassed a live following in England and parts of Europe, and was now entering the various circulations of press articles and music magazines. It was time for Jimi to leave the underground circuit to which his reputation had grown over the years and enter the mainstream consciousness of the record buying public.

Mike Jeffery and Chas Chandler needed instant exposure for The Jimi Hendrix Experience and arranged for them to perform at a daytime reception at the Bag O'Nails Club, in November 1966. They invited as many high profile celebrities and musicians as they could, as well as members of the music press and various showbiz dignitaries. The band astonished the crowd and received countless accolades from those present including John Lennon and Paul McCartney. Their performance at the Bag O'Nails established The Jimi Hendrix Experience as a force to be reckoned with.

At this point, in late 1966, rock and pop music was just beginning to stretch out from the conformity of *'guys in suits.'* The undisputed kings of pop, The Beatles, had developed a more sophisticated and complex technique, showcased on the album 'Revolver' released in August that year. They essentially became a studio band, more interested in the technology that this could bring, as opposed to a live performance. The Stones (who had never been into suits) had all but deserted their beloved blues and rock 'n' roll in pursuit of the "fab four" to become recognized as songwriters in their own right. Other British bands like The Who, Small Faces, Kinks and Yardbirds were also becoming more adventurous in their writing and arrangements. However, nothing had prepared Britain for the revolution that was The Jimi Hendrix Experience, with their brilliant fusion of rock, R&B, blues and psychedelic pop. Eddie Kramer remembers it fondly: *"Jimi destroyed everybody. Beatles, Stones, everyone came to see him and just freaked out because he was such an original"*.

The fact remained though that despite all this adoration, if a band didn't have chart success, then it simply did not take off. If you were a live band, regardless of how brilliant you could be, it made no difference in the 1960s. Without hits, the bookings didn't come and a quick fade away was inevitable. In the background Mike Jeffery was planning the next phase, which was his expertise; contracts to sign, and deals to be made. Who would essentially benefit from these deals, however, is a key point.

Everything Jimi had worked on to this point basically hinged on 'Hey Joe' having an impact. Something to build upon, something to gain that recognition to the masses that Jimi now needed. It was a huge gamble for all concerned, but the time had come for the first ever single by Jimi Hendrix.

Chapter 12

Where You Gonna Run to Now?

"Anybody can do anything; it's up to themselves. All it takes is the right intentions"

The release of 'Hey Joe' with the B side 'Stone Free' was released on 16th December 1967 in the UK, on Polydor Records. It was executed well; the release coincided with the performance booked on RSG! The popularity of the show was still huge, but it was coming to an end; it was good timing, the following weeks show would be the final one ever.

Jimi Hendrix Experience
- **Hey Joe**
- **Stone Free**

-Polydor 56139 (Eng) Release 16/12/1966-Single

Although The Experience performed 'Hey Joe' on the show, this wouldn't necessarily provide the recognition through the airways that was needed. Only when a track hit the top forty would the crucial airplay be guaranteed. It still needed to climb the decisive charts to achieve this. It's worth looking at the importance of the charts at this time; they were absolutely key to any band's success, and there was only one true chart that dominated in the UK and the USA. This was based on physical sales of records that were bought over the counter at various music shops. Today, the chart systems that track records is completely fragmented, having a number one record today is virtually meaningless in comparison. Songs are downloaded in the millions every day with very little going to the artists, music is seen as a free thing once a subscription is paid. The gatekeepers are the platform companies, who have ultimate control.

From the 1930s through to the 1980s the buying of a record, from a store, was the only way to purchase music, and it was this physical sale that was counted. This was vinyl, there were no alternatives; no cassettes, no CD's, which came into the mainstream later in the 1980s, you had to physically go to a shop and buy it. The chart system that was prevalent in the 1960s, 70s, and 80s is unfortunately no longer in existence.

During the 1960s, there were numerous allegations that this system was subject to manipulation. It was claimed that substantial sums of money were paid to artificially elevate a record's position on the charts, with individuals employed specifically to purchase records from stores to boost sales figures and, consequently, track rankings. Despite many denials of such practices, rumours persisted, notably regarding 'Hey Joe', where it was alleged that similar manipulations occurred, although these claims were equally denied.

'Stone Free' was chosen as the B-side to 'Hey Joe', this is an important aspect of a single released during the 60s, 70s and 80s. From a band's perspective it allowed them to add in something extra, you may have been familiar with the single itself, as you would have heard it on the radio, or saw a TV appearance, but adding an additional track on the reverse gave a glimpse into what more a band could do.

The charts didn't start until the 1930s, so in the early days there was no reason to value one side of a record over another. In addition, radio stations didn't broadcast any recorded music until later, in the 1950s, which was when the Top 40 moved onto network radio. This was when the term 'single' became common in connection with a song release. It was now that record companies started to increasingly present one side of the record as an A-side and the other as a B-side, but at this time it was almost a random choice between the two tracks. There was little thought to the process and one song wasn't favoured in any way over another. There were also 'double A-sides' released when record companies realised that putting both songs out as an A-side meant that they would both make an impact on the charts - a dual hit. Famously, The Beatles with 'Strawberry Fields' and 'Penny Lane' was an early example. Both songs could be played in equal measure, giving additional airplay on radio. There was also the possibility that giving radio the option meant that a certain station might play one track more than another.

A shift happened in the 1960s in relation to B-sides as record companies and music executives pushed aggressively in search of hits. To get a hit, the record companies needed radio stations to push a certain song. They needed to pay particular attention to one song and not be distracted. It needed daily airplay on heavy rotation to reach the ears of the masses. It was here that the true A-side, and as a result the lesser B-side, came into its own. Record companies now started to assign an A-side as an indication of what they wanted the radio stations to play, the main song. In this case play 'Hey Joe' not 'Stone Free'. Now, A-sides started to dominate the market in terms of sales; they were seen as more important than albums and gave a bigger return. The problem was, there was still another side to the single, a side that couldn't be left blank. If a 'double A-side' was decided against, and they didn't want to include an album track, then another song had to fill the gap. Step forward the trusted B-side. Moving forward to the 1960s and beyond, album sales had increased dramatically, and double-sided hit singles had become extremely rare. It now became the norm for record companies to use singles as a means of promoting forthcoming albums; they frequently placed album tracks that they wished to promote on side A, which was usually the most radio friendly song, with little attention to the flip side. As a result, the B-side became less important and usually had a simple, non-album, instrumental song assigned. It was purposely played down, so it would not distract from the main song, which remained the focus, the one to promote, the A-side.

Despite this, there were many B-sides over the years, initially regarded as less important than the A-side, that became uninvitingly more successful. Record companies, during the peak of double-sided singles, wanted to avoid a stronger track on the B-side so it wouldn't overshadow the A-side, for which there were expensive music videos and TV appearances. However, over the years there are many examples of listeners deciding that the so-called throwaway song on the reverse side was actually better, and as a result, more popular. Radio and clubs sometimes bypassed the plug track in favour of the flip side, and this is what gave a B-side such kudos. In the world of music no one was ever sure what the public would take to and what they wouldn't. It's why A and B-sides became so popular.

Many bands and musicians also used the flip side to release songs that would normally not see the light of day. Jimi had many later compilation albums released featuring these B-sides or throwaway tracks, often not endorsed or official, but still snapped up by collectors. The Beatles, The Rolling Stones and Jimi continued to showcase these B-Side tracks in the years ahead, and they would often be mashed together in some kind of compilation album. Moving forward, Prince was a notable example of this in the 1980s. One of the most prolific stars of the decade recorded so many songs that his B-sides were often as good as, or better than, the released single. There were so many, in fact, that Warner Bros released a whole album dedicated to them: The Hits The B-Sides was released in 1993 with the compilation featuring 20 songs of B-sides on disc 3, all from the hits of the 1980s. Prince was not alone; over the years record companies started to look back on these little gems hidden underneath the main tracks, and realised there was scope for release, and ultimately, profit.

As technology in the distribution of records increased, notably with the transition from Vinyl to Cassette, the B-side side of released singles was largely unaffected. The CD though, saw the beginning of the end as the additional songs became more remixes, or 'additional bonus tracks' than actual B-sides. It was a system that worked perfectly for several decades when the physical records were bought and sold. With the resurgence in vinyl, diehard fans will undoubtedly keep collecting singles, both old and new, and listen to both sides, A and B, including rare and collectable editions. It's simple marketing at its best: just two songs ready made on plastic. The B-side gave scope for more artistry and proved rock music to be more than just a fad when it became a massive part of everyday culture in the 1950s and 1960s - in every sense it was a true art form. The B-side compilation albums were packaged in similar ways to greatest hits albums, but instead, were intended to give hardcore fans the behind-the-scenes non-hits that got them closer to their beloved artists.

There was something special about flipping over a record to listen to a B-side. Something nostalgic, something intriguing, something curious. For a fan it was almost investigative. It became personal and secretive, just between you and the artist, and it brought you closer to them. It was a double treat, it was value for money, and it gave you a chance to own a song that the masses perhaps would not; and if the B-side was as good as, or better than the A-side, it was a musical bonus that a CD 'bonus track' or remix could never really replicate. From the 1960s through to the early 1990s the humble B-side sometimes stood for 'better'.

Here in the swinging sixties, music was as close to fashion and culture as any time in its history, and Jimi was now part of it. Musicians like Jimi stand as a testament to a cultural revolution that reshaped London and reverberated globally. Its influence on music, fashion, and societal norms continue to echo through the corridors of time, marking an era that will forever be remembered as a swinging symphony of creativity and change. The Jimi Hendrix Experience was now ready to make its mark on this era and rise to the top.

With the release of 'Hey Joe' and 'Stone Free', the hope was that the single would appeal to the public, and the B-side would intrigue them enough to look deeper, creating a fan base. Jimi was entering the music world as rock and roll and pop music were becoming increasingly popular. It was a phenomenon that was growing and leading to cultural change in 1960s London. The city had become a cultural hub in its own right, a new wave had emerged of styles, fads and people becoming more individual than ever before. Previously there was control from the establishment, particularly from the old Tory-Liberal establishment, but this was now fading away. They were losing their grip on societal control while simultaneously being replaced by actors, photographers, singers and bands. It ushered in a new social order that rejected the elite-dominated status quo, the young now wore bright clothing, strutted around the streets and listened to beat music, rock and roll, and talked openly about sex. Driven by the influential baby boomer generation, it brought a quick change in youth culture, pushing forward a brave artistic flare in music, arts and fashion.

Jimi was launching his career at a time when freedom and liberalism were becoming ever more popular, a cultural backlash for previous attitudes was in abundance. The young, embraced taboo subjects like homosexuality, abortion, drug use, and non-marital sex, this was elevated further through the expansion of film and visual art. In addition, the release of oral contraceptives in the 1960s, although initially only available for married couples, broke previous attitudes surrounding sex and sexuality. There was of course, a backlash against the promiscuous attitudes of the young in Britian, as many politicians and older academics interpreted it as disrespect to the traditional conservative and moral standards of the 1940s and 1950s.

Despite this, the movement of the 1960s was too strong for the traditions of the past decades. Prohibitions and other restrictions such as abortion, same sex relationships, sex outside marriage and contraception were now seen as outdated ideals, and were fading away as a new wave of freedom and culture was developing. Nowhere was this emerging more noticeably than in London. Jimi was in the right place at the right time.

Rock and roll had only been around for a short period to this point, it didn't really come into the mainstream focus until the mid-1950s, and now running parallel was pop music. It had an unstoppable emerging fan base of screaming out of control teenagers, adoring the individuals delivering it. This was what Chas and Mike were after, if the marketing machine was put in place correctly, then Jimi's natural talent should do the rest. 'Hey Joe' set a blue print for what was to come for The Jimi Hendrix Experience. The sound of his guitar was simply timeless, it stood out above the rest, it set the basics that shaped the world of rock music that continues to this day. The B side of 'Stone Free' gave another snapshot into how Jimi played, away from the traditional sound that was heard to this point. Prior to the release there was some press coverage that was favourable; NME announced that the song was *'Guttural, earthy, convincing and authentic'* while Record Mirror stated that *'Hey Joe would be a hit, should justice prevail.'*

On release, the single rose steadily. On New Years Eve it was at number 12 on the R&B chart and number thirty-eight on the national chart. It eventually reached the top 10 in January 1967, peaking at number 6. It was a great start, and of course a relief for Chas, it ensured Jimi even greater exposure in 1960s London. As a performer he was talked about and sought after relentlessly, and now he had a chart hit. Things were on the up and he was establishing himself very quickly as a rising star in Britain and Europe.

Going into 1967 things started to move quickly for Jimi. It was evident that this was the right sound, with the right band, at exactly the right time. There was a major shift in music during this coming year; This was the year of the first issue of Rolling Stone magazine, The Monterey pop festival would emerge and The Beatles would release Sgt Pepper, which expanded studio sound composition beyond recognition. The circus that came with released singles was now in motion and Jimi was quickly swept into the world of media, recording sessions, interviews, magazine articles and photography. It all started to pull him in different directions. The initial momentum had been slow, it had taken four months to get to this point, but now it was a continuous stream of performances booked, articles written, and different media demands that were alien to Jimi. Unlike the fragmented press in the USA, England's press was mostly national, which some viewed as an advantage. While exposure on TV or radio in England could reach a wide audience instantly, this was not possible in the US due to the lack of national TV, radio, or press. In England, once the momentum began, a musician's presence could be quickly established.

As far as marketing Jimi, the idea was simple, to shock. Chas had put Jimi out there as a wild man, an ugly individual, and an almost non-human rock star. It is easy to see why this approach would work, he played guitar unlike anyone before, and his onstage presence was utterly unique. The musicians around him already knew he was the greatest guitar player they had ever seen, but despite the press willingness to happily run with the *'wild black man from overseas' character*, when interviewed, Jimi was always honest and upfront with his answers. He was naturally timid; he was always polite and courteous but at the same time modest and shy. He would always talk openly, and he was especially candid about his career and his music. During interviews on the release of 'Hey Joe', he dismissed the track, calling it a cowboy song. He even went on to emphasise that the song *'Isn't us'*. *"We're working on an LP which will be mainly our own stuff, if I write something about three or four in the morning, I can't wait to hear it played. It's even a drag to wait for the other cats to arrive. It's like being addicted to music, music makes me high on stage, and that's the truth!"*

Jimi kept the interviews, and the press demands in place as 1967 progressed, one aspect he did hate however, was miming to performances. He was a live performer at heart, he was raised and had his musical apprenticeship in some of the best places on the planet, with some of the biggest figures in rock. Pretending to play was something he just couldn't relate to, he told NME at the time *"It's so phoney, I felt guilty just standing there holding a guitar, if you want to scream and holler at a record you can do that at home, I'm strictly a live performer. I know I can't sing; I'm primarily a guitarist, I've been working with myself and my ideas for 21 years, now I want to find out from everyone else if they are any good."*

The single was released in the United States shortly after, in May, but it failed to make any impact. The B-side 'Stone Free' became the second song the Jimi Hendrix Experience ever recorded and viewed as a counterculture anthem; it fitted in with Jimi's own outlook on life, that of free living and doing as you please without judgment. In addition to the B-Side placing 'Stone Free' was also later released on the Smash Hits compilation album. The track became a concert favourite with extended guitar work. 'Hey Joe' would also become infamous for being the last song Jimi performed at Woodstock, which in turn made it the last song of the entire festival.

Management in the 1960s was a separate entity to that of musicians. In Jimi's case he was not alone in his attitude towards his business activities. He was a musician first and foremost; his only real interest was in creating and performing. Business affairs were left for others. Following the success of 'Hey Joe', Jimi's team proceeded with careful planning to ensure his future, which ultimately also secured their own.

They negotiated a deal for Polydor to financially support Track Records. Chas and Mike also signed another contract, which was with Lambert and Stamps production company called New Action. They secured a £1000 advance with a promo film for every single released. It was agreed that Jimi would release four singles and two albums for every year the contract was active. There were some parts of the deal though that were questionable and likely unknown, or unnoticed by Jimi. Mike and Chas were free to arrange other publishing and recording contracts, and they never paid anything directly to the band members.

Chas was still weary of Mike Jeffrey, and with good reason, but had come to the conclusion, despite the way Mike had apparently ripped off The Animals, that he would be a good person to have on his side. Chas also had the additional reality that he was still under contract with Mike, which meant that he would have a claim for any money he earned should his new venture be successful.

The initial contract signed by the band was characterised as a production deal, designating Mike Jeffery and Chas Chandler as record producers. It was not a management contract per se, and notably, despite Jimi Hendrix's status and individual reputation at the time, the contract did not differentiate between him and the other two musicians. They were individually identified as musical performers collectively known as 'The Jimi Hendrix Experience'. Reports indicated that the deal allocated 20% of royalties and additional percentages of publishing rights to Mike Jeffery and Chas Chandler, whereas the band members collectively received only 2.5% of the royalties from record sales. This arrangement clearly favoured Mike and Chas, to the detriment of the musicians. However, it is important to note that at this early stage in the band's career, they had no foresight into the immense success they would eventually achieve.

It was also reported that the agreement with Polydor included a clause whereby all rights to the releases by The Experience would automatically revert to Mike and Chas once the Track Records deal concluded. Such agreements, often inadequately scrutinised by the bands themselves, frequently resurfaced to cause significant issues in later years. For instance, Noel Redding's career was marred by his ongoing efforts to reclaim substantial sums of money he believed were owed to him by various record, publishing, management, and production companies. This situation was likely exacerbated by the 'fame fog' or perhaps the 'purple haze' that clouded the judgment of many musicians during that era. Despite hundreds of millions of dollars flowing into the Hendrix estate over the years, Noel relentlessly pursued justice through the courts on both sides of the Atlantic, attempting to unravel the complex web of signed contracts, verbal agreements, questionable investment schemes, and financial arrangements often made with companies that either did not exist or more importantly, could not be traced.

These contracts and deals were the exact ones that Mike was pursuing now and getting ink on paper for. Not a second thought from the band members would be given to such signings, especially when they were performing night after night, hitting the charts and feeling that they had actually made it. The reality, however, was often very different. Noel, in the years ahead, went from one case to another and in turn suffered humiliation for his cause. There was even an unbelievable moment during a court case in the USA that was focusing on an early hit single by The Experience, the song was played, and he was asked to prove there and then to the court that the bass notes on it were actually played by him. As he said while relating this tale, *"On that basis Paul McCartney couldn't prove he played on a Beatles record!"*

Shortly after Jimi Hendrix performed a highly acclaimed concert in London, and with the success of "Hey Joe" well established, Mike Jeffery invited him to the luxurious Mayfair office of solicitor John Hillman, the creator and architect of Yameta. During this meeting, John and Mike presented Jimi with another legal agreement. This contract was not about the band; it was exclusively focused on Jimi Hendrix as a performer across all mediums. While this agreement theoretically seemed beneficial for Jimi, as it acknowledged his talent and stardom, he was unfortunately unable to fully grasp its implications at the time.

The deal allegedly gave Mike Jeffery a whopping 40% of Jimi's gross performance earnings, a huge figure by any show business standard. Jeffery explained that part of that percentage could pay for possible tour expenses. John Hillman told Jimi about the Yameta tax shelter and tried to impress him by mentioning the name of Yameta director Sir Guy Henderson who he claimed was a significant person in the Bahamas. He explained to Jimi that it was Sir Guy who was the original architect of Yameta. Jeffery and Hillman convinced Jimi that if he focused his attention on the USA, as well as England, then these Bahamas accounts would help him avoid paying too much in taxes, it would basically give him financial security for the rest of his life. At no point was Jimi offered any second opinion on these discussions or any opportunity to seek independent legal advice or to discuss the meeting and contract with Chas Chandler, who incidentally hadn't been present at that meeting. Jimi did raise some concern regarding his previous contract he signed in the USA, that of the Ed Chaplin contract he signed without any real thought. He was assured, however, from Mike, that the deal with Ed Chaplin could be dealt with. The agreement that Jimi Hendrix signed that day would seriously affect him for years to come.

With the Bahamas account in mind, Mike headed to the USA, he had made many contacts over there. He returned after just two months with a deal with Warner Brothers for $150,000. The deal gave him 2% producer royalties with 8% for the band and a large advance. The point to all this was that finally on the surface they now had money, however, where and whom it went to was a different question. On closer inspection of the alleged deals that were set up at this time, it's obvious where the cash was going.

With the release of 'Hey Joe' there was also strong rumours circulating that Mike Jeffery used his various talents to push the record forward, by any means necessary. It was common practice at the time, especially if you had someone like Mike Jeffrey at the helm, to get what you wanted by any means possible. As previously highlighted, there were certain practices that were allegedly going on within the chart system. Mike used all his underground skills to push forward with the cunning and deceptive notion of chart-rigging, consisting of different methods of paying someone to buy records from the record shops that the UK chart compilers sampled to calculate record sales, it was also known widely as seed money. Trixie Sullivan, Mike Jeffery's assistant has said: *"There was a guy that used to come around, all the business used him. He knew all the record shops, so he would go around and buy records to make the numbers up"*. Within the system Mike also whipped up the exposure by making a deal with the pirate radio stations to ensure that 'Hey Joe' would get plenty of air plays. Basically, he traded a part of Jimi's future publishing royalties in exchange for publicity.

During this frantic deal making period at the start of 1967, Mike Jeffery also wanted to extract Jimi from the contracts he'd signed before coming to England. This would of course give him ultimate control. He hired a team of lawyers to sort out the messy contracts and managed to resolve some of the contractual issues by 'buying off' various individuals. He also managed to secure the rights to seven songs that Jimi had recorded as a backing musician in 1965 while under contract. It was one of these lawyers that secured the record deal for the Jimi Hendrix Experience with Warner Brothers. Another key element here is that despite Mike explaining the benefits for tax avoidance to Jimi, and the financial security it would yield with dealing with Yameta, the fact was that the contract bypassed the band completely and was actually only between Reprise Records and Yameta.

Yameta was required to provide recordings *"embodying the performance of Jimi Hendrix or the Jimi Hendrix Experience."* The band themselves, that of Jimi Hendrix, Noel Redding and Mitch Mitchell, were not obliged to sign anything because they, themselves, were already exclusively tied to Yameta. As part of the agreement, Yameta and not Warner Brothers was to retain the ownership of the master recordings. So with this $150,000 deal, a royalty advance of $40,000 and a promotional budget of $20,000 this was an excellent outcome - for Mike Jeffery and Chas Chandler.

The above frenzy in signings and deals was without doubt outside of the band's control, and likely know-how. It was a complicated web of contracts where the band would have probably zoned out if it was explained properly. In hindsight, it's easy to read these dealings with a reflection of naivety on the band's behalf, the fact was though, that bands in the 1960s didn't get involved in these types of negotiations. The music industry would go on to be littered with legalities that put bands and artists at the lower end of the percentage scales, with managers and such like suited individuals walking away with a majority stake.

For Jimi he was just concentrating on his music, performances, and songwriting. He was fully aware that he was on the verge of achieving significant success. His management team was diligently promoting him, positioning him on the threshold of stardom. For Jimi he had no time for administrative tasks, he was never going to authorise any third-Party Risk Management or Due Diligence on what he had previously signed, musicians made music, that's the way it was.

Jimi had become a valuable asset, and a crucial entity needed to generate revenue, particularly for those in his orbit. He needed to focus on performing, and his schedule was set to become increasingly demanding in the years ahead. It would become challenging and arduous, in all aspects of creativity, it would push him to the edge. This however was just the beginning.

Jimi had evolved into an invaluable asset, essential for revenue generation, particularly for those surrounding him. He needed to concentrate on his performances, and his schedule was anticipated to become progressively more demanding in the upcoming years. This would be challenging and strenuous, testing his creativity to its limits. It was set to get worse for him, this was just the beginning. .

Chapter 13

The Moon Turned Fire Red

"I used to live in a room full of mirrors; all I could see was me...

Jimi continued into 1967 with gigs around England, expanding his reputation as simply the greatest guitar player anyone had witnessed. It was in March of this year that saw the release of *'Purple Haze'*, noted as the second single by the Jimi Hendrix Experience. It stood as the debut single for Track records. The infamous riff from the classic track came from Jimi fooling around with his guitar. Chas Chandler later said he heard Jimi playing it and told him to keep working on it, he thought it was a great riff, extremely catchy and worthy of working on. *"I heard him playing it at the flat and was knocked out. I told him to keep working on that,* saying, *'That's the next single!'."*

Jimi Hendrix Experience
- **Purple Haze**
- **51st Anniversary**

-Track Record 604001 (Eng) Release 15/03/1967-Single

The riff for 'Purple Haze' has become iconic; however, at the time of its release, it was an unusual and risky opening to a song, which is a testament to Jimi Hendrix's innovative spirit. For a track in the 1960s aimed at chart success, the introduction was highly unconventional. It was unlike anything typically heard of on the pop charts. The opening bars of 'Purple Haze' create a disquieting introduction, which was precisely Jimi's intention. From a musical perspective it was utterly unique, especially in rock.

It was on January 11th, 1967, that the band started the recording process. Both Mitch and Noel had not heard the song before they met at De Lane Lea. Per an account by Mitch, he and Noel learnt the song whilst in the studio: *"Jimi came in and kind of hummed us the riff and showed Noel the chords and the changes. I listened to it, and we went, 'OK, let's do it.' We got it on the third take as I recall."* Amazingly, the basic tracks were captured in just four hours. When the recording was completed and dispatched to Jimi's American label, a note was attached, it gave a specific instruction which points to Jimi's groundbreaking techniques at the time, it noted: 'deliberate distortion, do not correct'.

The infamous opening riff of the track falls into the musical tier known as 'Diabolus de Musica', Latin for 'Devil in Music', a technique that was actually condemned by the Spanish inquisition; during this period from 1478 through to 1834 around 150,000 people were prosecuted for various musical offences. There were also around 3,000 to 5,000 people that were executed. The medieval ear was used to hearing perfect fourths and perfect fifths - and impeccably in tune. Anything unpleasant was therefore viewed as labelled 'Diabolus de Musica' and comprehensively banned from church music. Jimi Hendrix, with the opening bars of 'Purple Haze', was lucky to be composing a song in the comparative freedom of 1960s swinging London. The chords also had additional names, such as the devil's interval, the tritone, the triad and the flatted fifth. As its Latin moniker suggests, it's an evil sounding combination of notes that's designed to create a chilling or foreboding atmosphere, deliberately written to sound unpleasant and off key.

The reason it was so controversial was the fact that to the ear it was a sinister type of sound, sonically unpalatable, listeners originally found it both undesirable and surprising. Before the tritone became a common tool in rock, listeners expected composers to create chords and patterns that were pleasing to the ear. When a tone wasn't harmonic and agreeable to listen to - such as the triad that was inserted into a musical passage, it was disconcerting, it was something that music didn't produce, put simply it didn't conform to the listeners' expectations. Although composers like Beethoven had used the technique previously - his 1805 opera Fidelio is riddled with triads - Jimi was the first musician of note to entwine the technique into rock, especially as the main riff. What's more startling is that he used the technique in the opening chords, the song literally starts with the sound, the so called *'Devil in Music'*. At the time it was an astonishing, unique and daring opening to a song.

Chas claimed that Jimi wrote the rest of 'Purple Haze' in the dressing room of a London club during the afternoon of December 26, 1966, before a gig. However, Jimi himself had never claimed that to be the case. Jimi was also circumspect about the song's meaning. When asked during this period on what the track was actually about, he gave a few different answers: he explained on one interview that it was inspired by a dream he had in which he was walking underwater, however on another occasion he went on to explain that it was about a journey through a mythical land, and on another he would claim that the song was of a real-world inspiration, though one that still had a metaphysical angle. He even stated on another interview to have based the lyrics on an experience he had in New York in which a woman he liked had put a voodoo spell on him.

It was left for the listener to decipher, which was mainly concluded that to be about a trip on psychedelic drugs. It's a plausible theory, given some of the lyrics and the overall psychedelic nature of the song's production. Although this is widely regarded as the real explanation, Jimi had never cited this in relation to the song's meaning, and Chas stated he did not trip at any point while writing 'Purple Haze'. On another interview, Jimi did point to one line in the lyrics which he found to be significant, at the end of the second verse: *'Never happy or in misery / Whatever it is, that girl put a spell on me.'*

During the late 1960s, technology was progressing fast, especially for recording music. It was seen as groundbreaking at the time. New multitrack recording technology allowed engineers to record and add additional parts for the final master, so after the basics were in place, the band had room to augment the song in any way they saw fit, meaning time pressures that were there previously were now alleviated. Chandler commented on the song's development beyond the basic stages: *"With 'Purple Haze', Hendrix and I were striving for a sound and just kept going back in (to the studio), two hours at a time, trying to achieve it. It wasn't like we were there for days on end. We recorded it, and then Hendrix and I would be sitting at home saying, 'Let's try that.' Then we would go in for an hour or two. That's how it was in those days. However long it took to record one specific idea, that's how long we would book. We kept going in and out."*

Although The Jimi Hendrix Experience was a band, it was essentially all about Jimi, and even though he respected his fellow band mates he was fully aware that this was the case. A key element to this dynamic was that Chas Chandler was a musician in his own right, and saw himself as a member of the band, there to add his creative input, as well as to make managerial decisions. He was getting himself involved both creatively and commercially. Famously, Noel and Mitch were not needed for the overdubbing process because Chas thought that between him and Jimi, they'd be able to finish the track in a more time-efficient manner. Wanting a better-quality cut, Chas took the four-track basic tape to Olympic Studios, where the overdubbing process was completed. This was to be a significant decision, as at Olympic, they were assigned the sound engineer Eddie Kramer, who would go on to be a defining influence on future tracks by Jimi.

It was during the first week of February 1967 that Jimi added new vocals and guitar parts, he was searching for something unique, striving to create something genuinely pioneering, Chas made use of the modern tech that was now available, utilising new effects and sounds that were on offer. They enriched background sounds by playing them back through headphones, which were moved around a recording microphone creating 'a weird echo'. Guitars were sped up and then recorded at half-speed, which raised the pitch. Additionally, they played around and experimented with panning, the process of distributing a sound signal into a stereo or multichannel sound field. This technique placed the sound, so it came from different directions giving the ability to position instruments or sound sources to the left, right, or anywhere in between. These new groundbreaking techniques in the studio gave Jimi and Chas a new dimension to the mix, it helped achieve the sound that Jimi was searching for. An iconic fantasy feel to the background noises.

These various progressions in experimentation gave birth to Jimi Hendrix's signature sound. The wailing guitar solo in 'Purple Haze' was the first use of the Octavia guitar effects unit. It was created by sound engineer Roger Mayer and developed using Jimi's input. Doubling the frequency of the sound that is fed in gave the sound outputted an upper octave. Moving forward, Jimi had found his style, and he was to inspire legions in the process. The studio experimentation, along with Jimi's unmatched musical ability, contributed to his recognition as a significant figure in music history.

'Purple Haze' was the first proper taste of all the wonders that were yet to come. As a single it would become the highest-charting single from 'Are You Experienced'. However, its legacy has more to do with the influence it had on album-oriented rock than as a hit single. The popularity of 'Purple Haze' ignited interest in 'Are You Experienced' and further pushed Jimi onto greatness. It was so significant, in fact, that some defined the track as the "debut single of the Album Rock Era."

It was when money came through from 'Hey Joe' that the transfer came to Olympic Studios. The management freed money so Jimi could expand further, this was a place where Jimi could really utilise the latest technology to hand. It was here that Jimi was matched up for the first time with an adventurous and experimental young sound engineer, the aforementioned, Eddie Kramer.

Eddie would go on to contribute to many of Jimi's future recordings. "*The studio manager said to me one day, 'You know, Eddie, there's this American chappie with big hair called Jimi Hendrix, You do all that weird stuff so why you don't do this; you know?' It was very English and very proper, and we hit it off. I mean, it was just a good feeling. He was very shy. When he stepped out on the studio floor and, you know, plugged in - oh, my God, it was just a revelation for me. You know, I'd never heard anything quite like it.*" There was a quick appreciation for experimentation that both Jimi and Eddie aligned with, basically there were no rules when they were together. Eddie continued, *"For example, who says you're always supposed to record at normal speed? There's a high-pitch guitar at the end of 'Purple Haze' that sounds almost like a mandolin."* Eddie explains that to get it, he set the tape recorder to half-speed: *"If you played a fairly rapid figure at half-speed, it would be really silly fast at high speed, and that's what it was."* Jimi had a unique, and many would say refreshing approach to his talent, it was something that many loved about him. *"He had such a deep understanding of the guitar that he knew his own solos backwards and forwards."* Eddie explained, *"And since he didn't have a day of formal musical training to his credit, Hendrix came up with his own method of teaching his songs to his band mates, a sort of large legal pad with copious notes"*, Kramer says. *"You know, the lyric content possibly, and then he would describe in detail where certain things would be happening in the song, 'OK, drum hits here, bass drum pattern here' and there would be a map of the song."*

As much as Jimi was a genius with his guitar, and revolutionary with the sound he was searching for, one thing that he was incredibly doubtful about was his voice. The second he had to approach a microphone in the studio he had issues. *"He hated the way he sounded. He thought he had the worst voice in the world."* Eddie recalled, *"He was embarrassed about his vocal performance; so much so that I had to build a series of screens - three sides - facing away from the control room windows so nobody could see what he was doing. We had to turn all the lights off in the studio, except for a little light where he had his lyrics, and he would do the take and we would stop and he would poke his head around the side of the screen and say, 'Hey, how was that? Was that all right? Are you sure it's OK?' And I'd say, 'Jimi, it was great, it was great. Yeah. Come on, let's go. Keep doing it. 'Oh, all right. OK. Well, we'll do one more then.'"*

Although the studio was where Jimi was truly free, his onstage antics were still raising eyebrows as the freedom he showed through his guitar work was analysed. In an interview from a 1973 documentary, Jimi explained he had no time for that kind of criticism. ,*"I don't care, man, I don't care what they say anymore. It's up to them if they want to mess up the evening by looking at one thing. You know, because all that is included, man. When I feel like playing with my teeth, I do it, because I feel like it, you know? All that is complete when I'm on stage, I'm a complete natural, more so than, you know, talking to a group of people or something."*

The track's blend of blues, eastern music, and psychedelic elements introduced the Octavia guitar effect, which added a higher-octave overtone to Jimi's guitar solos. He contributed hugely to the development of this unit. Regarding the song's lyrics, because there were various explanations in interviews about their origin and meanings, it suggests that the lyrics were likely formulated over different periods and combined into one cohesive piece. Contrary to popular belief, the song was not about an acid trip; those close to Jimi at the time stated he had not tried LSD at this point. In all the interviews regarding the meaning of the song, Jimi referenced many different explanations for the lyrics, but none related to drugs.

'Purple Haze' stands as a significant and pivotal track in the career of Jimi Hendrix, not only due to its widespread recognition, but also because it marks the first instance where Jimi experimented with new effects and sounds in the studio.

A modus operandi that he would utilise in his future recordings; the track was his gateway to significantly use the studio for new sound techniques and distortion.

On release the record was given a fantastic endorsement. Paul McCartney was one of many key musicians that was talking about Jimi Hendrix frequently, he was singing his praises even in these early stages of his career. He gave the record a fantastic pre-release review in Melody Maker. The song rose quickly and reached number 3 in the UK chart; it spent 14 weeks there. Jimi played the track several times to promote the song and forthcoming album, and during March 1967 he appeared on television on programs such as Top of the Pops, Beat-Club and Dee Time. He also performed live for German NDR and BBC Radio's Saturday Club. In the USA the song was paired with 'The Wind Cries Mary' as a sort of double A-side, this version was released in June. It entered the chart in late August but because of the increased airplay on the underground radio scene it made the actual album outperform the singles.

Jimi continued onwards with performances that were arranged by his team. A tour of Finland and other Scandinavian cities were not without issues. These were off the stage as well as on it, as Jimi's appearance was seen as a red flag for many hotels and establishments. There was one instance when one hotel refused him entry altogether, the Experience were forced onto the street and couldn't find anywhere to stay. They ended up flying back to Germany to continue. In addition, Jimi was booked onto TV shows which required him to lip sync, he often refused stating that he could never remember the lyrics, or how it was played and performed in the studio. This was actually true, Jimi had a terrible time reciting his own lyrics and performing them correctly, replicating the exact record that was released. He rarely performed any song the same way and often just flowed freely depending on the mood. In Helsinki, Jimi hit the headlines again from the Finnish press, who had taken the baton from the UK tabloids, the headline prior to a concert at Hesingin Sanomat ran with *'New Madman coming to Helsinki'*.

This was the first time in Jimi's career that he started to get fed up with the scheduling that his management team had organised. The constant TV shows, interviewers asking the same questions everywhere he went, and the cris-crossing of countries for a single performance or concert were starting to have an effect, even in this early stage of his accession. It would be a reccurring theme for Jimi as his team continued to book him in at any opportunity they could to gain him exposure.

Jimi had several sound issues during these tours, another frustration he found difficult to cope with. There were thousands of fans who were now pouring into the badly organised venues. The issue on the tour stemmed from the heat, which affected the sound coming from his guitar and the Marshall amplification. He would often not play until he got the sound just how he wanted, the crowd often didn't care and booed him, impatient with his need for sonic perfection. Australian writer Germain Greer wrote a report after one such concert: *"They didn't care whether 'Hey Joe' was in tune or not. They just wanted to hear something and adulate. They wanted him to give head to his guitar and rub his cock over it. They didn't want to hear him play. But Jimi wanted, like he always wanted, to play it sweet and high. So, he did, and he fucked with his guitar, and they moaned and swayed about, and he looked at them heavily and knew that they couldn't hear what he was trying to do and never would."*

At one point during a concert in Scandinavia, Jimi, on spotting the continuous agitated crowd movements and noise, yelled back; *"Fuck You, I'm gonna get my guitar in tune if it takes all fucking night."* He broke every string on his guitar and kicked an amp over before smashing the guitar completely, he fused the lights in the venue, and it plummeted it into darkness.

The main issue The Experience had was that the sound systems couldn't cope with the volume and the way that Jimi played, this was early on in the design of equipment that was made to withstand touring. The large protective cases we see today were flimsy by comparison and equipment was often damaged in transit. Jimi also pounded the whammy bar, also known as the Tremelo. In the 1960s he used it more than most and hammered it every night. Before Jimi Hendrix this was used mostly for subtle effect, but Jimi had transformed it into part of his signature sound. The downside to this was that it threw his guitar out of tune frequently.

Another aspect of Jimi's frustration was the actual crowd themselves. Jimi had come from an incredible place to hone his craft; he had played with the best, watched and learned the skills of the great performers in how to control a crowd, when to showboat, when to slow things down, to learn the pace of a show in its entirety. The repetitive nature of giving the audience what they wanted was frustrating for Jimi. He wanted to be heard as well as seen and often became impatient with crowds just wanting to see him showboat without actually hearing what he and the band were playing.

The punishing schedule the management team had in place, and the sound and performance issues he was having were giving him continuous irritation. This annoyance was starting to head into resentment and led the band to start to question what was going on behind the scenes. Jimi had signed a contract, which of course he had to honour, he was performing with The Experience at concerts and TV shows frequently and had the first taste of chart success in the UK, Europe and the USA. But he was also aware that there was a compromise to this frustration, that of being paid and earning money. With the contracts he had signed, along with Mitch and Noel, the band were asking questions. So, along with the irritation of concerts and touring, questions started to surface. Where is the money?

It was now the end of May and The Jimi Hendrix Experience had performed and travelled relentlessly since January, several of the concerts they had played were bringing in around £300-£500 per night, a large sum in the 1960s, so naturally the band were wondering exactly what was going on. It was Noel Redding that eventually stepped up. He wrote a letter that both Jimi and Mitch counter signed, and a meeting was set up with Chas and Mike back at the office. During these meetings Jimi was usually quiet, business talk was not for him, he had a very relaxed attitude toward money, as long as it provided him with enough to continue to create without issues, he was happy. In hindsight though, Jimi needed someone looking at his finances, someone who knew what should have been paid and to whom; for now though, Jimi was just rolling with his freedom. Maybe Noel saw the signs early on, which is why he was the most vocal in the meetings regarding the finance of The Experience and how money was distributed and controlled by Chas and Mike.

It was a complicated web that was in place, one that Jimi and the band would have a tough time following or tracking. The band were given cash, just to keep them quiet for a while, but the basic premiss was that all earnings were split 50/25/25, with Jimi obviously having the larger share. Noel and Mitch were not on a wage, and nothing was ever drafted or signed.

It was now time to concentrate on the album, This June would be a very important month. Mike and Chas had managed to keep the band happy, at least for now, and the carrot of fame and fortune was well and truly dangled. Their first album 'Are You Experienced?' was now completed and ready to go. Until now Jimi Hendrix was still a relatively underground artist, although his reputation as one of the best guitarists on the planet was continuously growing, he had only to this point garnered a couple of hits, and he had no album out to accompany them too. That was now about to change.

'Are You Experienced?' would go on to be one of the most important and compelling albums of all time. It is groundbreaking on multiple levels - technically, musically and culturally. Jimi knew it was good, but even he would have been surprised by its significance in the years ahead, it would even appear in the Library of Congress' National Recording Registry in recognition of its cultural significance to America and the world.

If fame was something that Jimi Hendrix craved when he played the broom as a child, or as a teenager with his first acoustic guitar, when he was playing guitar in the army, or even while touring the chitlin' circuit and the seedy bars of Seattle and New York, then his wish was about to come true. The question was though, would it be as electric as he imagined it would.

Chapter 14

Take Anything You Want From Me

"When I die, I want people to just play my music, go wild and freak out, do anything they want to do."

The debut album *'Are You Experienced?'* and its preceding singles were recorded over a five-month period, from October 1966 through to April 1967. The album was released the following month, in May 1967.

Are You Experienced?

UK & International Version:

Side One
1. Foxy Lady
2. Manic Depression
3. Red House
4. Can You See Me
5. Love or Confusion
6. I Don't Live Today

Side Two
1. May This Be Love
2. Fire
3. 3rd Stone from the Sun
4. Remember
5. Are You Experienced?

North American Version:

Side One
1. Purple Haze
2. Manic Depression
3. Hey Joe
4. Love or Confusion
5. May This Be Love

6. I Don't Live Today

Side Two
1. The Wind Cries Mary
2. Fire
3. Third Stone from the Sun (US edition spelling)
4. Foxey Lady (US edition spelling)
5. Are You Experienced?

The album utilised three separate recording studios over 16 sessions. These were CBS, Olympic and De Lane Lea Studios. Olympic hosted most of the recording sessions, preferred due to its superior acoustics; it was also the most modern, benefiting from the latest equipment, allowing Jimi to do what he loved the most, experimenting with sounds. As the album was a debut, Jimi was working with a limited budget to record with, as a result most of the pre-production work was done at a shared apartment to save costs. Although they were a trio, in essence this was a Jimi Hendrix album, and there was little input from Mitchell or Redding. Jimi, before recording, had all the tempos and sequences already worked out so it was just a case for them to follow his lead.

Jimi was just as much the band leader in the studio as he was on stage, he arranged the majority of tracks and knew exactly what he wanted from bass and drums as well as the guitars. Chas had taken the master copies across to Olympic previously to be mixed by Eddie Kramer, who would continue forward as a key element in getting the sound from Jimi's head onto record. While most bands' debut albums typically consist of original material that they would have played many times, both in the studio and live, Jimi preferred to teach his new songs to Noel and Mitch right before they recorded them. This gave it a fresh sound; they were not able to get complacent and it sounded raw and unaccustomed.

The album itself had a delay on release. Chas was very unhappy with Track records as the delay meant that the release was competing with 'The Wind Cries Mary' which was not long out. He feared that two releases so close together would cancel each other out. His concerns though were soon quashed, the debut album rose quickly reaching number three on the album chart by 10th June. It was more than likely kept from reaching the number one spot by Sgt Pepper.

The album even today is celebrated for being one of the most audacious debuts of all time. Jimi had already secured a formidable underground reputation and was universally admired; he was seen as a phenomenon, especially live. But on record he hadn't yet had any chance to display his skills, apart from on a few releases, and it's here that this changed.

Many were expecting an album that showcased Jimi as an incredible virtuoso guitar player, but the album delivered far more than that. It blended blues, R&B, pop, layers of psychedelia, heavy rock and even elements of jazz. It was presented in a contemporary way, unique in its offering, especially in the studio. Of course, the Beatles release of Sgt Pepper at this time was completely groundbreaking for a studio album, the difference was Jimi was able, and more to the point willing, to replicate the studio sound live. He had the ability; he wouldn't craft an album he couldn't replicate at a live performance.

It was a debut that felt like it was coming from a seasoned veteran, and in many ways it was. Although Jimi was still young, he'd worked the circuits in the USA, housed in blues. He'd studied and played alongside some of the most respected musicians working clubs and bars in major cities linked with musical excellence. Most of the bands in the charts at this time were not even close to the level of competence in musical styles that Jimi had. Lyrically, as well as musically, he was skilled, imaginative and visionary. He could be whimsical as well as eccentric, and his lyrical prowess fitted the music perfectly. And of course, there was his voice, a part of Jimi that he was never satisfied with, one that he would always laugh about in the studio, but something that was far underrated. He was a great vocalist: his timing, his voice, the rhythm he had in it - it was perfect for storytelling, and for the music he was making.

The tracks themselves feel more like a greatest hits package rather than a standard album: It feels more akin to an artist that was showcasing a back catalogue, like it was spanning an entire career for a musician or band that had been around for years. Such was the strength and quality of the record, 'Are You Experienced?' went on to spend 106 weeks on the Billboard 200, eventually selling more than 5 million copies in the US alone.

Successful trendsetting albums have to land at the right time, and for Jimi, 'Are You Experienced?' did just that, it was exactly what the public, fans and wider music loving communities wanted, and it delivered perfectly. It would be difficult for an album like this to even get the green light to be released today, the marketing machine that is in charge of album launches would have an impossible time trying to pigeon hole it into a genre. Senior suits in record label ivory towers and bespectacled marketing executives would have a fit trying to figure out how to sell it to the lucrative teenage girl market.

This was a summer of love debut, the madman and his band had delivered what sounded like divine psychedelia; 'Purple Haze', 'I Don't Live Today', 'Manic Depression', and 'Fire' were all punch drunk with finesse, they had an arrogant swagger that was equally honed with a skilled virtuosity. The music was wrapped around themes that were sprung from primal wondering, lust, and fear. The album was expansive in its feel, it made fans listen to it over and over again, finding new grooves and textures on every listen. It was a far-reaching combination of pop, rock, soul, jazz, funk and stoned experimentation that fitted perfectly within the hedonism of London in May 1967.

Jimi was evolving, he was becoming more accomplished, he said at the time when asked about his career so far, *"The real ambition, man, is like for us to be known for, for us to be respected as musicians and, you know, like songwriters, now that we're trying to get into that."*

The albums eleven tracks were all written by Jimi, it surprised many, especially with its musical diversity, notably Jimi's skillful writing that was away from the standard guitar work. Jimi Hendrix, the songwriter, had arrived. He had obviously gained incredible merit for his experimentations and revolutions, and in London at this time there were many outstanding guitarists on the circuit. When Jimi arrived in London and started playing in the clubs, effectively going toe to toe with the best of the best, he quickly rose to the top, his laid-back shy on stage persona only endeared him more to the professionals looking up at him. But Jimi now showcased himself, possibly begrudgingly, as an established vocalist, as well as a writer-composer of equal merit.

For a debut album, it landed hard as a statement. Debuts are usually, by their very nature, a stepping stone to bigger and better things, the trio here slammed down an album of eclectic content at a level bordering on excellence. It stood out from the rest by a country mile, mainly because of its reach into many styles of music, all mashing and crashing around the main content. It is, for example, only 15 seconds into the introduction of Foxy Lady before the listener understands the magic in the sound coming through. It almost sounds easy, but it's one of the most symbolic representations of Jimi's music. Its rhythmic guitar effects, with layers of feedback, gives something rarely heard on record. The demonic sensual interpretation, blending the charismatic, gives musical surprises that were simply not around before Jimi. It's still refreshing today, especially on vinyl, but trying to understand what the 1967 listener felt when hearing it is fascinating. In comparison, the top 10 singles in the UK charts at this time consisted of Lulu, Tom Jones, Nancy & Frank Sinatra and The Monkees. In contrast it was a stratospheric lunar experience.

This experience is precisely the journey it aims to be. 'Manic Depression', as indicated by its title, features melodies that are immediately catchy, underpinned by Mitch's rhythmic contributions, which infuse a jazz quality that can be extended into live performance jams. 'Are You Experienced?' predominantly incorporates elements of psychedelic rock, acid rock, and hard rock. Blues, however, clearly serves as a primary influence, as exemplified in 'Red House', a true homage that showcases Jimi in his element. This track relies heavily on traditional influences both in technique and subject matter, allowing Jimi to naturally express his roots without forcing or replicating them. He asserts his distinctive touch, combining contemporary blues and rock foundations with his exceptional guitar demonstrations.

The album excels across all tracks, including 'Can You See Me', 'Love or Confusion', and 'Remember', which adhere to the innovative formula developed by the trio. Side one concludes with the immersive 'I Don't Live Today', which contrasts sharply with 'Red House' through its experimental construction and integrated innovations. Throughout, Jimi demonstrates his ability to captivate listeners with varied quotations and meaningful messages. Beyond the feedback and dynamic guitar work, he delivered the sumptuous ballad 'May this be Love', highlighting technical and acoustic complexity. In 'Third Stone from the Sun', he merges psychedelic and prototypical jazz rock with futuristic spoken word elements. Conversely, 'Fire' offers an accessible experience with a strong bass line and catchy choruses, illustrating the trio's ease in exploring soul and funk that transcended initial perceptions of mere experimentation. It exceeded anything heard or seen in 1967 and represented a balance of mystery and genius, elevating Jimi from an underground guitarist to one of the most talented guitarists of all time, swiftly surpassing Eric Clapton and others. Additionally, he emerged as a songwriter, poet, and versatile artist, quickly achieving unprecedented stardom - a status that left him both uncomfortable and perplexed, despite his own recognition of his talent.

During the album's recording and release, few artists were producing what would become the standard three-minute track within this genre, particularly in 1966/1967. Jimi uniquely unveiled the concept of writing concise rock songs packed with enough hooks and twists to engage listeners and leave them wanting more. He elevated the genre significantly; rock music was irrevocably transformed. Previous decades had offered some progression, especially acoustically within blues, folk, country, and jazz. The Beatles had pop well and truly mastered for short songcraft, but it was the electrification revolution of the 1940s that catalysed the birth of rock & roll a decade later, pushing it into the mainstream.

Despite Jimi's ability to showcase cross genres with the guitar, it was the solo where he was most at home, the grooves and the fundamental rhythm were always heading that way. His solo on 'Manic Depression' sounds like it had beamed in from another dimension altogether and of course 'Red House' made the jaws of London's musical elite drop when he was given freedom to perform it on stage. It's an embroidery of music which indelibly watermarks the album. On record, Jimi's ability to showcase his guitar skills, either by grooves or complete solos, within the structure of a pop song, was utterly unique. Even more impressive is that it rarely detracted from the stand-out, casual brilliance that is so abundant.

Going back to the London elite at this time, it was widely acknowledged, and even conceded, that Jimi's sound was the future arriving fast, transiently coming into focus; tacky, awkward, inspirational, exciting, perplexing and sometimes contradictory for sure, but the future, nonetheless, was landing. Jimi's love for jazz was always spoken about during his interviews at this time, he appreciated the players that mastered the genre and showcased it night after night in bars and clubs around the music hubs of major cities. Elite players that were unrecognised by mainstream media, even to this day: Jimi stated at the time; *"I like different jazz, not all the regular stuff. Most of it is blowing blues and that's why I like free form jazz, the groovy stuff instead of the old-time hits."*

The Jimi Hendrix Experience's debut album is a celestial marvel beaming with exemplary creative practice in every facet. The trio channeled unbridled virtuosity, with Jimi at the helm, to the forefront of rock innovation. As a collective they had the ability to weave jazz and contemporary psychedelic styles into a unique and accessible product. For Jimi himself, he had proved that he wasn't just a wizard on the fretboard, as some had previously claimed, he had cemented without any doubt, songwriting ability where he could create compelling lyrics inspired by his life experiences and literary diet. It was an incredible start, unprecedented in terms of its reach, quality and overall standard. Furthermore, Jimi was a live performer that had established his reputation before the album had even been released, and it was here that Jimi's next move would be just as groundbreaking.

Ben Shapiro and Alan Pariser were two young Hollywood entrepreneurs with big ambitions. Alan Pariser was a well-known figure in the rock music scene; he had frequented Los Angeles and the wider area since the mid-sixties. He had a few management roles, notably with singer songwriting duo Delaney & Bonnie and English singer songwriter Dave Mason, amongst others. He also had his eye on festivals, noticing the business potential a wide scale event could bring in. It was here that the first plans were laid down for Monterey Pop. Famous for being a jazz festival since 1958, organisers started assembling plans to completely revitalise Monterey and bring a significant Pop festival to the scene.

Large-scale festivals, like the one initially planned at Monterey, were not common for various reasons. There was minimal demand for extensive gatherings, particularly for rock or pop music. Additionally, equipment and technology in the 1950s and early 1960s were inadequate for projecting sound over a vast outdoor area, and there were no screens to transmit imagery to distant viewers. Consequently, attendees far from the stage could neither hear nor see effectively, presenting immediate challenges for the organisation of large outdoor events. This situation was about to change.

Over the past decade in the United States, a significant development occurred in how music was presented, which subsequently expanded to many countries. This evolution transformed the presentation of popular music, enabling much larger venues to host concerts and ultimately leading to the inception of music festivals, where hundreds of thousands of attendees could watch multiple bands perform. Previously, music was predominantly showcased in bars, dances, and underground clubs. Although larger concerts existed, they often faced sound quality issues. Notably, The Beatles highlighted these challenges, prompting them to return to the studio and focus on experimentation rather than live performances, culminating in the creation of one of the first ever concept albums, the classic Sgt Pepper.

It was the issues with live concerts that prompted the Beatles to effectively retire to the studio. By the time they began their 1966 tour of the United States, it was only Paul McCartney that was still relatively happy with touring. Paul continued pushing the band, persuading them to carry on. At the time it was standard practice for bands to tour regardless of the challenges it would bring, especially in larger venues. He believed it gave them more kudos and would make them stronger musicians. After a miserable show in St. Louis, though, even Paul admitted that this was the last straw, and they needed to stop. It was reported that it was here that the band decided to end all live performances.

After missing their first ever show due to bad weather in Cincinnati, The Beatles flew to St. Louis for a concert at an open-air venue, this concert was even worse, it was a complete wash out with heavy storms. Open air concerts were notoriously bad at this point, both in sound and logistical set up, but if the venue had extreme weather, it made it virtually impossible to perform. Beatles road manager Mal Evans said in The Beatles Anthology. *"When it looked like rain in the open air, I used to be scared stiff. If rain was on the wires, everybody would have been blown up, yet if they'd stopped the show, the kids would have stampeded. Although they continued with the show in St. Louis, they were deeply unhappy with it."* Paul also commented on the St Louis concert *"It rained quite heavily, and they put bits of corrugated iron over the stage, so it felt like the worst little gig we'd ever played at even before we'd started as a band, We were having to worry about the rain getting in the amps and this took us back to the Cavern days*

- *it was worse than those early days. And I don't think the house was full. After the gig, I remember us getting in a big empty steel-lined wagon, like a removal van, there was no furniture in there - nothing. We were sliding around trying to hold on to something, and at that moment everyone said, 'Oh, this bloody touring lark - I've had it up to here, man.' I finally agreed. I'd been trying to say, 'Ah, touring's good and it keeps us sharp. We need touring, and musicians need to play. Keep music live.' I had held on to that attitude when there were doubts, but finally I agreed with them."* John Lennon also reflected on the last few dates of touring with the band; *"One night on a show in the South somewhere, somebody let off a firecracker while we were on stage. There had been threats to shoot us, the Klan were burning Beatle records outside and a lot of the crew-cut kids were joining in with them. Somebody let off a firecracker and every one of us - I think it's on film - look at each other, because each thought it was the other that had been shot. It was that bad."*

While the show in St. Louis was something The Beatles wanted to forget, the ongoing accumulation of chaotic concerts meant they had simply had enough, they were ready for a break. The band decided to play their final show, at Candlestick Park in San Francisco. Paul McCartney asked press officer Tony Barrow to record the concert, and they photographed themselves afterward. *"We placed our cameras on the amplifiers and put them on a timer,"* George Harrison said, talking afterwards to Rolling Stone, *"We stopped between tunes, Ringo got down off the drums, and we stood facing the amplifiers with our back to the audience and took photographs. We knew: 'This is it – we're not going to do this again. This is the last concert.' It was a unanimous decision."*

It wasn't just The Beatles that encountered substantial challenges while touring as their popularity increased. When the venues grew in size, issues related to substandard facilities and inadequate equipment became more prominent. Jimi was among those experiencing frustration due to these limitations; however, a considerable change was on the horizon.

Up until this point, individual bands managed their own crews and moved from venue to venue. Plans were being developed to centralise pop music performances into larger-scale events at single venues, capable of accommodating thousands of fans over several days. This ambitious initiative required a collective effort to integrate the necessary technology and logistics. Ambitious entrepreneurs such as Ben Shapiro and Alan Pariser had recognised a strong demand for such events and were well aware of the need for careful planning and coordination to bring this vision to life.

Music was on the brink of intersecting with an unprecedented counterculture movement, characterised by a rapid demand for freedom through music and art. A place where individuals from diverse backgrounds could gather in unity to appreciate this common collective. The response to the demand would give rise to the music festival, an event that would become inseparably linked, with Jimi Hendrix.

Chapter 15

Killing Floor

"When the power of love overcomes the love of power the world will know peace."

It is widely conceded that the catalyst for Monterey was the 'Human Be-In'. One of the first large scale gatherings of pop music to gain media attention. On January 14, 1967, more than 20,000 hippies and other participants in the counterculture movement gathered in San Francisco's Golden Gate Park, the plan was of course to do more than simply 'be together', but music was the headline. The event would put the Haight-Ashbury district of San Francisco well and truly on the map as a hub of activity around the growing appetite for anti-establishment get togethers. With an event on this scale, it's easy to understand that entrepreneurs would quickly seize on the moment to capitalise on the thousands of people determined to travel to such events.

The Human Be-In had a considerable impact that sparked the appetite for future events. It attracted significant media attention and featured notable countercultural leaders such as Allen Ginsberg, Timothy Leary, Gary Snyder, and Jerry Rubin, each addressing an enthusiastic crowd of thousands. Each speaker's address was intentionally kept to approximately 15 minutes to prevent the event from becoming a rally and causing disruption among attendees. Musical performances included rock bands from San Francisco, such as The Jefferson Airplane, Big Brother and the Holding Company, and The Grateful Dead.

Copies of the San Francisco Oracle were freely distributed; this underground newspaper published 12 issues from September 1966 to February 1968 in the Haight-Ashbury neighbourhood. The Oracle was an early member of the Underground Press Syndicate, part of a network of underground newspapers established in 1966 that featured countercultural news stories, government policy criticism, and cartoons. Also hitting the press circulation was a parachuter - widely rumoured to be renowned chemist and LSD manufacturer Stanley Owsley III. He was reported to have distributed over 100,000 free doses of LSD, undercutting the black market; a generous contribution to peace love and unity.

The organisers of the event were basically trying to bring common ground to diverse groups. They believed that there was a growing fracture within certain parties, and this was leading to potentially harmful movements: Notably the lifestyle hippies of Haight-Ashbury and the politically oriented anti-establishment movement in Berkeley. The aim was for these opposite groups to come together, to become more familiar with one another, to see that they were of similar mindsets, and, as the name suggest, to simply be together. Larry Freudiger of Austin's The Rag wrote of the Be-in: *"The revolutionary and the asocial elements have long needed to bridge the artificial boundaries between them, and judging from recent news, they've done it."*

This basic strategy, to bring everyone together, would be the first of a series of countercultural Be-ins, or Love-Ins as they were also known, that would follow all over the country. There were countless underground papers that acted decisively in organising, advertising, and documenting what happened at all of these gatherings, and these in turn encouraged the next event. Be-ins and love-ins became one of the central ways for participants opposed to social norms to get to know one another, and to create culture together. They were also central for making their political presence felt in cities and towns with much smaller communities than the larger popular cities such as San Francisco or New York.

Although the creation of a pop festival was a new concept, Jazz festivals had been around for many years. In Boston, in 1954, the Newport Jazz Festival took place. It was, as the name suggests, a pure jazz showcase with performances from Billy Holiday, Ella Fitzgerald and others. It was billed as the first Annual American Jazz Festival and was held at Newport Casino, in the Bellevue Avenue Historic District of Newport, Rhode Island. The festival also had academic panel discussions in addition to live musical performances. It was the first time that an event of this size had brought people together with many different acts performing, these acts were only permitted if they had an association with jazz.

Following the success of the Jazz festival, The Newport Folk Festival followed in 1959, with performances from Joan Baez, Brownie McGhee and Pete Seeger, and from here things started to change. Quickly, the gatherings became political, and a force for legislative change: Constitutional and social comment started to become a large part of the festival. It was a concept of integration and performance, fusing together. These early concerts affected the presentation of music; before these two events, the festival itself, as it would become known, was pretty unheard of. The Newport Jazz Festival and The Newport Folk Festival paved the way for what was to come. Soon the idea spread across to England.

The National Jazz Festival in Richmond, England, became one of the first in the UK following on from Newport. The jazz festival, as a concept, became well known within the jazz community itself, but had not crossed over into the rock and pop world. In an unusual twist, The National Jazz Federation actually ran the famous Marquee Club in Oxford Street, London, which would go on to host some of the biggest bands in the UK at the time. This meant that the National Jazz Festival moved slowly into other areas of music. Now, music by bands and musicians that had performed at the Marquee Club had a gateway into the event, reaching a large audience. This evolved quickly as the festival gained ground and the transition slowly moved it into a more R&B and rock gathering. Blues-infused groups were now becoming prominent and started to move in, and of course this changed the demographic of the audience as its popularity grew. The whole concept of a music festival was now taking hold and becoming something that the younger generation would flock to in their droves.

One aspect that the organisers of Monterey noticed when planning the festival was that most of the potential attendees were white kids from affluent backgrounds, numbering in the thousands. This represented untapped potential for any aspiring entrepreneur. Initially, Shapiro and Pariser raised $50,000 and hired a publicist, Derek Taylor, who had previously served as the press officer for The Beatles. Despite the significant sum raised, which was considerable for the 1960s, the festival encountered difficulties early on; the plan was to hold a three-day event, but booking acts required substantial upfront fees and it quickly exceeded the budget. Additional funds to secure performers would be needed. Various options were discussed, such as shortening the festival to one or two days; however, a unanimous vote determined that it should remain a three-day event. Paul Simon was another artist approached; however, due to high upfront costs, he couldn't be secured.

Derek proposed a suggestion that was eventually accepted: the event would be non-profit, allowing the acts to effectively select themselves and cover their own expenses. All proceeds would be donated to charity. A committee was established, which primarily served to generate significant publicity. The committee included notable figures such as Paul McCartney, Mick Jagger, Brian Wilson, and Smokey Robinson. During the initial planning stages, it was actually Paul McCartney who suggested that the festival would not be worthwhile unless it featured Jimi Hendrix. Determined to get him involved, Paul flew back to London.

Jimi agreed to the festival, after all he had proved himself beyond measure in England and Europe and was, when Paul invited him to perform, riding high on the success of his debut album. He performed a final concert at the Saville Theatre, with Paul McCartney in the audience. Jimi celebrated his last gig in London before he flew to the US for Monterey. At the end of his performance, he smashed his guitar and threw the shattered white pieces of the fender into the crowd. When the broken guitar was retrieved it was discovered that written on the back was a poem written by Jimi, it read; *'May this be love or confusion born out of frustration wracked feelings, of not being able to make true physical love to the universal gypsy Queen, true free expressed music, darling guitar please rest. Amen'*. Paul and many others were convinced Jimi could be an international star, not just confined to the UK and parts of Europe. Monterey would be his opportunity.

The event would turn the sleepy little Monterey, California, into the epicenter of rock-and-roll music. The team had been assembled to bring the idea to life, and they had succeeded. They could not have predicted, however, the true impact it would have, especially for Jimi, whose performance was, even by his own ridiculous standard, above and beyond what anyone would have expected. The team consisting of musician John Phillips, manager and producer Lou Adler, promoter Alan Pariser and publicist Derek Taylor were about to change the course of live music forever. The festival and the way it was presented, would be born here.

Jimi had travelled from the UK in style. He sat in the back of Mike Jeffery's Rolls Royce and then boarded a TWA flight. He chatted at length in first class with stewardesses and watched TV. On arrival Jimi visited Broadway and the many music shops, buying countless albums along the way. That evening Jimi tracked down his old haunts, especially Café Au Go Go, which that evening hosted a performance by Richie Havens, who was still yet to be a star. Jimi was still to this point relatively unknown in the mainstream in America, he did however dress and act like a true star. That evening he wore white trousers with a bright floral multi colored jacket; to top it off he wore a bright emerald, green scarf. On the back of the jacket were the words 'Champion Bird Watcher'.

It was reported that yet again Jimi had difficulty getting a cab that evening, and the ones that did stop threw him out; basically if you were black, dressed strangely or looked like a hippie they would rarely stop. Jimi ticked all the boxes. Keith Altham who was following Jimi for the NME was with him that evening; *"Not only would they not stop for him, but they would also try and run him over, so we had to keep him in doorways, and then go and stop a cab. Even then the cabby told him to get out. Jimi would just say 'Just get out and don't say a word'. A year or so later of course they couldn't do enough for him."*

The three-day Monterey International Pop Music Festival would bring together a collection of major acts that fitted the demographic and the overall feeling that was needed: Simon & Garfunkel, The Grateful Dead, and The Mamas & the Papas to name a few. The event would also introduce the music world to others that would become icons in their own right, ones yet to be discovered in the USA. The Who and Jimi would be watched for the first time on a grand scale and presented to American audiences, the event also turned Janis Joplin into a star overnight, the famous scene where Mamas & Papas singer Cass Elliot is watching Janis sing open mouthed is a classic visual from the festival. Otis Redding, who only 15 months prior, had recorded his legendary 'In Person at the Whisky a Go Go' in Los Angeles, performed incredibly at the event and was widely acknowledged. Otis would tragically die just six months later in a plane crash in Wisconsin.

The line up also had a twist in the tail, it was attended by four members of the infamous 27 club who were at this festival at the same time: Along with Jimi was Brian Jones, Janis Joplin and Jim Morrison. It was actually Brian Jones himself that introduced Jimi to the stage, introducing him as *"the most exciting guitar player I have ever heard."*

The festival preparation had proved to be an unequivocal success and paved the way forward for others in its wake. With it being such a huge event it obviously wasn't without its issues though, and many had to be overcome as things progressed in the run up. There were frequent concerns that the youths and hippies would descend in their thousands causing chaos to the sleepy town and surrounding area, it could potentially be a hotbed for trouble. This was one of the reasons why the mainstream pop acts were largely avoided, and the tact shifted to welcome a more mature crowd. The business side of the festival also proved difficult as managers like Mike Jeffery were wanting advances, while the event itself was angled towards charity and an improved society for all citizens. It was focused towards love and peace, encompassing everything that was appealing to young people in 1960s free liberal culture.

John Phillips officially opened the festival at 9pm on Friday evening, at that point there was an estimated 30,000 people in the showground, with around 7,500 in the arena itself. This rose over the weekend to around 90,000 people, because of this number the police force kept a low key, they ignored drug taking, letting things happen, staying as invisible as possible within the event. There were even reports of police officers walking around smiling happily, as the marijuana smoke wafted around them.

Although The Stones were discussed to attend the festival, they were not permitted to enter the USA at the time due to pending drug charges surrounding Mick Jagger and Keith Richards. Mick was, however, part of the committee alongside Brian Wilson and Smokey Robinson. Brian Jones was unaffected by the charges and attended alone. The general line up was structured to have pop acts on Friday evening, Californian bands on

Saturday and the true superstars finishing the festival on Sunday, scattered between were various MC's.

Once the momentum grew, there was also a growing list of bands who wanted to play but for various reasons were not permitted, mainly because of fear of how the crowd would react. It had to be harmony throughout, no one behind the scenes wanted to risk any trouble or negative reaction to anything presented. The Monkees were one band who wanted to play, Peter Tork of the Monkees, who was the only credible musician in the band, pushed hard for an appearance. The conclusion was though that they would go down badly, they were a manufactured band and could not be taken seriously amongst the more seasoned acts that were already scheduled to play. The Jimi Hendrix Experience were down for Sunday night and Jimi and the band enjoyed the time they had before their performance. Brian Jones spent a lot of time with Jimi prior to this, and rumours circulated of LSD and other substances including STP, known to stand for, *Serenity, Tranquility and Peace* being frequently taken. It was rumoured to give an 18-hour trip on just 3 milligrams.

Monterey had a real Californian vibe; and despite the fears of the organisers it set the standard for future festivals. It embraced peace and hope, and from a music perspective it made stars out of many acts, in the USA it made Jimi Hendrix. It was the benchmark for a festival of like-minded, open-minded people. An advert of free spirit. Monterey was a revolution for pop music and how it was observed to a wider audience; it captured a counterculture movement using music as the foundation within a new environment, and it gave force to a community that bound everyone together. In many aspects the festival going audience was more important than the music and the bands themselves.

Prior to Jimi hitting the stage he chilled out and tried to relax as much as possible. He got high for most of the afternoon and enjoyed sitting in the crowd and watching Ravi Shankar. It was a cloudy Sunday afternoon when sitar maestro Pandit Ravi Shankar played his mesmeric four-hour set, he was accompanied on stage by Ustad Allah Rakha on the tabla and Kamala Chakravarty playing the tanpura. Ravi was a huge favorite of The Beatles and fitted the 'Love-in vibe' perfectly. He later recalled; *"The Monterey Pop Festival was the real beginning. All the young people were so fresh and so passionate and so drawn to my music. From the moment I started my first stroke on the instrument (sitar), I knew that we were connected. I saw some very famous people in the field of rock and pop music. It was very strange. They were just sitting there, listening to me, swinging away and enjoying themselves. I had seen them perform the night before and they were so different. I was scared after that because their way of presenting* the show is so different from ours. I didn't realise it then, I was excited, but later on so many people told me how it did change their life, which was very touching," he added.

This unfamiliarity was not just lost for Ravi Shankar. Jimi himself would have been acutely aware that apart from some minor radio airplay in the USA, many had not seen or heard his music before. Less would have been familiar with his guitar playing when it came to live music on this scale. His hits to this point had been in the UK only, which had the benefit of one or two mainstream channels, the USA was far more fragmented so only a few US radio stations, with new FM frequencies, were playing him. This would be his first major US debut. Jimi had a great spot at the festival, giving him star status and a tremendous impact when he would enter the stage. There was a reported heated exchange, however, backstage with Jimi and The Who guitarist Pete Townshend.

This event marked a significant debut for The Who, underscoring their pursuit of American stardom alongside Jimi. Both The Who and The Jimi Hendrix Experience had established reputations for their dynamic performances up to this point. Consequently, neither Jimi nor Pete were willing to follow the other on stage. Due to their similar tactics of concluding performances by smashing equipment and making dramatic exits, both artists refused to perform after the other. It was reportedly resolved with a coin toss. The Who lead singer Roger Daltrey recalled the standoff; *"Jimi was playing Sgt. Pepper on his guitar, but, and this was the amazing thing, he was playing all the parts. He would go from a bit of orchestration to a vocal part, to a solo – the whole thing on one guitar. The others stood and watched, accompanying Hendrix by beating out a rhythm on anything close to hand. At one point Jimi stood on a stool in front of Pete to show off on the guitar, as if to say, 'Don't fuck with me, you little shit.'* In the end, John Phillips suggested they toss a coin." Pete won, The Who would go on before Jimi.

For UK bands such as The Who, this was a crucial time for gaining recognition in the expansive American market. The British invasion had been solidified, but at this point, only The Beatles and The Rolling Stones had consistently achieved significant chart success. It was widely known that the event was now being organised for an upcoming film, making it a prime opportunity for performers to gain guaranteed exposure. Pete instructed his band to deliver a performance that would make a lasting impact on American music.

Winning the coin toss allowed The Who the first chance to showcase the raw energy of rock music, and they did not disappoint. Their performance was exceptional, and the band's intense playing style captivated the audience. They concluded their set with the iconic 'My

Generation' and the customary smashing of instruments. As the stage lay strewn with broken equipment, conversation throughout the grounds centred on The Who's remarkable performance. They had delivered a superb show, but Jimi was waiting his turn backstage.

Jimi wasn't too concerned about playing after The Who, he had selected four Fenders and sat to paint swirls on them, one of them would be sacrificed during the performance; Jimi spoke with Eric Burden prior to hitting the stage; *"I'm looking forward to tonight man, I'm so high, living on my nerves. The spaceships gonna really take off tonight."*

After The Who had performed Jimi couldn't really go on immediately afterwards, the crowd were still digesting what they had seen, and of course there was lots of clearing up to do. It was agreed that The Grateful Dead would go on next, giving Jimi time to tune up backstage in an area sectioned off with some VOX AC 30 amps. Unfortunately for The Grateful Dead it was a bad move, they were sandwiched between a prime The Who and a wound-up Jimi Hendrix. They openly admitted afterwards that it was dreadful. Even Phil Lesh, the co-founding bassist, admitted several years later that the Dead's performance at Monterey Pop stunk. *"We have a tradition of blowing the big ones,"* Lesh said. *"It was a famously bad performance, stuck as it was between two acts that absolutely shattered rock expectations."* Frontman Jerry Garcia agreed ; *"It was one of the classic bad scenes for us. We came onstage just after The Who finished smashing their equipment for the first time in America. Theres this 'aahhh', the audience is devastated. The Who were beautifully theatrical, there's clouds of smoke and explosions and they're clearing away the debris. And so we came out and played our little act - ding ching ding ding - and then Jimi Hendrix comes on after us. We were erased from existence."*

After a short break, the announcement came over the PA: *"And now the next act, one of the hottest bands from England. It's led by an American - Jimi Hendrix. And here to introduce him - he's all the way over from London... Brian Jones of The Rolling Stones. Ladies and gentlemen, Brian Jones!"* Brian swaggered on stage to large applause and introduced The Jimi Hendrix Experience. *"I'd like to introduce a very good friend, a fellow countryman of yours.... He's the most exciting performer I've ever heard...The Jimi Hendrix Experience."* With that Jimi walked on to the stage.

Although the band were introduced as a new outfit, they were of course anything but. They had already played as a collective over countless gigs in and around Europe, and were playing the psychedelic scene like seasoned veterans, full of swagger and assurance. Mitch Mitchell and his jazz infused style of drumming complemented the beat perfectly, he was able to add his own footnote instead of just keeping time, while the bass of Noel Redding was equally impressive, playing almost like another lead guitar as opposed to backing up the band, as is often the case; he was contributing not just supporting.

The key driver to all this of course was Jimi himself. He was dazzling and electrifying throughout, showcasing a seductive reinvention of musical traditions. Wearing his ruffled shirt with feather boa, red trousers and hair teased into perfection he was the very essence of rock and roll. He was a vision of ingenuity and pomposity in equal measure, ironically an outfit he was forbidden to wear on stage only a year or so before was now the very substance of his presence.

The Jimi Hendrix Experience had maximum impact, settling into the set they blasted into their high-octane take on Howlin' Wolf's 'Killing Floor' followed by 'Foxey Lady', the latter introduced by Jimi with a self-assured: 'Dig this'. Their first big American gig might have been a touch belated, but the kaleidoscopic performance and on-stage antics were well and truly honed. Mitch's drumming was not fazed by Jimi's constant flights of fancy, where he drifted away letting the guitar take any direction it wanted to, Mitch in turn was able to make a few excursions of his own while still holding the groove. Noel's liquid playing approached the bass as another lead instrument, contributing ideas and changes rather than simply holding a bass line for continuity. The threesome meshed superbly on what is widely regarded as one of the best festival sound systems ever - the crowd had a hard time acknowledging it was just a trio. When listening back afterwards to the Live at Monterey album it's easy to understand why, Jimi was almost casual in the way he utilised feedback and fuzz with power and originality.

His relaxed almost spoken vocals were wonderful, and he played in a way that no one had ever witnessed before. It was unconventional but strangely familiar, rolling around the floor, humping the guitar and speakers, and of course the sacrificial burning of the guitar at the end. These tricks never once obstructed or faded the actual musicianship and skill that was on offer; it was true magic. Jimi Hendrix at Monterey exemplified the counterculture's musical revolution. He had arrived at Monterey as a relative unknown, and he would leave as the absolute embodiment of everything a festival represented.

Many musicians throughout history have covered songs, and these covers have been so powerful that they take the song as their own, they become forever associated with it, owning the updated version. Jimi would of course have 'All along the Watchtower' as a staple of his catalogue to come later, but he, for now, had 'Wild Thing', a song that felt it was literally made for him, to perform live. The finale brought an electric feral version of the track, and it became a key moment of his set. A plethora of unorthodox guitar-playing, even watching this today the performance is unique, unmatched in its theatrical delivery and technical skill.

The highlight of Jimi Hendrix's Monterey performance occurs during the midpoint of his set, featuring the songs 'Hey Joe', 'Can You See Me', and 'The Wind Cries Mary'. During this segment, Hendrix focuses solely on his musicianship, devoid of any theatrical showmanship or distracting gimmicks. These 12 minutes effectively establish Jimi Hendrix as a key figure in achieving the festival's objectives. While the rock elements, particularly Hendrix's solos, are prominent, the essence of blues remains central to his performance. He demonstrated profound respect for the blues through his playing, viewing it as a dynamic and evolving entity rather than a static tradition. Hendrix's mastery conveyed the blues as a spirit rather than a rigid form, infusing it with renewed vigour that resonated deeply with the audience. His performance was not only musically appreciated, but also wholeheartedly embraced by the spectators, who recognised the alignment with their progressive ideologies.

The trio performed under intense scrutiny, not only from the captivated audience but also from observers on the sidelines. Their ability to synchronise and complement each other was natural and instinctive. Mitch was an exceptionally captivating drummer, performing alongside Jimi rather than merely providing background rhythm. His role was crucial in the power trio format, offering essential support to the overall sound. Aware of his limitations following The Who, Jimi understood he could not replicate the dramatic equipment destruction for his finale. However, the deliberate sacrifice of a guitar at the conclusion of 'Wild Thing' remains a landmark moment in live music history, showcasing premeditated brilliance in showmanship and theatre.

Prior to this though, Jimi had something to say, he knew he had nailed Monterey, he knew America was now in his grasp and he paused for thought… *"You know, everybody says that, man, but this is something else, man, like, it is no big story about we couldn't make it here, so we go over to England and America doesn't like it because you know, our feet's too big and we've got fat mattress and golden underwear. It aint no scene like that brother, you know, it just, dig, you know, laying around. And I went to England and picked up these two cats and now here we are. Man, its so groovy to come back here this way and, you know, really get a chance to really play, you know. I can sit here all night and say thank you, thank you, thank you, but I could just as well grab you man, but I just can't do it, so,*

I'm gonna sacrifice something here that I really love, okay. Don't think I'm silly here doing this, Cos' I don't think I'm losing my mind. Last night, oh man, god, this is it for everybody, this is the only way I can do it. So, we're gonna play the English and American anthem combined, Okay. Oh, don't get mad, I want everyone to join in too, alright, don't get mad, there's nothing more I can do."

The speech prompted Jimi to engage in an intense session of guitar playing. The tritone was back to the fore, matching the mood of the event perfectly. Mitch performed vigorously on the drums with exceptional skill, and the trio seamlessly transitioned into the initial bars of 'Wild Thing'. For the conclusion of the set, Jimi displayed all his showmanship, including playing the guitar between his legs, with his teeth, and behind his back. He interacted with the speakers, managed the feedback, and even executed a somersault.

At the close he stood alongside his guitar, holding it astride; he hit the whammy bar constantly, like an angry father smacking a disobedient child. He then walked to the back of the stage and came forward once more. He sprayed the guitar from his crotch, lighter fuel spurting forward and drenching the doomed Fender about to be sacrificed. He then lit the fuel, igniting the fire. What followed is one of the most iconic images of Jimi Hendrix, a ceremonial kneeling, a ritual sacrifice over a fender Stratocaster: He beckoned and encourage the flames upwards, only stopping briefly to squirt more liquid fuel onto the bedevilled instrument. It was the perfect ending to his performance. The flames rose, Jimi then lifted the burning guitar and proceeded to smash it into pieces, valiantly tossing it into the crowd as it emitted its final inevitable doomed sounds.

Monterey was his.

Chapter 16

Light your Fire

"I've been imitated so well I've heard people copy my mistakes."

The Experience walked off stage to an astonished audience, what had they just witnessed? Not only was this an incredible live band, but the relatively unknown guitar player, the enigma of a front man that had just performed, was something else. At Monterey, 90,000 spectators had just witnessed a performance so unique it was a moment to behold, a passage in time for the watching crowd to forever remember, reminisce and share.

Writing about Jimi's Monterey Pop Festival performance when reviewing the CD release of it back in 1986 Rolling Stone said:
    With the Rainbow Shriek of his flaming Stratocaster at the 1967 Monterey International Pop Festival, Jimi Hendrix dramatically announced the arrival of the new Aquarian age of peace, love and spiritual aspiration. At the same time, he liberated rock & roll guitar once and for all from the choke of Top Forty dictums. The way he tore into 'Purple Haze', scratching the song's elephantine funk intro with sawtoothed distortion, and calmly skated up the shimmering, ascending chorus of 'The Wind Cries Mary' had no precedent in rock guitar and, even at Monterey, no equal. The American debut of the Jimi Hendrix Experience at Monterey is still a revelation. An orgasmic explosion of singing feedback, agitated stretches of jazzy improvisation and recombinant R&B guitar. Sucking the crowd into his hurricane sound, Hendrix dragged Dylan's 'Like a Rolling Stone' through Mississippi-blues mud, attacked his own 'Can You See Me' with amphetamine impatience and, egged on by Noel Redding and Mitch Mitchell's rhythmic frenzy, drove 'Wild Thing' head-on into a wall of white noise.

After the iconic performance backstage it was chaos, high fives were exchanged, and amazed glances were traded back and forth. Heads nodded and overall appreciation for what had just happened was systematically applauded. Chas desperately tried to get back-stage from his position in the crowd; it took him over half an hour to battle through. Once there he found Jimi and the band basking in the glory of what they had achieved.

Everyone conceded that what had happened was beyond success, it was an historical moment, especially when you reflect back to the fact this was one of the first major pop festivals to be presented in such a way. The only section of the backstage ensemble that would have had any doubts were perhaps The Mamas and Papas who were due on next to close the festival with their folk-rock vocals; a band perfectly placed for such an event, but also a band that was given the worst slot in music history. A mental note was subconsciously added here by all bands, *do not ever follow Jimi Hendrix.*

Monterey was potentially Jimi's most together gig so far, although the crowd were relatively new to The Jimi Hendrix Experience it was nevertheless as hit-crammed as possible. Other shows he had performed were louder and contain more rarities with extended free flowing guitar breaks, but Monterey was recorded when both festivals and Jimi were unfamiliar, and more ebullient. He spoke freely, in a relaxed way, almost before every track, and seemed cheerful rather than stoned-cool. All of this made a substantial contribution to his perception from the crowd, he single handedly reclaimed the very essence of chilled out blues and rock.

His union of psychedelic funk, rock and blues became one of the crucial bridges between the black arts movement of the early 1960s and funk itself, it created a renaissance that emerged at the end of the decade. It made Monterey Pop the most significant festival to date, marking the moment the previously regional and segregated hippy scenes came together in unanimity. Culturally it enabled this freedom to expand. Jann Wenner, who was present during The Experience's performance at Monterey, and would later go on to launch Rolling Stone magazine wrote; *"Monterey was the nexus - it sprang from what the Beatles began, and from it sprang what followed."*

The festival's success and exposure turned the US music business upside down. Music executives started to realise the cash cow that had been sleeping, it was here that rock as a standalone genre came into its own, surpassing the traditional genres of pop and rock'n'roll. They even started to dress differently, emulating the very bands they wanted to attract and represent.

Things had changed rapidly and dramatically, the performances by The Who and The Jimi Hendrix Experience showcased what a festival can bring; elite performances, and a fully engaged audience basking in the glory of music, love and peace. Jimi had arrived as a relative unknown to become the personification of organiser John Phillips' intention for three days of inclusivity and adventure, during the Summer of Love in 1967.

Jimi was now fast becoming famous on both sides of the Atlantic, talked about and discussed by the musical elite and music fans alike. Mike and

Chas started to lay down plans to exploit the momentum. New material was key in continuing his success, the management team quickly prepared for him to start recording again, but first there were more gigs to attend. Jimi would have little to no time to dwell and enjoy his rising fame.

It was not just Monterey that he was scheduled to perform when he flew to the US. Jimi was booked even before he left England on a US tour; a wide misconception is that he performed at Monterey and then retreated back triumphantly to England to continue recording and performing. Another was that he was booked in quickly around the USA solely 'because' of his performance at Monterey instead of coming back, again this was not true.

Jimi was scheduled for a set of performances at Bill Graham's Fillmore West. Without any time to rest after his Monterey success, he flew with his band to San Francisco for six shows, two per night, plus an open-air gig in Golden Gate Park. Jefferson Airplane were the main headline booked at Fillmore. They had previously headlined Monterey on Saturday night so were now fully aware of Jimi Hendrix. When the lineup was announced they realised they were scheduled to go on stage directly following Jimi. They now flatly refused to go on stage after him, no doubt learning from the predicament that presented itself to The Grateful Dead. In the end, they declined to perform altogether. As a result, Bill Graham paid The Experience a $2000 bonus for adjusting the order at the top of the bill.

Jimi was now in hot demand, not just in respect of performing when and where his management booked him, but also with the rock 'n' roll elite and celebrities of the time. He spent time with Peter Tork at his estate in Laurel Canyon, the bass guitarist and keyboardist for The Monkees. He was the only real member of the manufactured outfit that was a competent musician in his own right and was still trying desperately to get the band some kind of musical direction. Jimi also spent time with Cass Elliot, Judy Collins, Joni Mitchell, David Crosby and Mike Bloomfield.

Whist in Laurel Canyon Jimi also became acquainted with Devon Wilson, a groupie of sorts that had been on the music scene for many years, she was associated with many tours and key musicians, in today's world she would have been referred to as a socialite of the highest echelons. At this time, Devon stayed with Jimi in a house that was previously owned by escapologist Houdini, unfortunately for Jimi there was no escaping from his increasingly gruelling schedule. Devon would also become an individual that would be significant in Jimi's final hours, but that's for later. The schedule in place wasn't helped by the constant partying and drug use that was now part of his everyday scene. Jimi was now existing on drink, drugs and constant travel. His life was chaotic and unbalanced, with music becoming his only real focus and stability.

On January 16, 1964, a small club on the Sunset Strip opened its doors for the first time; it was Whisky a Go Go. It would later become the first live music venue to be inducted into the Rock and Roll Hall of Fame and the most iconic club of the strip. It was owned by Elmer A. Valentine, a self-described crooked cop who fled Chicago to start a new life on the Sunset Strip. The venue was an immediate hit, with headliner Johnny Rivers attracting celebrity-studded sold-out audiences. In 1977 critic Robert Hilburn wrote; *"For much of the '60s and early '70s, Elmer Valentine's Whisky was the most important rock club in town, It was an incubation spot for local bands and a showcase for highly touted visiting groups."* Jimi made his debut on July 2nd, 1967. On the bill that evening were Sam & Dave, who Jimi had played with previously, they fired him of course for the standard reasons of dress code and not towing the line. Here though, things were different, Elmer asked Sam and Dave if Jimi could play with them, he recalled: *"The people started lining up, Sam and Dave arrived that night and thought it was for the. When Jimi finished his set, the place cleared out, nobody stayed for Sam and Dave."* Jimi had had his revenge.

Places like Whiskey a Go Go were perfect for Jimi, they were made for him. A club where he would effortlessly leave an enduring impression on all those fortunate enough to witness the magic unfold. The Jimi Hendrix Experience served as a testament to the ability to captivate audiences and push the boundaries of musical expression. Jimi's performance that evening left an indelible mark on the history of Whiskey A Go Go, solidifying its standing as a venue that hosted some of the most memorable moments in music.

Despite the magnificent performance, the band were feeling the effects of the schedule. Bassist Noel Redding recalled: *"We were tired and too intoxicated to care. We could hardly stand up, and it didn't help that we had a 10am flight to New York the next day."*

In addition to his ongoing travel and live performances, Jimi was frequently encouraged to compose new songs so that they would be ready for recording when studio time was scheduled. Rapid recording was essential to minimise costs for management. One of the songs initiated during this period was 'The Burning of the Midnight Lamp', although it was temporarily shelved to be revisited later. This particular track was written during a challenging period for Jimi, as the demands of his lifestyle were beginning to take a toll. He was constantly in transit, moving between flights, venues, and hotels. His natural lack of sleep was exacerbated by the partying and substance use, which adversely affected his health, mood, and overall well-being. Additionally, he faced a lack of control over decisions made behind the scenes regarding touring, selecting singles, choosing hotels, and arranging numerous flights. This was something Jimi had accepted, he had little choice in decisions and business matters, he rarely saw any money, and what was made was hastily redistributed on forward projects. It was a whirlwind existence with little to no supervision. Although Jimi was somewhat used to this lack of control to this point, one decision that Mike Jefferey was about to make took him completely by surprise, in fact it was a decision that made him furious. Mike announced that he had agreed, arranged and booked The Jimi Hendrix Experience on a nationwide tour across America, where they would be supporting; The Monkees.

For Peter Tork, accustomed to rubbing shoulders with elite musicians, this was an excellent opportunity. He was aiming hard for The Monkees to be taken more seriously, to move away from the teen market and into an area more respected. For Jimi of course it was a disaster, over the previous years he had worked tirelessly to build up a credible following, gaining notoriety and respect within the musical circles he was frequenting. To be part of a tour with a manufactured band aimed at teenage girls was nothing more than an embarrassment. He had said previously; *"I'm so embarrassed that America could make something stupid like that, they could have least done it with a group that had something to offer".*

Simply put, Mike Jeffery had prioritised profit over musical integrity, sacrificing it for Jimi's teen exposure, which he thought was needed. He saw Jimi as the main asset in his business empire, and this decision proved that. Despite Jimi's feelings and fury, the plans went ahead for a full-scale US tour. The record companies and promoters also saw no issues. They saw The Jimi Hendrix Experience and The Monkees as similar acts attracting teens, completely ignoring Jimi's remarkable background. It was the screaming teenage girl market where they saw the ultimate gain.

At this point in the USA the only band to rival The Monkees was The Beatles, who had recently decided to quit touring, so looking at it from a touring and exposure perspective it was concluded that this would be good for Jimi, from a purely business sense. One Warner Bros executive, Stan Cornyn said at the time: *"Anything beyond Dean Martin fell into one category, and The Monkees and Jimi Hendrix were beyond Dean Martin, so nobody at the time had any issues with pairing them."*

With arguments continuing behind the scenes Jimi moved on with his current tour and headed to New York. Here he encountered the same issues he had previously, something he was now all too familiar with. The band were laughed at and mocked coming through the airport because of their clothes and Jimi was again refused entry to hotels. Jimi was always cool in these situations, despite the frustration of his band mates. At one hotel, a guest erroneously assumed he was a porter and requested that he carry her luggage to her room. Despite the hardship Jimi felt, the first phase of the US tour for The Experience went well, they also played to an 18,000-capacity crowd at Rheingold Festival in Central Park, co headlining with the Young Rascals. It was though not far around the corner when the inevitable happened.

On July 8th they took a flight to Jacksonville to officially start the Monkees tour. A great recollection of the tour was when it reached North Carolina, described by Mike Nesmith for Guitar World Magazine at the time, he recalled; *"The hallway was lined with probably five or six on either side of southern police with the big beer belly and different color blue shirts, I was standing in the hallway for no particular reason, just couldn't sleep or something. A door opened and there was this eerie kind of blue-red light that came from it because of the exit sign over it. Hendrix appeared in silhouette, with this light in the back of him. And he took a step forward and it was like it was choreographed, Noel and Mitch came up either side of him and they made this perfect trio, it looked like the cover of Axis. They started walking down, and none of those guys was very big, and all those cops were like 6'5, and Hendrix just started walking down the hall, with these pinwheels in his eyes. And to see him walk under the nose of those cops and these guys looking at him going by was something to see. They didn't know what in the world had landed, it was pretty spectacular, wall to wall hair brushing against pot bellies, Jimi was in absolute control."*

Chas was equally frustrated with the tour; he saw it from the same perspective as Jimi. It was after all Chas that discovered Jimi playing to a small crowd underground in New York. He knew Jimi's pedigree, understood he was the greatest guitarist the world had ever seen, and knew that The Monkees were a manufactured bunch with nothing to offer, other than exposure to teenagers. From a music perspective anything The Experience would do, no matter how brilliant they played, would be completely lost on the audience. Chas had tried to change the tour, he pushed to get Jimi on something decent with an agency tour alongside Frank Barsalana, renowned as one of the best agents for rock bands at the time. Mike Jefferey was having none of this and had pushed ahead, the deal was done, to the frustration of everyone.

As anticipated, the tour proved to be challenging for Jimi. The audience did not appreciate The Jimi Hendrix Experience and perceived their music as noise. Teenagers were eager for their favourite pop band, impatient with any band performing before them, Jimi's blues and solos were largely dismissed, and the band's talents went largely unrecognised and underappreciated. Backstage and during travel, it was equally frustrating. The Monkees' tour resembled a circus, with large sections of hotel floors reserved and cordoned off. Security personnel were ubiquitous, bearing 'The Monkees' on their uniforms, contributing to an overly extravagant atmosphere. Despite having around 400 fans at each hotel, as opposed to the thousands that The Beatles attracted necessitating police escorts, The Monkees maintained similar security measures, which seemed unnecessary. This environment appeared completely over the top to Jimi and his band. They were merely passive observers amidst the overhyped spectacle.

As expected, Jimi quickly started to resent the tour, if a crowd was unresponsive to him, he would rush through the set and leave, or purposely play bad, because what did it matter, they were not listening anyway and had no interest. The Experience were to play around 20 to 25 minutes, but even Jimi couldn't handle it, he started to turn his back on the audience and even refused to sing as the tour progressed. Monkees fans, mostly young kids dragging along parental chaperones, had no idea what to make of The Experience. *"Jimi would amble out onto the stage, fire up the amps and break into 'Purple Haze,'"* wrote frontman Mickey Dolenz in his autobiography, *"and the kids in the audience would instantly drown him out with, 'We Want Davy!!' God, it was embarrassing."* Although Peter Tork was overjoyed to have Jimi and the band on the tour, he later recalled the pairing as a singularly bad idea: *"This is screaming, scaring-your-daddy music compared with The Monkees. It didn't cross anybody's mind that it wasn't gonna fly. And there's poor Jimi, and the kids go, 'We want The Monkees, we want The Monkees.'* Noel got frustrated with Jimi's refusal to play the sets properly, accusing him of being unprofessional, eventually the inevitable happened and Jimi refused to continue. He was done with Monkeemania."

Chas and Mike would have to quickly sort it out, it was an issue, and inevitably it came to blows. Chas had made provisions prior to the tour, despite him not having his way with Frank Barsalana he had the foresight to make a deal with Dick Clark that if anything should happen, or Jimi refused to carry on, then they could leave without any financial penalties, and here they were with The Jimi Hendrix Experience playing just eight of the 29 scheduled tour dates. Jimi spoke with NME after he played his last gig on July 16th; *" Firstly they gave us the death spot on the show, right before the Monkees were due on. The audience just screamed and yelled for The Monkees. Finally they let us go on first and things were much better. We got screams and a good reaction, and some kids even rushed the stage. But we were not getting any billing, all the posters for the show just screamed out The Monkees. Then some parents who brought their young kids complained that our act was vulgar. We decided it was just the wrong audience. I think they're replacing me with Mickey Mouse."*

To smooth things over in the press, and no doubt to avoid any negativity aimed at The Monkees, a story was told to satisfy any tabloid intrusion that may arise. The publicity team behind the tour developed a story that, 'outraged parents' had demanded Jimi be taken off the tour, to 'protect' their innocent children. Of course the press in part new this was completely fabricated; it did however do nothing to increase Jimi's wild man reputation. Chas and Mike came to blows over the tour ending prematurely, Chas claimed afterwards that it took him all day and night to convince Mike to get Jimi off the tour, he claimed that Mike had said *"Just remember Jimi is signed to me and you don't have a fucking contract with him"*, which was an interesting claim. Mike then left the USA and went to Spain.

Jimi returned to New York with Noel and Mitch after the abandoned Monkees tour. They visited the Mayfair recording studio and recorded their new single, the previously unfinished 'Burning of The Midnight Lamp', before playing some further gigs at Café Au Go Go. Jimi jammed freely, many nights until dawn alongside seasoned musicians such as John Hammond and Eric Clapton. As well as Café Au Go Go they also jammed at Gaslight on MacDougal Street playing blues tracks.

While in New York, Jimi naturally hooked up with his old friends and acquaintances, those that played with him before he had hit the dizzy heights he was now about to reach. One such acquaintance was Curtis Knight. Curtis later claimed that Jimi had approached Mike Jeffery at this time asking for some money but was turned away. He eventually went to Ed Chaplin asking for a loan, and the two went for dinner. It was here that Ed allegedly told Jimi that he intended to sue everybody surrounding Jimi, because it was his belief that Jimi was still under contract with him. The claim stated that PPX had issued writs against Polydor and Track to stop them recording Jimi until the PPX contract expired, which was set at October 1968, over a year from this point in time. He claimed there were also writs being prepared against Warner Bros.

Despite this announcement, Jimi entered the studio with Curtis and Ed, and they recorded approximately six tracks. However, if Jimi had been discussing ownership and rights to his recordings, this only exacerbated the complexities of Jimi's contractual obligations. It is reasonable to assume that Jimi was highly frustrated with Mike and chose to go into the studio as a form of defiance against his current situation. In both the studio and on stage, Jimi had absolute freedom - the freedom to create and perform as he wished. While this afforded him artistic liberty, it raised questions regarding the rights and ownership of the recordings once completed, it convoluted the tangled web of his recorded work. At times, Jimi seemed indifferent to these matters.

It appeared also that Ed had an agreement with Capitol of America, whose sister company in Britain happened to be Decca. Decca in Britain had previously tried to release Curtis Knights version of 'Like a Rolling Stone', renamed 'How Would You Feel?', which featured Jimi. This would have countered against the release of 'Burning of The Midnight Lamp' however, so the release was cancelled under a threat of counter litigation from Track/Polydor. The wranglings behind the scenes were a world away from the blues bars and creativity of Jimi, Mitch and Noel. Jimi was indeed struggling for cash, which is quite astonishing when you look at his tours and record sales to this point, but the very notion of recording with others only made matters more complicated as his status grew further.

Jimi Hendrix Experience

- Burning of The Midnight Lamp
- The Stars That Play with Laughing Sam's Dice
    - 51st Anniversary
    - Label: Polydor – 59 117
    - Track Record 604001 (Eng) Release 15/03/1967-Single

'Burning of the Midnight Lamp' was now released on Track Records in the UK. It was widely acknowledged that most of it was written on the plane when Jimi travelled previously from Los Angeles to New York - a low point for Jimi - and this comes through in the feeling of the track, and the reflective nature in the writing. Jimi said of the song; *"There are some very personal things in there. But I think everyone can understand the feeling when you're travelling that no matter what your address there is no place you can call home. The feeling of a man in a little old house in the middle of a desert where he is burning the midnight lamp ... you don't mean for things to be personal all the time, but it is. That's really a song I'm proud of. Some people say this is the worst track we have ever done. I think it is the best. Even if the technique is not great, even if the sound is not clear and even if the lyrics can't be properly heard, this is a song that you often listen to and come back to. I don't play neither piano nor harpsichord, it just come to me that's all, I just pick out little notes and it comes from there, I had managed to put together all these different sounds. It was the starting point."*

Jimi introduced the wah-wah pedal on this track, an innovative piece of equipment at that time. Vox created the wah-wah pedal by accident during the design of the Vox Super Beatle amplifier in 1966. Jimi would later extensively use it at Woodstock, becoming closely associated with the effect and mastering the technique. The pedal was invented amidst the musical revolution of the 1960s and became known as psychedelia's non-psychotropic aid. When rocked up and down, the pedal produced sounds resembling human vocal cries, thereby connecting music and vocal communication. The wah-wah pedal gained recognition through various artists, including Eric Clapton and the theme song for the film 'Shaft', establishing itself as one of the most influential technologies in music history. It continued to be a staple in rock guitarists' repertoires, bridging the gap between rock, heavy rock, and psychedelic funk. In many of Jimi's releases, such as 'Burning of the Midnight Lamp', the wah-wah pedal became a distinctive element of his music.

The brutal schedule now began to affect Jimi's mental wellbeing, and those around him noticed the change. It was demanding and unpredictable. He was consistently booked into hotels, buses, flights, interviews and venues. To cope with the chaos, he upped his use of various substances, including LSD. Outside of this, or because of it, he developed an interest in concepts such as the universe and the meaning of life, influenced by the hallucinations he experienced. Jimi explored different theologies and read about astrology, the occult sciences, and I Ching, an ancient Chinese divination text. He found these practices intriguing, and the use of drugs enhanced his interest. The B-Side of 'The Stars That Play With Laughing Sam's Dice' was thought by some to be linked to LSD, although this was not widely recognised at the time. During this period, interestingly Jimi advised others around him to be cautious with substance use, noting that he had a higher tolerance.

The new single had a somewhat mixed bag of reviews on release. It was a different sound to what he had put out previously, it was seen as a slightly harder listen. It certainly wasn't commercial, especially when you consider this would have been released during a tour with The Monkees; a commercial aim from Mike Jeffery to get Jimi the teenage fan club he thought he should have. The single was a world away from the 'pop poster in the bedroom' of teenage girls, unless of course they were bad girls rebelling against parental control. Jimi was reflective and the music complimented his vision perfectly. It would have been lost on the demographic his management team wanted him to pursue. He was right to leave the tour and get back to songwriting and expression in a way he knew best. The song appears to start in a standard way but soon dissolves into an extended hedonistic jam and guitar solo with someone jabbering away in the background, it's both manic and great in equal measure. It's a mystical sound, magical and yet melancholic, the two songs played together give the impression that 'Lamp' is almost the downer that follows the crazed high of 'Stars' on the reverse. The low before the high. The music buying public however were not ready for the single in a way that the commercial suits would have wanted, it became Jimi's first UK single to stall outside the top 10, peaking at number 18. This was of course when chart positioning was absolutely key, there was only one chart, and it was all that mattered.

The marketing machine behind the scenes soon sprang to life, less than a week later 'Purple Haze 'and 'Are you Experienced' both entered the billboard charts. The US version included different tracks that were tailored for the US market, which was considered distinct from the UK market. The Reprise release had different versions to that of Track. Leaving behind 'Remember', 'Can you see Me' and 'Red House', Warners decided to release 'Hey Joe', 'Purple Haze' and 'The Wind Cries Mary'. They also changed the cover, which was originally shot by photographer Bruce Fleming. The new cover was more inclusive of the band, and shot in New Yorks Kew Gardens, although a little dull, just featuring the band standing.

Despite the frantic scramble of new releases in the USA, by the time it was all completed and charts were being punctured, the band were flying back to England, in hindsight it could have been more beneficial to exploit the US market in their own terms with a solo tour. The decision was already made, however, and The Experience touched down at Heathrow to continue in England at Jimi's favoured Olympic Studios in London to begin composing new material.

Jimi was scheduled for TV appearances in England, including the notable 'Top of the Pops', a crucial show for self-promotion. The show was a strange one, and continued to be over the years, mainly because of its shift towards either miming or playing, something the show toiled back and forth with over its time. At this juncture the show required live singing over a recorded backing track. Something Jimi was never comfortable with, he performed it never the less.

Not long after landing back in London, news started to filter through that stunned the music fraternity, and the wider public. On 27th July 1967, during two scheduled shows at Saville Theatre, Jimi and the band got the news that Brian Epstein had committed suicide. It was a major shock to the music world: the reports came in fast through the media. One such report read:

The Beatles' manager, Brian Epstein, has been found dead at his Belgravia home in London. It is not yet clear how he died. Friends found his body in bed after his housekeeper raised the alarm. Mr Epstein, 32, was due to travel tomorrow to Bangor in north Wales to join the Beatles at a meeting of the International Meditation Society. Paul McCartney and his girlfriend, Jane Asher, drove back to London in a chauffeur-driven car after hearing the news. The other Beatles were also returning to London. Before leaving Bangor, John Lennon said: "Our meditations have given us confidence to stand such a shock." George Harrison said: "There is no such thing as death, only in the physical sense. We know he is ok now. He will return because he was striving for happiness and desired bliss so much." Brian Epstein's housekeeper became worried when she did not get an answer after knocking on his bedroom door in the middle of the afternoon. Friends, who had called round to see him, broke into the room and found him dead. The police were called. One of his business colleagues, Don Black, described his death as "a terrible and stupid accident". Another colleague said: "He has been unwell for some months. The reason for his death is at present unknown, but there were no untoward circumstances associated with it." A concert at the Saville Theatre, London, headed by Jimi Hendrix, was cancelled tonight in tribute to Mr Epstein. He owned the theatre's lease. Mr Epstein brought a number of singers to fame. Apart from the Beatles, his other protégés included Cilla Black, Billy J Kramer, The Dakotas and Gerry and the Pacemakers. Mr Epstein discovered the Beatles when they were still performing in blue jeans and leather jackets at the Cavern Club in Liverpool. He encouraged them to smarten up their image, wear suits and stop swearing and smoking in public - in order to broaden their appeal.

In January 1962 the band agreed a five-year contract with Epstein, although he refused to sign it, saying their mutual regard for one another was enough. He got them their first record deal with EMI in October 1962 and by autumn 1963, Britain was engulfed by Beatlemania. Mr Epstein was a director of Northern Songs, the company which owned the copyright to McCartney and Lennons' songs. He was also a major shareholder in Nems Enterprises, which in turn was a big shareholder in Northern Songs.

The death of Brian Epstein deeply effected Jimi and the band, as well as the rest of the music world. He was a high-profile manager, steering The Beatles to become the biggest band in the world at the time. After a short pause of reflection, The Jimi Hendrix Experience were booked into Olympic to continue to record. The tracks the band were working on at Olympic would end up as 'Axis: Bold as Love', the second studio album by the Jimi Hendrix Experience. The band concentrated on the sessions and purposely kept live gigs to a minimum while recording. They did however take a trip to Sweden and played two shows at Tivoli Garden in Stockholm, both the 8,000 capacity shows were completely sold out and the reception for Jimi was incredible.

In the UK, pirate radio had now been banned and removed from the airwaves; a new pop radio station was now introduced, BBC radio 1. It was launched on September 30th, 1967, with DJ Tony Blackburn playing 'Flowers in the rain' by The Move. The station was established at the request of the British Government; they wanted pirate radio completely removed and introduced a legal pop music radio network for the UK. At the same time the BBC's other radio networks, called the 'Home', the 'Third' and the 'Light' programmes, were renamed Radio's 4, 3 and 2. Many of the previous pirate radio DJ's successfully transitioned across to the legal network, including John Peel.

John hosted a radio programme named 'Top Gear' and a week later had booked 'The Jimi Hendrix Experience' on to the show. These sessions would take over 20 years to be released officially, when they appeared on the album 'Hendrix Radio One Sessions' in 1989. Another great fact about this session was that Stevie Wonder was also in the studio at the same time, waiting to be interviewed. He was reported as being very nervous and actually sat in with Jimi and the band, he played drums alongside Jimi to calm his nerves. They jammed on the song 'Aint too Proud to Beg' by The Temptations.

Jimi spent his time at Olympic fully immersed in the recording sessions. What was interesting however was just how free flowing he was with his creativity; he had basic ideas for songs and used these as foundations to build upon rather than sticking to any preconceived plans. Engineer Eddie Kramer went on to comment on working with Jimi at this time; *"There were no meetings in advance and Jimi created things in a very loose sort of fashion. He knew in his own head what he wanted to do, and he wanted to create. He had pages and pages of lyrics to choose from, but he knew exactly what he was doing. Every overdub, worked out, in his head, in a very private sense. I was not to know what he was going to do until he walked into the studio. I don't think anybody else did. Take any backward guitar solos, and there are quite a number of them, when the tape was put on backward, with the music rushing by you, and he knew exactly in his own mind as he was doing the solo what it would sound like afterwards. The point is the man had a firm grasp of what he was doing and what its end result would be."*

Jimi also wrote additional lyrics as he went along, the tracks were laid down very roughly and then he would pull everything together, often retreating to the control room and finishing lyrics, trying them out in his head, it was a very natural process. The band rehearsed briefly before recording. This was something of a challenge for any studio, especially in the late 1960s, although technology was fast making things easier. Jimi wanted as close to a live sound as possible, so everything was turned up to the max. As usual the equipment struggled and reached its capacity, with Jimi pushing all the technology of the time to the absolute limit.

The sessions were not as seamless as the debut album; Jimi actually lost the master tape for the first side of the LP after he left it in the back of a London taxi. The band were forced to remix most of side one in a frantic overnight session. Despite their efforts they couldn't get the sound quality that they originally had on the track 'If 6 Was 9' as the master was lost for the song. Fortunately, bassist Noel Redding had saved a tape of this mix. The tape was ironed out due to wrinkles, and Jimi then doubled his vocals for the verses with a guitar line played an octave lower. Despite this he was very disappointed with the finished song and vented his anger when the label refused to give him more time to work on the tracks.

When completed, Jimi was reflective with the album that he'd produced, it was more introspective, more mystical, and smoother all round in its presentation. He said at the time; *" It's made with stereo in mind, and I hope everyone can dig it in stereo because that's what it's all about. The album was made over a period of sixteen days and we all helped in the producing it with Chas Chandler, and I mixed it as well so it really is us. Weve tried to get most of the freaky tracks right into another dimension so you get that sky effect like they're coming down out of the heavens, you know."*

'Axis' is far more creative than its predecessor, it demonstrates Jimi as an artist, rather than a full-on guitarist blasting out solo's. It is both thoughtful and caring and reveals a whimsical side to his character. It does though, lack quality in its sound and the production is often lacklustre in comparison to both albums before and after it. That said, as a concept, the album sits progressively well as a follow on from his groundbreaking debut effort, with a solid collection of great tunes and intuitive interactive playing between himself, Noel, Mitch, and the use of the recording studio itself.

Keeping the team in place, Jimi was also on familiar ground, with manager Chas Chandler producing and Eddie Kramer as engineer. Jimi only had to look through the glass to be reassured that his recognisable team were around, one that understood his creative process. Jimi expanded his musical range compared to the first album, developing further and wider as a songwriter. He was still full of trippy hedonistic ideas, spacey rockers like 'You Got Me Floating', 'Up from the Skies', and 'Little Miss Lover', all feel like they are next phase contenders to hit radio stations as a follow on to the commercial heels of 'Foxey Lady' and 'Purple Haze'. Jimi's strength on Axis, as songwriter and lyricist are evident in the slower tracks. Wistful, dreamy ballads 'Little Wing', 'Castles Made of Sand', 'One Rainy Wish', and the title track showed incredible growth in his artistry. The hooks and melodic nature of the songs, alongside beautiful studio improvision give a lyrical imagery. You cannot help but become immersed in Jimi's opulent psychedelic musical vision.

These slower numbers are liquified with Jimi's most avant-garde tracks yet, 'EXP' and the proto-fusion jazz blowout of 'If 6 Was 9'. The instrumentation on 'Axis' is of the highest quality. As a trio, The Experience exhibited remarkable synchronisation and creativity, demonstrating a visceral understanding of each other's rhythms.

The label, Track Records, first released it in the United Kingdom in December 1967, which was only around seven months after the release of the group's highly successful debut, 'Are You Experienced?'. In the United States, Reprise Records delayed the release until the following month.

Axis: Bold as Love

Side One
1. EXP
2. Up from the Skies
3. Spanish Castle Magic
4. Wait Until Tomorrow
5. Ain't No Telling
6. Little Wing
7. If Six Was Nine (US edition spelling If 6 Was 9)

Side Two
1. You've Got Me Floating (US edition spelling You Got Me Floatin')
2. Castles Made of Sand
3. She's So Fine
4. One Rainy Wish
5. Little Miss Lover
6. Bold as Love

For radio airplay, Axis' didn't automatically offer instant radio friendly tunes; this was an album in the form of a concept, 'Where Are you Experienced?', as outstanding as it was, felt more like a greatest hits collection. This album is a beautiful collection of songs that, while not featuring any standout radio singles, flows seamlessly as a cohesive entity, it follows its predecessor with remarkable ease.

Jimi had moved to another phase in his career, after proving what a truly innovative and progressive guitar player he was with his first record, or more to the point demonstrating he was the greatest guitar player anyone had ever witnessed. 'Axis' is a much more mature, relatively laid-back album by comparison. Although it includes several ballads, the performances also incorporate a mix of rock elements with a more polished execution. Caught between two undisputed rock cornerstones, Jimi's second album is his most focused and song-oriented work of the three albums he would create, before he reached 27.

Despite the technology available at the time, the trio successfully recorded their performance live in the studio and replicated perfectly the sound they were after. They produced an innovative blend of psychedelic rock, dynamic soul, and early metal. Over the coming years many admirers praised Jimi Hendrix for obvious reasons - his genius for the guitar is, of course, well documented and accolades for his performances were in abundance - but his talent as a songwriter often seemed under-appreciated, and 'Axis' might be the best example of his lyrical talents. It was a pure merger of rock and R&B-style posturing that produced a bizarre trippy stream-of-consciousness imagery.

He was again experimenting in the studio, using technology to its utmost for what was available at the time, helping him stretch out lyrically as well as musically. He reached out further here than the first album, but even more so as a songwriter. Lyrical symbolism meets mystic hyperactivity, producing another side to his grand decadent musical vision. A vision that fitted perfectly with the social and counterculture movement of the times. Jimi again covers several musical styles, but more than likely unintentionally, demonstrating organic growth as a major star. It draws on his foundations performing with rhythm and blues bands, which would remain in his live repertoire throughout his career.

The album cover, which draws on Hindu religious iconography, was designed without Jimi's approval, and he publicly expressed his dissatisfaction. Jimi later said that the cover, which the record label spent $5,000 producing, a sizeable amount in 1967, would have been more appropriate had it highlighted his 'American Indian heritage' He said: *"You got it wrong ... I'm not that kind of Indian."* Despite his displeasure at the cover imagery the album went on to be certified platinum in the US and silver in the UK. Upon its release in the UK on December 1, 1967, where it peaked at number five, it spent 16 weeks in the charts. Shortly after, in February 1968, 'Axis: Bold as Love' reached number three in the US.

By the time the album was released Jimi was on another tour of the UK. This time though, he was headlining in his own right. The tour had commenced at The Royal Albert Hall in November with a substantial supporting roster, The Move, Pink Floyd, Amen Corner, Outer Limits and a band associated with Mike Jeffery and Chas Chandler named The Nice. The Experience were finally realising that they were now superstars, they were the headline act, with a second album flying up the charts on both sides of the Atlantic. They were increasingly nervous to be performing; Chas told NME later that; *"Noel and Mitch were shaking like leaves and even Jimi was petrified to go on stage. They realised that they were part of something bigger than themselves and I had to get a bottle of scotch to restore some courage all round."*

Despite the nerves, the trio continued the tour. The reality was that Jimi was now a star, with fame becoming a significant part of his life within the past year, the roller-coaster world of celebrity, and the trappings that surround it, had finally arrived. He had reached remarkable achievements at a very young age.

On 27 November 1967, The Experience performed two shows at Whitla Hall in Belfast as part of their 'Festival '67' programme. Before the shows, Jimi was given a birthday cake by the festival organisation to celebrate his 25th birthday, this was the only night The Jimi Hendrix Experience played in Ireland, and it was clear that the sheer volume of noise the trio created was something that the audiences were not used to.

The Belfast Telegraph commented on the two shows shortly afterwards; *"The noise being blasted out at the Whitla Hall last night during the Jimi Hendrix concert was the loudest I have ever heard. It was so bad you could feel your insides - and even your chair - resonating...in tune, naturally...the group were fine on record, and just as good at reproducing a similar sound 'live' but the enormous amplification swamped everything. Their performance received a polite but cool reception."* The Belfast Newsletter publication wrote later on 28th November: *"Jimi received an enthusiastic response from the two 1,000 strong audiences... were grasped entirely by this way-out brand of music, obviously exceptionally skillful, if you appreciate that sort of thing... With Noel Redding and drummer 'Mitch' Mitchell, Hendrix captured his audience."* Another report got straight to the point on the volume Jimi created; *"It is now an acknowledged fact that a Pop Concert should be ear-splitting and kaleidoscopic. Last week's Jimi Hendrix concert fulfilled both criteria. On stage, amplifiers dwarfed and deafened the performers; in the gallery frenzied amateurs feverishly juggled with six squares of coloured cellophane and two spotlights. Fifteen hundred people sat in the 'Whitla' and waited for their minds to be blown...It was Hendrix's birthday. The audience sang 'Happy Birthday' in a feeble and slightly embarrassed fashion. The compére hurriedly initiated a cry of 'We want Jimi.' The lights dimmed and weaved; Hendrix exploded on to the stage; 'Plug your ears, it's gonna be LOUD.' the ensuing welter of noise, confusion and flashing lights could not obscure the fact that Jimi Hendrix is a guitarist of considerable talent and though it is at times difficult to separate sheer gimmickness from genuine musical expression.*

He played the guitar in fifty different positions from the Kama Sutra, made an indecent assault upon the amplifier, and in a final frenetic gesture smashed a Fender Stratocaster against the wall (having first displayed method in his madness by unplugging it). It was as though he had finally succeeded in identifying the instrument with his own arrogant virility and subsequently, frustrated with the latter had involved it in the final act of destruction. It is now as important to smash a guitar as it is to play it. Hendrix did both with admirable expertise. Offstage, Hendrix is incongruously mild, affable, and unassuming. He sat in the dressing room, temporarily detached from the bevy of road managers, and munched birthday cake. He constantly strummed a guitar covered in psychedelic patterns."

The comment above, observing Jimi as temporarily detached and surrounded by managers, is a telling one, and one that is common during this period. Jimi was now a full-on commodity and it was him, and him alone, that was the major asset. Many people were earning vast sums of money from him, profiteering from his talent, at times it was full on exploitation. He was now a full on rockstar, and the trappings that came with this were evident. Unfortunately the quiet celebrations Jimi had on his birthday wouldn't be around for long, as many darker days and struggles lay ahead.

Chapter 17

Gold and Rose

"Who are you to judge the life I live, I know I'm not perfect and I don't live to be. but before you start pointing fingers, make sure your hands are clean."

x

With his increasing interest in studio work and advancing technology, Jimi began to spend more time behind the mixing board. He aimed for perfection in his work, which conflicted with Chas's preference for quick and straightforward recording methods. This initiated ongoing conflicts between Jimi and Chas in the studio.

Additionally, Jimi started having more individuals around him. Despite his shyness, he recognised his talent and had a natural inclination to entertain. He did not refuse when other band members wanted to spend time with him. This environment led to increased drug use and drinking, which continued persistently. Jimi was often distracted by visitors in the studio, especially women, and would frequently arrange meetings at clubs, bars, or restaurants and forget about them. As a result, visitors would arrive unexpectedly during sessions, and he would allow them into the studio, this naturally caused ongoing frustration from those who were present.

Jimi began to consume a significant amount of marijuana; it helped alleviate the increased pressure from those around him as his fame augmented. The more popular he became, the more demands and commitments he needed to fulfil. Chas had a different perspective on the stress and artistic challenges Jimi was facing; he was often unsympathetic and openly questioned why musicians feel pressure by stating simply, *"You're doing what you love, so what's the problem?"* Jimi continued to make attempts to discuss his contractual matters in an effort to regain some control, particularly over what was released and the sound of the recordings. Ultimately, he was aiming to manage his affairs both within and outside the studio.

In the 1960s, managers often exercised significant control over their artists' finances, creative output, and touring schedules. This was a common practice that many accepted. The limited aspect of recording sessions as well as chaotic touring schedules were increasingly difficult for any band, but because it was relatively normal for those involved it was very difficult to break away from. To cope with these demands, many bands, and Jimi included, increasingly turned to drugs, which of course were readily available. As a result, as tours continued, so did the parties, and the pressure on him became more apparent. The constant demands became increasingly aggravating, and the trappings of fame affected him from multiple directions. The entourage surrounding him grew larger wherever he went, hangers on, all wanting to be part of the ever-growing circus. The trio was now expected to tour constantly, perform night after night, party afterwards and record as required, while simultaneously keeping recording costs down.

The studio should have been a place that Jimi could retreat to, a sanctuary of creativity, but this was also becoming unbearable, he was increasingly dissatisfied with the recording process. Jimi's pursuit of perfection in the studio was starting to create challenges, especially for managers accustomed to a quicker production pace. Jimi now wanted multiple takes, to experiment, and not to be rushed or settle for what he perceived to be anything substandard. He was searching for something more fulfilling in his creativity, and also wanted time to reflect, he said at the time, *"I'd like to take a six-month break and go to a school of music. I'm tired of trying to write stuff and finding I can't. I want to write mythology stories set to music based on a planetary thing and my imagination in general. It would be similar to classical music; I'd use strings and harps with extreme and* opposite *musical textures.... I'd play with Mitch and Noel and hire other cats to supplement us."* In another interview he confirmed just how frustrated he was getting with the recording studio process: *"It makes me so mad. We record it and everything and then all of a sudden something happens and it just comes out all screwed up. You just get so mad, you just don't want to know about it anymore. Like our next LP, every track is gonna have to be right, or else, you know. It depends on so many things, the cutting of it, you can get in there and mix and mix and mix and get such a beautiful sound and when it's time to cut it, they just screw it up so bad. It comes out all bad cause they go by levels and all that. Some people don't have imagination, when you cut a record, because of the really deep sound, the depth, you almost remix it right there, the cutting place. And ninety percent don't do this. They just go, 'oh turn it up there, make sure it doesn't go over there, make sure it doesn't go under' and there it is. It's nothing but one dimensional. Our new LP was made in sixteen days, which I'm very sad about."*

At the start of 1968 Jimi was arrested during a European tour, accused of possessing illicit drugs. As well as his marijuana use, he was also taking LSD, amphetamines and heroin. Jimi was now, with the effects of this, becoming more aggressive and agitated; increasingly hostile towards those around him, he wasn't in a good place, and began behaving irrationally. In typical rock and roll style he even started to trash hotel rooms.

One such event happened when they landed in Gothenburg during their short tour. After the concert Jimi went to Klubb Karl with Mitch to party, and they returned to the Hotel Opalen around 2 am. Once back, Jimi discovered he wasn't alone, there were hangers on in his room who had come to continue the party, Jimi had no idea where they had come from. According to a statement later given by Noel, Jimi was in mid-conversation in his room when he just started smashing it up, he was reported to have been in a 'frantic and uncontrollable rage'. A fellow hotel guest called reception to complain about the obvious noise, and the night receptionist opened room 623 with a spare key to find it completely trashed. The hotel window was also broken and blood was everywhere. Lying on the bed was Jimi with his hand, bloody, caused by smashing the window with his fist. Nothing in the room had survived the onslaught. Because of the seriousness of the damage, the police were called. Jimi told them that he believed his drink was spiked, and conceded he did go a little crazy when he had drank too much. He also stated how he wanted to be alone, to have some peace, but there were people in his room who wanted to party. Jimi was cuffed and charged with criminal damage; he was then taken to hospital to get stitched up.

The hotels claim for damages was never processed. Chas intervened and paid 8000 crowns (about £500 then, equivalent to £9000 today) directly to the hotel.

The police immediately placed a travel ban on Jimi, keeping him in custody for two weeks. They ordered him to check in at the police station every day at 2 p.m. until his court date on Jan 16th, 1968. Despite this, The Jimi Hendrix Experience were still allowed to perform their remaining shows in Sandviken and Stockholm.

After those gigs, Noel and Mitch went back to England while Jimi returned to Gothenburg to appear in court. On Jan 16th, he was fined 3,200 Swedish Crowns. £200 then, equivalent to around £4000 today. The previous payment made by Chas to Hotel Opalen for the room damage turned out not to be a good will gesture. It was later discovered that this payment was taken back out of the bands gig money.

The smashing up of hotel rooms was not uncommon for bands, and in some ways, it did enhance Jimi's reputation as a wild man, a reputation that was initially fabricated for press advantage was at times like this seemingly true. With the ongoing accolades coming in continuously it wasn't long before the media started to gain an ever-increasing interest in him. Music magazines had been around for a while but one in particular, that was recently created, was gaining momentum. It would become arguably one of the most prominent music magazines in history, it would now feature Jimi for the first time.

A year earlier, in 1967, Rolling Stone magazine was founded in San Francisco, California, by Jann Wenner and music critic Ralph J. Gleason. It was initially known for its rock music coverage and political reporting, particularly by Hunter S. Thompson. Although it changed over the years, it has since returned to its traditional content mix, encompassing music, entertainment, and politics. The inaugural issue of Rolling Stone magazine featured John Lennon on the cover and was published biweekly. The magazine was renowned for its provocative photography and cover photos showcasing musicians, politicians, athletes, and actors.

Naturally it wasn't long before Jimi was spotted and featured. In 1968, Rolling Stone magazine honoured Jimi with the title of *Performer of the Year*. Such endorsements, particularly from a magazine of Rolling Stone's stature, were significant affirmations of Jimi's position among rock legends. It became evident that Jimi Hendrix was not merely another musician, but a transformative figure reshaping rock music.

Additionally in the same year, in recognition of his contributions and burgeoning fame, Jimi's hometown of Seattle, honoured him with the keys to the city. This symbolic gesture underscored not just an acknowledgment of his celebrity status but embraced his legacy. It highlighted the substantial cultural impact he had made in such a brief period. This however was seen by some in his inner circle as a contentious award. After Jimi's death, the connection the city claimed they had was at odds with opinion, one that some completely disagreed with. Jimi was of course initially from Seattle but there were many close to him that had the opinion it wasn't a happy place for him. His only connection was that it was where his family were, and where he had his childhood, which wasn't a happy one. It certainly wasn't a place some thought he called home. It was a city that he didn't have an affectionate connection too, and definitely somewhere that he shouldn't be laid to rest in.

The increasing entourage was often a mystery, especially to Jimi. It had grown steadily before but now it was notably larger than any tour previously. They were described as dodgy undesirables with an aggressive edge: drug dealer types, scroungers and hangers on, all wanting a piece of the now worldwide star.

Jimi's long-time partner and friend Kathy Etchingham was shocked when she caught up with him after not seeing him for many months. She observed that his appearance had altered significantly: his hair was deteriorating, and his skin appeared unhealthy, *"He looked like he had aged ten years in just two, He was clearly under pressure from all angles"*, she recalled.

The band continued to sell out venues across Europe, exhaustingly moving forward with the chaos and incoherent touring. This wouldn't have been so bad if they were making decent money, but the fact remained they received minimal payment for their performances. It was in the USA where the money was to be had, and of course Mike Jeffery was on to this quickly. Now Jimi had appeared in Rolling Stone, Mike promptly commenced preparations to facilitate Jimi's return to America for his inaugural headline tour.

Jimi's record sales were now becoming huge. 'Are You Experienced?' had now topped over 1 million record sales and had been in the charts for two years, it would continue to peak to over 2.3 million copies. 'Purple Haze' as a single had moved over 250,000 copies alone, and now 'Axis' was also riding high. Jimi was a major star. Mike moved to gain further control, to fully capitalise on the fame. He founded Jeffery and Chandler Inc. and hired Gerry Stickells to manage the tour. He engaged a law firm and advocated for managing all concert promotions himself, rather than delegating them and potentially losing significant percentages of revenue. Exactly how much of these percentages went to Jimi, Mitch or Noel, is another question.

Prior to the tour Jimi did the usual press conferences that had been organised for him as well as interviews for various magazines, this was part of a promotional campaign called *'The British are Coming'*. It didn't go to plan however, as most of the other bands that were also scheduled on the tour failed to make it to the press conference organised by Michael Goldstein. It mattered not however, there was only one person the press had come to see, Jimi Hendrix.

One interview that Jimi conducted at the time was for a Jazz and pop magazine. Jimi was asked specifically about the comparison between himself and Eric Clapton: *"That's one thing I don't like, the notes might sound like it, but it's a completely different scene between those notes. You can have your own blues; it doesn't mean that folk blues is the only type of blues in the world. I heard some Irish songs that were so funky, the words were so together and the feel. That was a great scene. We have our own type of blues scene. We do the blues on Axis, it's called 'If 6 was 9', that's what you call a great feeling of blues. We don't even try to give it a name. Everybody has some type of blues to offer, you know".*

Jimi was very vocal in his interviews in the way 'Axis' had been created. He was clearly upset, and felt the album had been rushed, in hindsight he was dissatisfied with it, and it was clear. Previously, on its release, he did state he was happy with it, but clearly as time went on his annoyance with the way it was created was increasing. It's an interesting predicament; and not one the marketing executives would have been too pleased with. Jimi was about to embark on a major US tour, the first of which was his in his own right, as a headline act, yet the very album he was promoting was something that agitated him. He commented several times that his next album would be "just the way he wanted."

Despite Jimi's dissatisfaction with 'Axis', the media in general overlooked his reactions, they didn't really pick up on his comments too much and reported the usual standard information to the public. The tour commenced with four nights in San Francisco at The Fillmore to incredible reviews, also performing here were John Mayall, and Albert King and Soft Machine. Janis Joplin with Big Brother and The Holding Company supported for the final night. The tour continued on to Arizona before heading back to California in February.

Things didn't go too well during this stage, it became apparent that the stage gear used on the tour was being shared with all the bands, so Jimi's usual set up was not in place when he hit the stage. The roadies who worked for a particular band were tasked with looking after the equipment between gigs, and back in the 1960s the protective aspect for equipment was not as good. Therefore, they protected their own bands gear, over and above any other. In addition, to keep costs down during the tour, equipment was often shared, with the priority given to the bands that roadies were connected to. This caused many issues with equipment failure as the set up for each band was different, so this had to change for each performance on the night. Jimi liked his equipment set up in a certain way and on more than one occasion it caused amps to blow. On one performance he was so agitated by this he only sang a few words and eventually left the stage altogether. Noel was very upset that Jimi had walked off, and a heated exchange happened backstage. Jimi was furious with Fender, who had loaned guitars and gear for the tour. After more difficulties, mainly because Jimi insisted on turning everything possible up to ten, he went back to using Marshalls.

The next venue was a personal one for Jimi, it was a concert he was no doubt waiting for as the tour was planned. He was returning to his childhood city. On February 12th he would be performing as the headliner at Centre Theatre in Seattle. He hadn't seen his father or extended family in nearly seven years. During that time, his father remarried a Japanese woman, and they had a daughter named Janie. Jimi must have been a little nervous, he had stated previously in an interview that *"I'm scared to go home, my father is a very strict man."*

Jimi was greeted at Seattle airport by his brother Leonn, along with his stepmother and stepsister, whom he met for the first time. The press talked to Al prior to the show while Jimi stayed in the background, spending time with his extended family and chatting with his brother. In Seattle, there was controversy when it was announced that instead of playing the agreed Boyd Grafmyer's comfortable Eagles Auditorium, the venue would change to the concrete bunker-like Seattle Centre Arena at 225 Mercer Street. The show would be run by Seattle's Concerts West company, headed by KJR radioman Pat O'Day.

Pat O'Day was an American broadcaster and concert promoter in the Pacific Northwest. He was the afternoon drive personality at Seattle's KJR 950 radio station in the 1960s and would eventually become the programme director and general manager. Pat was highly influential in the 1960s and helped to bring the Seattle music scene to national prominence.

Jimi was obviously apprehensive about playing in Seattle, he had not played publicly in his hometown since leaving to join the military in 1961. Although he did pass through when he was playing backing guitar for Little Richard. Despite Jimi's Seattle connections The Experience were advertised as a London-based band with a reputation for noise at the highest order, in fact the show would be quoted afterwards as *"An avalanche of sound, generated by Jimi and his band. An incredibly expressive guitar style augmented from time to time with vocal interludes".*

Not everyone was happy with the change of venue. Seattle writer Tom Robbins was upset that the concert venue had been moved; he wrote that the Hendrix concert had been greatly anticipated, *"But the atmosphere is different now because Hendrix will not be heard in the easy looseness of the Eagles auditorium; no, he's been sucked into the Pat O'Day syndrome with all of the phoney baloney implicit in that milieu".*

The week before, which was when Pat O'Day allegedly persuaded Jimi to change venues, Jimi's new LP was listed *as 'Up and Coming'* at the bottom of the KJR Top 40 album charts. Now, with ominous suddenness, the album shot into the No. 2 spot in the ratings and KJR began playing Jimi Hendrix records for the first time.

Pat O'Day's recollection was rather different: *"Yes, Boyd had actually booked him, but at that point in time Jimi was running with different promoters and was dissatisfied. Some people weren't paying him the money he thought he should have"* Pat said a connection with Concerts West occurred via Ron Terry, a talent agent in New York. According to Pat, Terry was a person "*who recognised the power of this new idea called Concerts West. Because having a touring company that paid for everything in advance, and covered all the costs of the group, and planned all of the outdoor and indoor dates, and then settled up with them at the end of the tour -- that had never been heard of before. And that's what we did. We created a new idea in the delivery of concerts, and as a result, Jimi Hendrix was very appealing to us, and as a result we worked through Ron Terry and got hold of Jimi's attorney and made a deal where we would get to handle all of his appearances, and in return, we would finance all of his touring and travels"*

It's interesting that this is what could have persuaded Jimi to move venues, the fact that he was in some way controlling his own affairs, and his money. In his hometown, he had decided to move venues and in turn took back a little control, that favoured him and the band.

The concert went well, Al was obviously extremely proud, seeing his son as the star he now was. Jimi kept theatrics and gimmicks to a bare minimal, he played straight, no humping of the guitar or smashing up equipment. Aware of his family watching, Jimi kept the show low-key, making it perfect for the situation.

In April 1968, as Jimi began working on his next album, which would become 'Electric Ladyland', Track Records released a compilation album called 'Smash Hits'. The UK version featured all four of the group's singles and four extra songs from the UK edition of 'Are You Experienced?'

Smash Hits

UK edition

Side One
1. Purple Haze
2. Fire
3. The Wind Cries Mary
4. Can You See Me
5. 51st Anniversary
6. Hey Joe

Side Two
1. Stone Free
2. The Stars That Play with Laughing Sam's Dice
3. Manic Depression

4. Highway Chile
5. Burning of the Midnight Lamp
6. Foxy Lady

The USA version was tweaked slightly for release.

US edition

Side One
1. Purple Haze
2. Fire
3. The Wind Cries Mary
4. Can You See Me
5. Hey Joe
6. All Along the Watchtower

Side Two
1. Stone Free
2. Crosstown Traffic
3. Manic Depression
4. Remember
5. Red House
6. Foxey [sic] Lady

If 'Axis' was an album Jimi couldn't really get behind, especially when he reflected back on the process and was interviewed after its release, Smash Hits' gave a perfect round up of his career so far. It was essentially a greatest hits album. In addition to singles, it included B-sides and served as an advertisement for Jimi's notable tracks up to that point. It reached number 4 in the UK and number 6 in the US. The compilation attributed to The Jimi Hendrix Experience, was released in April 1968 in the UK and July 1969 in the United States respectively.

The album also included several tracks that were previously unreleased. This strategy, which originated in the 1960s, was designed to attract individuals who already possessed the tracks in the same format. It quickly became a prevalent and winning formula that continues to this day with the release of 'Greatest Hits' or similar compilations. These often include unreleased or rare tracks, as well as remixes and alternative versions. An approach that has become a standard practice to encourage music enthusiasts and collectors to make additional purchases.

On the UK version, 'Fire', 'Can You See Me', 'Manic Depression' and 'Foxy Lady' are included from the album 'Are You Experienced?' In the US version, 'Fire', 'Manic Depression' and 'Foxey Lady' (US spelling) also come from 'Are You Experienced?' while 'Can You See Me' and 'Remember' are sourced from the UK edition of 'Are You Experienced?' Although 'Axis: Bold as Love' was released before 'Smash Hits', the compilation does not include any tracks from it in either version.

After Jimi performed in Seattle the tour continued on throughout the USA, 'Axis' was climbing up the charts well, and it was good timing. Previously when 'Are You Experienced?' was released in the USA, Jimi headed back to England and Europe, now it was a chance to capitalise on the albums rise by actually promoting it with a US tour. Money was at last starting to come in, and the concerts were fast becoming sell outs, Jimi was voted *'Best Musician in the World'* by Disc and Music Echo magazine. The weekly music magazine, published between 1958 and 1975, was one of the key publications during this period, in competition with Melody Maker, New Musical Express and Sounds.

Despite the success, the band started to become more distant as the tour progressed, one notable aspect of this was when the band played at Fort Worth at the Will Rogers auditorium. They were notably becoming estranged and communicating less with each other, ironically just as this started to materialise, they received their biggest pay out to date, around $25,000. This was allegedly due to Chas and Mike opting to receive percentages of the gate money, which proved to be a shrewd move.

Another significant aspect of this concert was that, for the first time, the band members were in separate dressing rooms backstage, having achieved individual stardom. However, this separation did not help improve the relationship between Jimi and Noel. The band's rigorous schedule, with the consistent touring, playing, rehearsing, photo shoots, interviews, and soundchecks, was continuing to take its toll. The schedule itself was as usual extremely poorly planned, with constant flights between gigs and hotel rooms often booked for single nights. Jimi and his entourage were spending nearly 24 hours a day together, and the presence of drugs and alcohol added to the stress, contributing to issues behind the scenes. If any of the three were feeling unwell, drugs were given to get them on stage and perform. If they couldn't sleep, drugs were given to knock them out, and again if they were bored, due to long flights, bus rides or simply waiting around for the next gig, it was drugs and drink that bridged the tedium. It was a constant and consistent merry go round to keep going, just to simply function.

As well as drugs there were women of course, groupies hung around the band in nearly every city they played. Jimi frequently socialised with women, taking advantage of opportunities to meet and spend time with them. He was now a bonafide rock star and, as well as drugs freely available, so were women. They were backstage, in the recording studio and even in his hotel room when he arrived back from a gig. There were countless stories of Jimi's entourage waking him in a hotel to go to the next city, only to find several naked women in his bed alongside him. In the next city it would continue again.

It wasn't long before Jimi was scheduled to return to the studio. After the success of the US tour, Jimi returned to England for a short break before flying to New York to begin recording. This album though would be different; Jimi had stated many times during the end of 1967 and into 1968 that his next album would be done *'his way'*.

He was determined that this one would be just how he wanted it to be, he wouldn't be rushed, he was now a superstar, he could call the shots. It would though inevitably cause issues, especially within his relationship with Noel and Chas. Jimi was serious about his previous claims for perfection on his next project, especially about being rushed. Previously on Axis, he mentioned continuously about the limited days he was given to record, with no time for production tweaks or revisiting tracks. Now, things had changed, in an act of recording defiance, he block booked the Record Plant on West 44th New York. For three whole months….

Chapter 18

The Magic Carpet Waits.

"Happiness is within you... so unlock the chains from your heart and let yourself grow- like the sweet flower you are. I know the answer- just spread your wings and set yourself free."

Despite the frantic nature of the past tour, it was still only around five months after the release of 'Axis' that Jimi was back working on tracks that would form the classic 'Electric Ladyland'. He had, as well as the tour, jammed frequently, his way of relaxing after concerts. He talked about jamming to Eye Magazine around this time; *"Any chance we have, we jam. That's what playing is all about. When you're creating music with other musicians, that's what you live for. You can't express yourself by jabbering and talking all the time. We have a certain little crowd which is great, we'd like to bring in other jammers, but then after playing a while you feel the flow that goes through music and you can follow each other, and finally you're there, jamming. You can be more together than on a record you might have worked on for two weeks. Like changes of key and timing and breaks and licks. It can be one of the most beautiful things if you have time to hit it."*

Jimi was true to his word when the recording process began, especially with his fascination with the mixing board. One engineer commented at the time; *"I recollect watching him at the board one night, adjusting the sound, fiddling with equalisers to get more highs and lows, some echo button here, setting dials there, throwing switches, calling plays. Satisfied, he got up and walked into the studio. Before he even picked up his Fender, the engineer jumped into the just vacated seat and started to retwist everything"*. Another recollection of Jimi in the studio was from Jack Adams from the Plant; *"Jimi knew nothing about the board, but he was brilliant alright. Sometimes he and the band would come in and jam all night, one song would just blend into the next one. On remixing, he'd have such a set idea of what he wanted a record to sound like, that he'd remix a song about 300 times. No fooling, we'd remix a song for ten hours straight, all week. I'd get tired and say to hell with it, I'm going home. He'd smile and ask if he could phone me if he had a question."*. On Electric Ladyland, Eddie Kramer was asked to engineer the album, he duly agreed and flew over from England.

As well as this initial time spent recording at The Record Plant in New York, the album would also be worked on at several other studios in the US and UK between July 1967 and January 1968. It became a difficult environment for Chas. Now Jimi was able to call the shots, not be molded or persuaded to change from any initial decision. He recorded as many times as he wanted, often the same tracks multiple times. He would also arrive at the studio with a growing entourage of people who Chas and the others had never met before; it changed the atmosphere. Back on the scene at this time was socialite Devon Wilson, becoming a sort of blend between a PA and a groupie. She would do anything Jimi asked, even arranging women for him, but at the same time staying as close to him as possible. Jimi's drugs use continued and became a regular part of his routine. He was mixing various different drugs, including acid. At this time Chas's wife was pregnant and Jimi would regularly drop by his flat with spaced out characters he'd met that evening. Understandably this caused issues and eventually Chas had to stop Jimi coming over completely.

The basic tracks for the new album were formulated with Jimi and the band during the frenzied US tour. When the trio wasn't in the studio, they were on the road, fulfilling the demands of promoting 'Axis', and of course 'Smash Hits', which sneaked its release during the same period. It helped meet the increasing demand by rock audiences to absorb the impact of Jimi's guitar necromancy. The recordings were also at the behest of Jimi totally, when The Experience were in the studio (primarily the Record Plant in New York City), there were copious distractions and frustrations to go around. Jimi would wander in as the spirit moved him, sometimes hours after the rest of the band and was often accompanied by an entourage. Noel was increasingly frustrated, he spoke later in a 1997 documentary about the making of the album, recalling that he had to fight these assorted groupies for couch space in the control room. Once the sessions got underway, they could be frustratingly slow with Jimi's desire for both control and perfectionism. He is credited on the sleeve of Electric Ladyland as both producer and director.

Prior to the studio sessions one song had already been completed, which was 'Burning of the Midnight Lamp'. It was released as a single in the UK in August of '67. Even though Jimi had laid down the basic framework for a handful of other tunes via a demo tape he had put together in a hotel room in New York, he still spent a lot of time at the Record Plant simply jamming. This was Jimi's musical home, his favourite form of music creativity. Here he could play with ideas fluidly, lighting the fuse of a nascent idea until the fire was lit. This was where he wanted to be, the sessions were long and fruitful as a result.

'Electric Ladyland' became an absolute classic amongst rock music fans and remains so to this day. More than any time before, or even the short period he was still on this planet afterward, Jimi managed to seamlessly fuse his myriad of musical influences into one hybrid force that inebriated the rock world. He had achieved an incredible rise; in just two hectic years he had gone from playing Greenwich Village nightclubs for food money to the unofficial head freak of the musical underground. Two albums of psychedelic amalgamation later, he had alerted the public not only to his Strat-mangling prowess, but also his innate grasp of great songwriting.

By 1968, however, the situation had begun to deteriorate further. Jimi found himself in dire need of respite, which unfortunately for him was not forthcoming. He was growing weary, not only in touring but also in the incessant demands for performance stunts, such as playing the guitar behind his head or with his teeth. He was also tired of the timescales required, with the constant and continuous requests for new material. During the recording sessions for 'Electric Ladyland', it was common for Jimi to be out at clubs and bars, arriving at the studio around 3am, while some band members had been waiting since 6pm. This led to understandable frustration among them due to the long hours spent waiting. Furthermore, the presence of numerous acquaintances during recording sessions, whom Jimi would often bring from his favoured venue, The Scene Club, further exacerbated the situation. The hangers on gave no input, but simply sat around, stoned or tripping. Despite his difficulty in refusing people, this practice increasingly irritated his band members and others who were focused on completing the record.

Kathy Etchington visited Jimi in New York and remembered this time; *"The change came around in late '68, when you had all these hangers on. I went to the United States and this guy came around and he put a bag down on the floor, and the bag gapped open and there was white powder in it and right on the top sat a gun, a silver-colored handgun. And I think that was the breaking point, I saw that, and I wanted to go home."*

It wasn't just the band though that were at breaking point during this period of recording. The man who had rescued Jimi from obscurity in New York and brought him to London, was, himself, getting sick of the entourage surrounding Jimi's every studio session, and the call for endless takes which accompanied the herculean intake of chemicals. Chas Chandler had quite literally had enough.

Early into the recording of 'Electric Ladyland' at New York's Record Plant he walked out. This left Jimi creatively free, but with no one to rein in his more self-indulgent tendencies, this was a key turning point. Managers like Chas Chandler were innovative, they were open to conceive and nourish ideas. Chas later reflected on his time with Jimi when he went into the studio to begin work on the Electric Ladyland album, stating that he had come to realise that it was time to break up the association while the going was still good.

"Why?" says Chandler, *"Well, Jimi and a guy who'd been involved with us started to take an awful lot of acid. I thought it was a disaster area. They were sniffing a lot of coke too but I didn't find out about that until long after I'd split with Jimi. I had no idea about it; I thought he was just doing acid, pot and some booze. The pair of them were really into a lot of drugs and it had really become an ugly scene. They were getting out of their heads. Jimi would turn up at the studio with about 10 or 12 hangers-on and, instead of making a record, he'd be wanting to play with them. Because of all those drugs, the environment became peculiar. I was married to my first wife at the time - she was expecting a baby - and I just looked at things and thought... I don't want my kid to grow up in this fucking set. It was as simple as that. Good bit of judgement I think."* But, despite the drug abuse, Chandler continued reflecting on Jimi as a musician, *"We shared a flat for two years, and Jimi was terrific. He was great company and intelligent. We never had an argument, we just used to talk music 24 hours a day. We'd go to gigs; I'd stand in the audience and then go backstage and we'd compare notes at the end of the show. We'd be in the studio and then come back home and play the tapes all night until we'd figured out exactly what we were going to do the next day. We just lived and breathed his career for two years. He was the easiest guy in the world to manage. He used to get erratic at times - but he was a pro; he'd been playing in bands for years; he knew the discipline of the road. He'd blow off steam and things but when I was working with him, he never failed to turn up for a show - and he was never out of it during one. 15 months after we parted, Jimi was dead, I've never really been able to talk about it, it's hard to when that happens to somebody so close. It's all still locked up inside my head."*

After Chas left Jimi's management he continued in the music industry: He went on to manage and produced the British rock band Slade, and did so successfully for 12 years, during which they achieved six number one chart hits in the UK. He also bought IBC Studios which he renamed Portland Recording Studios. He ran it for four years before selling it on to music manager and agent Don Arden. He also ran several labels including Barn Records, Six of the Best and Cheapskate Records. Later during the 1990s he helped finance Newcastle Arena, the 10,000-seater sports and leisure venue that opened in 1995. Chas Chandler died a year later of an aortic aneurysm at Newcastle General Hospital on 17 July 1996. He was posthumously inducted into Hollywood's Rock Walk of Fame in May 2001 as a member of The Animals.

Jimi had always been a Joni Mitchell fan. He loved the way she played guitar, her genius for lyrics, melody and thought-provoking storytelling. The opportunity arose to see her live when Jimi's own tour reached Canada. Even more intriguing was he recorded her performance while seated in the front row. Unfortunately, these tapes were stolen and presumed lost until they resurfaced decades later in a private collection, they were subsequently donated to Library and Archives Canada. These recordings have been featured in Mitchell's 2021 box set, 'Joni Mitchell Archives Vol. 2: The Reprise Years (1968-1971)', within an extensive 10-LP collection. It was on March 19, 1968, that Jimi arrived at Le Hibou Coffee House in Ottawa, Canada, where Mitchell performed two sets that night, his recordings captured 22 songs.

Cameron Crowe interviewed Mitchell for the liner notes of the box set, wherein she recounted meeting Jimi before the show. Joni recalled, *"They came and told me, 'Jimi Hendrix is here, and he's at the front door.' I went to meet him. He had a large box. He said to me, 'My name is Jimi Hendrix. I'm on the same label as you, Reprise Records.' We were both signed about the same time.* He said, *'I'd like to record your show. Do you mind?' I said, 'No, not at all.' There was a large reel-to-reel tape recorder in the box."*

Joni recalled how Jimi knelt near the stage, which was only a foot tall, diligently twisting knobs throughout the show. She noted, *"All during the show, he kept twisting knobs. He was engineering it, I don't know what he was controlling, volume?"* Despite being recorded in front of an audience, Mitchell felt compelled to perform for Jimi directly during her set.

Four days after Jimi recorded Joni, she released her debut album 'Song to a Seagull', produced by David Crosby at Sunset Sound in Hollywood. However, the recording of her debut album sounded distant, it became known for possessing a spartan production. By comparison the recording that Jimi made was exceptional, there was minimal reverb. While it is not a high-fidelity capture, his proximity to the stage allowed fans to experience what it might have been like in the front row. Jimi's diligent adjustment of the equipment portrays his desire for perfection.

These recordings also highlight Jimi's admiration for Joni Mitchell, whom he described in his diary as a 'fantastic girl with heaven words'. He was particularly impressed by her lyrics, which intertwined seamlessly with her melodic guitar style, a trait that was admired for anyone encountering Joni for the first time. Jimi was sais to have had a particular fondness for the song 'The Dawntreader', featured on her first album. The song addresses themes of love, freedom, and escape through vivid imagery of the sea, subjects that undoubtedly resonated with Jimi...

"Peridots and periwinkle blue medallions, Gilded galleons spilled across the ocean floor. Treasure somewhere in the sea and he will find where. Never mind their questions there's no answer for": The Dawntreader by Joni Mitchell

Jimi was now left with Mike Jeffery, who began to plan another tour, there was no thought process here to where the tour went or how is was scheduled. Mike was about cash, he was plain and simply a business man. He was there to make money, mostly for himself, and that was the end goal. He decided the easiest way to do this was for Jimi to go on long tours, record albums as quickly as possible, and keep costs down. It was completely at odds with the way Jimi was creating his music at this time. That said, Jimi was arguably at his creative peak, despite his manager walking out, he was still focused enough to turn 'Electric Ladyland' into as close a perfect album as possible.

Recording the album In New York, Jimi did however enjoy the familiar surroundings, this encouraged tracks like 'Long Hot Summer Night', 'Crosstown Traffic' and 'Come On' to retain their sense of psychedelic pop, it also drew more heavily on the soul and blues music of his homeland. His restless search for new sounds had both his studio engineers and various tech bods running to catch up with his vision of 'consciousness expanding music'. The results were both spectacular and, to this day, just about as cosmic as anything ever placed on magnetic tape.

Two epic tracks demonstrate the two sides to Jimi during this period: That of the traditional bluesman and the spiritual planetary gypsy. 'Voodoo Chile' is a 15-minute superstar jam, included here are Traffic's Dave Mason and Steve Winwood, also hotfooting in was Jefferson Airplane's Jack Cassidy, who replaced an increasingly alienated Noel Redding on bass. It's late-night looseness at its best. The sound, however, never leans too far away from Jimi's astoundingly ingenious soloing. The other side of Jimi, albeit just as effortless, is '1983...(A Merman I Should Turn to Be)'. The song is dope stewed perfection, amongst the layers of backwards tape, jazzy interludes and groovy lyrics trip towards a world end with lashings of underwater connotations.

Electric Ladyland would become the third and final studio album Jimi released before his death. It would be an album that solidified Jimi's prominence completely, with its release he was now seemingly untouchable in the music world. It would be an album that was way ahead of its time, and ironically probably still is to this day. As with all classic albums, Electric Ladyland broke rules, it pushed boundaries that musically had not been shifted this far before. The album is arguably Jimi Hendrix's crowning achievement. He expanded his musical palette like never before, playing many other instruments. Apart from the obvious incomparable guitar work, he added anything wherever he could; he even played the harpsichord: the intro to 'Burning of the Midnight Lamp' showcases his skills here. There were also areas of experimental guitar work that were unusual for the time; an example of this was where Jimi would play at 7.5 ips, the recording speed of inches per second, and then play back at 15 ips, which in sound terms made it record at half speed. This made his guitar sound like it was speeded up, almost like a mandolin, which many people thought it was. These experimental techniques were littered all over the album: nothing was an accident and it was all pre-planned. Jimi said later that every single sound on Electric Ladyland was thought through, nothing was just thrown together. Vocally there were additional voices, notably that of Sissy Houston and the Sweet Inspirations who were Aretha Franklin's background vocal group; they can be heard beautifully on 'Burning of the Midnight Lamp'.

Sessions for the album actually started in England at Olympic Studios, the basic tracks for 'Crosstown Traffic' and 'All Along the Watchtower' were recorded there. The latter was of great inspiration for Jimi, it stands out as the main contender sitting on the playlist. The divine cover, if you can call it that, shows the time and effort Jimi put into the track. It sits perfectly placed, giving assurance that Jimi knew exactly how to sequence an album. A huge Dylan fan since he first arrived in New York, Jimi was always reading Dylan lyrics and listening to his work, he even kept a Dylan songbook in his flight bag, referring to it frequently.

'All Along the Watchtower' was a superb example of Jimi's ability to direct and orchestrate a band. It is widely celebrated as one of the greatest cover songs of all time. During the sessions, the assembled musicians had not heard the song before, Jimi orchestrated the track with them, showing them how it should sound, directing the whole recording. All the small intricate sounds and the attention to detail were guided by him. Incidentally, during the recording of 'All Along the Watchtower' Brian Jones visited the studio and decided to help out; his piano playing and percussion can be heard on demo tracks and run throughs, although the finished recording omitted his efforts.

Jimi was always open to anyone coming into the studio, if they had something to contribute to a song or a recording, they were welcome. While in England, there was a story of Jimi travelling to the studio one day in a London taxi where the taxi driver mentioned he could play the bongos. Jimi invited him to the studio and he turned up and played them. It was reported that the taxi driver had widely exaggerated his bongo skills, it turned out he wasn't that good, nevertheless he did get to play with Jimi Hendrix. It was always an open session when Jimi was recording, often to the ongoing frustration of his management and band members. He was open to ideas from anyone, always looking for something different. One irritation Jimi had with the recording session for 'All Along the Watchtower' was the slide guitar section, this caused arguments and disagreements as things progressed. Jimi was frustrated with the sound; he couldn't replicate what was in his head; he eventually did of course - the Hawaiian sound in the center of the track is achieved when Jimi slid a cigarette lighter along his guitar. Another example of his ingenuity was on 'Crosstown Traffic' where he used a piece of cellophane over a comb to make the famous kazoo sound.

Despite Jimi's continuing frustrations with the consistent travelling and tour dates he had little to no choice but to continue, engulfed by its disorganised and chaotic nature. Now that Mike Jeffery was running things this was set to get worse. There was little or no structure, which made it exhausting for the band. Jimi would be playing on one side of the USA for a single gig and then the next day on the other side. In nine weeks, one roadie said that there was almost a gig per night with barely a night off. He recalled that on one nine-week window alone he had recorded in his diary over 19,000 miles of driving, not to mention flights in between. It was both physically and mentally draining for all involved; During this period it was normal for the band to go to bed at 4am, leave at 8am and then travel on two planes to the next gig. This also included press interviews and all things surrounding a tour that were booked in around the gigs themselves. It was a tumultuous existence with everyone wanting a piece of him.

In addition to his performances in America, Jimi was now booked by Mike for several concerts in Europe. Prior to these engagements, he was set to perform at the Miami Pop Festival. Although the festival was anticipated to be a significant event, torrential rain led to performance issues. The first night of the festival was highly successful, with over 25,000 attendees. The event was due to hold over 100,000 over its duration. However, the second and third days experienced heavy rainfall, resulting in the bands opting not to perform due to concerns about potential electrocution. In The Road to Woodstock Michael Lang wrote; "*As rain pelts the roofless stage, the crowd is turning ugly, with tempers rising as high as Miami's humidity. I can't put any of the electric acts onstage, though a madman British vocalist announces that his band, the Crazy World of Arthur Brown, would like to perform and hopefully experience electrocution. 'It would be beautiful!' he insists. I'm thinking the sight of Arthur frying would not be beautiful. What we need is a powerful acoustic act. Just as the rain subsides and the crew starts clearing water from the stage - a pair of flatbed trailers - I spot John Lee Hooker, cool as ever, smoking a cigarette, sitting backstage waiting for his slot. He's my man."*

The morning of Saturday, May 18th, appeared serene. No clouds were visible as three stages were assembled on flatbed trucks. Miami had experienced a drought for 30 days, which would soon be ending abruptly. Forty miles southwest, local government agencies-initiated cloud seeding in the Everglades, resulting in rainfall across Miami and surrounding regions. While local farmers undoubtedly welcomed this development, the Miami Pop Festival prepared for its repercussions.

Miami Pop can be regarded as a transitional event between the pioneering Monterey International Pop Festival of 1967 and the iconic Woodstock Music & Art Fair of 1969. The festival adopted several production strategies from Monterey Pop, such as filming the concert for a subsequent festival film, which were later utilised at Woodstock. Miami Pop also predicted many challenges encountered later at Woodstock, particularly relating to adverse weather conditions. The rains that drenched festival goers at Woodstock were foreshadowed by Miami Pop, offering future organiser's insights on managing a festival amidst delays and wet conditions. Due to the entire planning occurring during Miami's 1968 drought, the organiser's neglected to secure rain insurance, posing immediate challenges when light rain began to affect Saturday's crowds. Nevertheless, the audience's enthusiasm persisted, the staff even went so far as to issue a false shark warning for the rising water near the stage to ensure safety.

Helicopters played a crucial role in both festivals to try and mitigate performance delays, transporting artists directly to the crowd. On May 18th, a helicopter from the nearby airport descended onto the green of Gulfstream Park, delivering the headliner, The Jimi Hendrix Experience. Jimi's performance is perhaps the most memorable aspect of the festival. Arriving in style in the helicopter Jimi was naturally highly anticipated, and despite frequent interruptions due to weather conditions, The Jimi Hendrix Experience delivered one of their best performances. Attendees and enthusiasts particularly refer to this live rendition of 'Purple Haze' for its extraordinary improvisation.

Miami Pop was also unique in its presentation. It was the first rock festival to have two entirely separate 'main' stages, that were several hundred yards apart. This was the Flower Stage and the Flying Stage. Both operating simultaneously and offering performers of equal calibre, this for the first time gave festival goers the choice on where they wanted to be, they could plan the event how they wanted too. It set the blueprint for others to follow.

Frank Zappa had a noteworthy experience that was rumoured to have occurred during Jimi's performance. The rumour states that when Jimi concluded his set, he went through the same ritual as Monterey. He soaked his Fender in lighter fluid, set it ablaze, and smashed it up, he then threw it off stage. Zappa, who stayed after his earlier performance, retrieved the guitar, extinguished the flames, and later repaired it. He then continued to use it for four years. It's a great story, but as usual accounts vary. Some claim that Howard Parker, one of Jimi's road crew members, gave the guitar to Zappa, while some attendees claim Jimi never burned the guitar at all.

Unfortunately, for the remaining attendees of Miami Pop, Jimi only performed one set at the two-day festival, as Sunday faced the full onslaught of the extreme weather. This included torrential rain, hail, lightning, and winds up to fifty miles per hour, resulting in four inches of rain. All was not completely in vain though, when Jimi was in his car returning from the cancellation he wrote in his notebook: 'Rainy Day, Dream Away'. It would later form into the track of the same name, *'Hey man, take a look out the window and see what's happening, Hey man, it's raining, It's raining outside, man, Aw, don't worry about that, baby, Think that's gonna be everything. We'll get into something real nice you know, We'll sit back and groove on a rainy day, Yeah, hmm, Yeah, I see what you mean brother, Lay back and groove. Rainy day, dream away. Ah, let the sun take a holiday, Flowers bathe and I see the children play, Lay back and groove on a rainy day.'* This, in hindsight, was a lyrical highlight for many who witnessed Jimi here, as the song was written when everyone was leaving during the soaked aftermath at the end of the cancelled festival.

Once the event was officially cancelled, many who had a financial interest turned there attentions to some kind of compensation, wherever or however they could get it. The company, Joint Productions, were due to be out of pocket by an estimated $60,000. This was an era when cash was King, the takings that were there at the end of day one had to be guarded by cops. It was reported that in a desperate attempt to recoup losses the actual security truck was stopped on the way out and held to ransom as it tried to take the cash to the bank.

Official recordings of Miami Pop performances were unavailable for years, but naturally there were some bootleg versions circulated amongst enthusiasts. The festival's impact, especially in its planning and organisation, was felt a year later during Woodstock. The festival offered valuable experience to future organisers, including Michael Lang and recording engineer Eddie Kramer. Despite an unexpected storm cutting the event short, Miami Pop undeniably paved the way for the greatest festival of them all.

Chas now made it official that he had left Jimi's management. He knew he could no longer convince Jimi to work at speed. He was frustrated with the hangers on and felt constantly sidelined. He worked things out financially with Mike and sold his partnership to him for a reported $300,000. At this point Mike had complete control over The Jimi Hendrix Experience, and crucially over the money. Yet another US tour was again booked in, but beforehand it was time for the pre-booked concerts in Europe.

This short tour of Europe was just that, just three dates were played in Italy and two in Switzerland, where Jimi headlined with Eric Burdon and John Mayall. There were now continuous fractures within the trio, between Italy and Switzerland Noel and Mitch flew to London while Jimi flew all the way back to New York for meetings regarding the law suit with Ed Chaplin. These were the law suits that were raised in mid-1967 when Ed first issued the writs against Polydor, Track and Warner Bros, they were now coming to fruition. Since that point there was a back-and-forth legal battle regarding the release by Ed Chaplin through Capitol Records, of material Jimi had recorded with Curtis Knight. At the time Jimi obviously knew he was being recorded but saw it as just bits and pieces on tape, many believed that he never wanted those jam sessions actually released. Curtis had a different perspective: *"There was never any hard feelings whatever between Jimi and me. If there had been, would he have recorded with me when he came back from England, when he was already a success?"*

Interestingly however, Warner Bros decided to settle, the rationale was thought to be Jimi's future earning potential. A litigation could go on for months, even years if it was dragged on far enough, this would inevitably put a freeze on releasing any new material while the case was potentially being fought. It therefore made commercial sense to settle, which would be far cheaper than the loss made from a freeze in releases over the same period.

After these meetings, and the short tour of Europe, Jimi was now scheduled again for the next US tour. He flew to London first, just to hang out there, he couldn't stay for long though. He then headed back to the USA, landing at JFK, before heading south. The tour started in Louisiana, which was a completely different environment to what he had become accustomed too. While Jimi Hendrix was widely celebrated as a rock icon in major cities such as London, New York, and Los Angeles, his experiences in the southern United States were markedly different. Outside of his performances, he was often treated with indifference or hostility. As a result, he frequently avoided any situations where he anticipated mistreatment, even declining to leave his vehicle or enter establishments where he expected to be ignored or be subjected to racial prejudice.

As the tour reached its mid-point Jimi started to rebel somewhat against his persona, against what the crowd were expecting him to do. The very thing that had made him famous, at least on stage anyway, was now something he was becoming bored with. Kathy Etchingham was with Jimi in London before he headed back to the US for this tour; *"He started to hate his image, he would sit on the edge of the bed almost in tears, trying to explain to me how he felt, how he was fed up with his stage act and what people expected of him".* In contrast to how Jimi was treated in the deep south of the US, when the band reached the West Coast on the next leg of the tour, the reception for Jimi was incredible.

In October, from the 10th to the 12th, The Jimi Hendrix Experience played at Winterland in San Francisco. Tracks taken from these concerts appeared later on the Live at Winterland and Jimi Hendrix Concerts albums. Cream at this point had split up, as a result Jimi had taken to adding his own version of 'Sunshine of your love' into The Experience set. Ironically during this period the trio were acutely aware that their own band was coming to a close, separately they were making individual plans. Noel in particular had made contact with other projects, which Jimi was aware of, and they all knew it was just a matter of time before they also went the same way as Cream.

Despite the need for a well-earned rest, Mike had scheduled the band to immediately tour Europe again after the final date in the USA. When the tour reached Germany Jimi played two concerts in Dusseldorf, on the second, watching in the crowd, was an Ice-Skating teacher from an affluent family, her name was Monika Dannemann. She would go on to be a pinnacle part of the final days of Jimi Hendrix.

Various connections gave her access to the show, although she was not really interested in Jimi prior to the concert, in addition she had read various reports on Jimi's on-stage antics that had made her a little hesitant to attend. Once Jimi hit the stage, however, things changed. She was mesmerised with him the second he started to perform. They met the following day at Jimi's hotel bar. She recalled the initial meeting; *"We didn't stop talking for over an hour, until they had to leave for Cologne, which was the next concert. I changed my mind about him, I realised he was a very gentle, kind person, very considerate and not what you would imagine a rock star to be like. So* when he asked me to come to Cologne, I agreed. I followed him later in my car, and on the way there I realised I had fallen in love with him."* Monika stayed with Jimi during the remaining tour of Europe, Jimi then asked Monika to come to London in February, where he was due to play at The Royal Albert Hall.

Mike Jeffery was now only interested in venues that paid considerably, in addition to this it transpired that Chas still had some loose connections that gave him an ongoing interest in The Experience. It was a vague clause giving him some financial gain in what they did going forward, it was, in essence, in his interest to keep The Experience together.

Monika kept her word and arrived in London, she did, however, miss the concerts. Jimi spent time with her, as well as Kathy Etchingham. Jimi desperately needed a break from recording and touring, he was at burnout. The news broke about The Experience break up around November. Noel reflected on this time later in 1993: *"We were a very spontaneous group - just plug in and play. Except for the occasional riff Jimi would ask me to double, I was free to come up with my own basslines. For the most part, I would anchor the tune while Jimi and Mitch Mitchell went off on tangents. Playing chords helped to fill out the sound while he was soloing, but no matter how far away they went, they knew I'd be there when they got back. I went off on a few tangents myself, but overall I preferred to keep it simple. I think that's the job of any good bass player. The recording sessions were chaos, and on stage, it was getting ridiculous. The audience wanted us to play the old Hendrix standards, but Jimi wanted to do his new stuff. The last straw came at the Denver Pop Festival when Jimi told a reporter that he was going to enlarge the band. I went up to Jimi that night, said goodbye, and caught the next plane back to London. Jimi phoned and asked me to come back, but I said stuff it."*

Jimi had to answer the obvious questions regarding this, he said during an interview with Melody Maker, *"Mitch and Noel want to get their own thing going, not a group: so very soon, probably in the new year, we'll be breaking the group, apart from selected dates. We're just like a band of gypsys moving about everywhere".* The confusing but philosophical statement sent Mike Jeffery into a fury, worried and angry that the mixed message could damage sales and future concert attendance.

In October 1968 Electric Ladyland was officially released. It became Jimi's biggest achievement to date.

Electric Ladyland

Side One
1. ...And the Gods Made Love
2. Have You Ever Been (To Electric Ladyland)
3. Crosstown Traffic
4. Voodoo Chile

Side Two
1. Little Miss Strange
2. Long Hot Summer Night
3. Come On (Part 1) (Come On on UK edition)
4. Gypsy Eyes (Gipsy Eyes on UK edition)
5. Burning of the Midnight Lamp

Side Three
1. Rainy Day, Dream Away
2. 1983... (A Merman I Should Turn to Be)
3. Moon, Turn the Tides....Gently Gently Away

Side Four
1. Still Raining, Still Dreaming
2. House Burning Down
3. All Along the Watchtower
4. Voodoo Child (Slight Return)

It flew up the various charts in England and America, as well as other territories around Europe. Jimi was unhappy with the record label's choice of cover for his album, amazingly this wasn't something he had seen himself until the actual release. Previously he had chosen the album cover photo, and thought it was a done deal. It was taken by Linda Eastman (soon to be Mrs. Linda McCartney) featuring the three members of The Experience and some children sitting on an Alice in Wonderland statue in Central Park. The company instead used a blurred red and yellow photo of his head while performing at Saville Theatre, which was taken by Karl Ferris. Even more controversial was a cover image by photographer David Montgomery: he shot the inside cover portrait depicting nineteen nude women lounging in front of a black background. The women were told that they would be meeting Jimi and happily went along to the shoot, and sat topless, but of course he wasn't there. The cover was banned by several record dealers as "pornographic", while others sold it with the gatefold cover turned inside out, or in a brown wrapper. Regardless of this the scandal didn't deter sales, and Jimi Hendrix was now one of the biggest selling artists in the US.

Jimi was desperately trying to do things the way he wanted, and often this wasn't in a conventional fashion. It was at this juncture that his recordings changed somewhat. After Chas Chandler and Noel Redding left, Jimi dismissed the standard structure, insisted by Chas, on how songs should be recorded: the radio friendly three-minute pop song. Now the intros were often this length, the rules of how a song should be structured were now in the hands of Jimi himself and he allowed his creativity to determine the song, without any kind of rules or leaning towards commercialisation. It didn't matter how obscure the sound or idea, if Jimi liked it, it was now pursued and included. This is one of the key attributes that made Electric Ladyland such an artistic masterpiece.

Naturally, Jimi's drug taking continued, which was another source of creativity. It was never said that this hindered his recordings in any negative way, but the relentless and continuing touring, prior to and in the wake of his newly released masterpiece, was definitely taking its toll on his mental health and general well-being.

In May 1969 he was arrested again in Toronto for possession of narcotics, and this effectively sealed the end for The Experience trio as a band. He was detained while a small lab was set up to test the cellophane packs of white powder and a small tube full of a dark resin found in his flight bag. The testing came back positive, the resin was hash and the powder heroin. Jimi was charged with possession and swiftly taken to the nearest police HQ. He was released later for bail of $10,000. Jimi was concerned that the scheduled concert he was booked to play may now not be permitted to go ahead, it was rumored however that a detective told him *"Oh, don't worry, we'll get this done as quick as we can, my kids have got tickets for the concert and they'll kill me if I don't get you out."*

The tour continued on, with heavy travelling and nightly concerts all over the south. Eventually it made its way back north and returned to New York once again, Jimi immediately booked himself into the relative sanctuary of The Record Plant and was joined by Billy Cox. Jimi had him lined up to replace Noel on bass, but as the tour was still ongoing it didn't make sense to replace him just yet. The much-needed seclusion of The Record Plant was good for Jimi, here he had no interviews, no one bothering him, just music and recording in relative peace.

Noel took a flight back to London for a few weeks once the tour had concluded in Hawaii, before plans were put in place for a large payday for the band to perform at the Newport Pop Festival, it was reported for a fee of over $100,000. It was a magnificent array of acts; Tina Turner,

Creedance Clearwater, Jethro Tull, Eric Burden, Marvin Gaye, Steppenwolf, Joe Cocker and the Byrd's were just some of the artists confirmed as performing over the three days, from June 20th to 23rd. Jimi was the headline. One reporter wrote a wonderful account after witnessing Jimi during the concert: *"He seems to know the instrument and its near limitless possibilities better than any electric guitarist who ever lived. He stopped only now and then to let other performers lay down some business, and he never repeated a riff. His creativity was awesome as he switched styles from Blues to jazz to rock to rhythm or whatever, all with ridiculous ease. Hendrix was Wes Montgomery, B.B. King, Eric Clapton and you name it, all rolled into one package of artistic fury. It was as if Hendrix had broken through the most profound musical dimension available to mortals and was being guided by the perfect, instantaneous teachings of improvisational composing most exhaled spirit. Man, Hendrix was playing out of his mind."*

The last performance of the original Experience line-up took place the following month on June 29th, 1969, at Barry Fey's Denver Pop Festival, a three-day event held at Denver's Mile High Stadium. It was another large payout for the band, and the last for Noel, he left and returned to London, *"I was planning to leave Hendrix this year anyway, because I was getting very bored. And then on our last tour of America, in fact in Denver, we read about Jimi augmenting the band, and the rumors about me splitting which even I never heard about. So, I just quit then."*

The band had essentially split months before, what had annoyed Noel was Jimi not telling him directly, this way it appeared to be his decision, and he had some control over it. Even though they were going their separate ways, touring remained in place. They were persuaded to carry on, Mike had secured lucrative concerts and he was not going to allow them to miss any, but this was coming to an end. The time was right, they could now move on. Mitch reflected later to sounds in 1971; *"The Experience was over with completely by then. The only thing that was going to happen is that maybe there would have been a band whose running, I was quite prepared to handle and leave Jimi alone to play and do the writing. That seemed to me like the obvious thing to do. Jimi was one of those people who pushed their lives to limits further than other people, so this band seemed a way of doing it. Jimi went off and did one thing and I did another and then when we came back and played together again, he was playing differently from when I left him. That was fine with me, there was a kind of rapport. There was always some kind of rapport there. At one point I was in the States doing a tour with someone else, but we were still working together on an album, just the two of us. One thing I will explain is that on a lot of the albums it was done with just two people with Jimi playing bass and playing guitar. It was faster working that way"*.

Jimi now planned a new band, and with this he had a different concept in mind, He was obviously nervous about losing Noel and Mitch but was moving towards a more open and inclusive approach. He wanted to exit the 'Rock Trio' and adopt a loose jamming format. Drafting in musicians from various sources he envisioned a collective that would be receptive to ideas, they didn't have to be the best around, he was after togetherness and inclusion rather than absolute perfection. It was time to welcome: The Electric Church.

Chapter 19

Gypsy Sun

"My goal is to be one with the music. I just dedicate my whole life to this art."

In August 1969 Jimi Hendrix was the world's highest paid rock musician. The previous litigation regarding Ed Chaplin had now been agreed, and part of this granted Ed the distribution rights to an album of original Hendrix material. Jimi decided that they would record the LP, Band of Gypsys, during two live appearances, which were now planned. First however, Jimi turned his attention to another festival, one that would solidify his reputation forever. It would become arguably the most legendary festival of all time. Made more so by the presence of Jimi himself. Preparations were in place. For Woodstock.

Throughout the summer the momentum and anticipation for the event was growing, and Jimi prepared himself well for it. He saw it as a great opportunity to showcase his new ensemble; they were jamming constantly but the agreed festival gave something to prepare for, to focus on. Jimi's new band, a fluid one that was open to all musicians, was now called Gypsy Sun and Rainbows. The drummer was the only real question mark. Intermittently Jimi still had Mitch, and in reality, didn't want to lose him. The issue here was Mitch was very hard to pin down, and he had a habit of missing rehearsals, as a result Buddy Miles was often holding the sticks, ready to take the spot if needed. As things got closer, and the rehearsals continued, it was Buddy that moved into the position, with Jimi teaching him the standard compositions from his back catalogue. Alongside this, Jimi was also creating and recording new material, he sat in on several sessions as well as the usual jamming sessions at clubs, a favored venue at this time was the Tinker Street cinema in Woodstock itself.

The initial idea for Woodstock started out very differently. As a basic concept it was first discussed in 1969, then just an idea from Michael Lang, who worked previously at the ill-fated Miami Pop Festival. Michael and his partner Artie Kornfeld, who was an ex-record executive, had concocted a vague plan to build a sort of studio complex within the Woodstock area, an affluent area where many musicians lived - Jimi included at this time. Once the idea developed, however, it soon shifted when two wealthy investors, Joel Rosenman and John Roberts, came on board looking for investment opportunities. As soon as this happened the previous plan was ditched, and the ambition for a full-scale rock festival was put in place. Not only that, once this momentum took hold, they realised they had an opportunity to deliver the largest festival in history to this point. Eventually there were 32 bands secured over the planned three days.

Lang and Kornfeld partnered with Joel Rosenman and John Roberts to form Woodstock Ventures Inc., splitting profits evenly. They planned a concert to fund a studio in Woodstock, the folk music hub. Initially set for Mills Industrial Park in Wallkill, NY, however the permit was rejected due to non-compliance with toilet codes. Elliot Tiber then suggested his 15-acre property at El Monaco Motel, but it wasn't large enough for the expected 50,000 attendees. Tiber then proposed using Max Yasgur's 600-acre dairy farm, which Lang accepted.

The slogan 'Three Days of Peace and Music' was used to promote the event. Originally profit-driven, with 186,000 tickets sold at $18 each, famously the concert became free due to overwhelming demand, exceeding 200,000 hungry festival goers. Woodstock's iconic fence-tearing would go on to symbolise the very essence of this peace and freedom, marking its place in music history.

The main observation most had on arrival at Woodstock was the vast number of people that were there, and the amount of weed that was there. It was literally being handed out for free. The summer of 1969 presented an ideal opportunity to organise an event. This period marked a significant transformation for an entire generation. The counterculture movement was widespread, driven by music, rebellion, and individuals seeking an alternative path, striving to discover something greater than their own existence and the conventional offerings of life. The surrounding area, once a humble dairy farm, would dramatically transform into images that captured the very essence of a movement. Over half a million people gathered there, it would become the most legendary festival in rock history.

Everyone knew when they travelled further towards the venue that this was no ordinary festival, this was something special, something magical, and a festival like there had never been before. It was almost a pilgrimage of like-minded people with one purpose. The organisation for the event was extremely chaotic, even before the festival was set up there were over 30,000 people camping around, without tickets. As a result, and because of the sheer number of fans descending, it became an almost free entry. Only those that had bought tickets in advance actually paid to get into the festival, this was estimated at around 60,000 fans, the actual number attending was said to be a staggering 400,000 to half a million.

Not everything ran as smoothly as planned, over the four days this festival of peace was anything but for the organisers. The two sides of the stage could not have been more paradoxical. In front, there were beautiful images of free love, with people huddled together, smoking weed with flower crowns; behind there was logistical nightmares, dangerous conditions, and moments of pure chaos. As far as event planning was concerned it was a huge miscalculation. The festival's organisers had underestimated nearly every aspect, this ranged from food, medical supplies, and even the sheer number of people expected to attend. To make matters worse, it rained, and within a matter of hours the fields turned into a mud bath. Flashbacks of Miami were coming thick and fast, and basic sanitation was virtually impossible to maintain. For those that were there, Woodstock simply became a test of endurance, just to get to the end of the festival would be an achievement in itself. While no official records exist, stories circulated that between one and four babies were actually born during the festival itself.

As far as the music was concerned this became even more of a headache for those organising the festival. With the chaos that was surrounding the event, many confirmed acts demanded payment upfront to secure their cash, as doubts descended whether they would be able to perform at all. Simply getting bands to the stage was virtually impossible as the crowds swelled beyond anyone's comprehension. The ticket barriers were quickly overwhelmed, which of course gave way to more people turning up as the word spread that it was now an unofficial free festival. The sheer volume of people was overpowering to anyone trying to keep any sort of order, which meant that the standard routes for bands to enter and leave were completely blocked. Many of the bands had to rely on helicopters drafted in to get them backstage as all routes on the ground were obstructed. It meant that most bands performed several hours later than scheduled, including Jimi.

Woodstock was also one of the first festivals where normal people were able to film what was going on: video cameras for the first time were made available for the general public to use, not just for major TV companies; they were designed for home footage, but people took them to Woodstock. This is one of the reasons why so much footage emerged from the festival, and crucially why so much footage was shown from the crowd's perspective. Many hours of footage was captured, not just of the acts performing but of the build-up and the actual audience themselves.

As Woodstock got underway, and news circulated from bands and various management sources of the sheer scale of the event, Jimi started to have doubts. He hated massive crowds; it wasn't helped by the then governor of New York declaring the event a disaster zone. Jimi was scheduled to hit the stage at midnight, and on that evening, he was still saying he wasn't going to perform. Janis Joplin had previously complained, stating the crowd was simply too big, and that she could only reach a small section. Jimi was to be paid well for his performance, a reported $18,000, he was promised an additional £12,000 to allow the organisers to film him. Despite Jimi's refusal to take to the stage it was Mike Jeffery who assured the organisers that Jimi would be performing. Mitch commented on the struggle to simply get to the stage; *"It was a shambles for us, it took us hours to drive up there in a couple of estate cars. There were no facilities for dressing rooms or anything. In the end we ended up trekking across this muddy field for half a mile to this little cottage with no heating, nothing. Playing wise, you couldn't hear a bloody thing"*

Jimi arrived on stage around 8am, only around 30,000 people remained to witness him. *"We're nothing but a band of gypsys"* he announced as he started his performance. They were actually introduced as The Jimi Hendrix Experience. Jimi quickly informed the audience of the band change: they were now Gypsy Sun & Rainbows. The band, however, would be a short-lived formation after Woodstock. The group performed just twice more before disbanding.

Jimi was the last act to close the festival, no one would have anticipated however that he would be coming on just as the sun rose. Jimi had earned his reputation, he was the major star on the scene, no one would have argued against him holding the traditional headliner's position - playing last – but even more than that it would have been inconceivable to think that due to the technical and weather delays the festival would stretch into Monday morning. With Jimi performing at sunrise.

One benefit of the delay was that the morning light made for excellent filming conditions, which may be part of the reason this particular Jimi Hendrix performance is so well known. By the time Jimi walked on stage most of the Woodstock crowd, malnourished and no doubt suffering from the immense ordeal both spiritually and physically, had already made their way in whatever direction they could. The band for this legendary performance were Jimi on guitar and vocals, Billy Cox on bass, Larry Lee on rhythm guitar and vocals, Mitch Mitchell on drums and Juma Sultan and Gerardo "Jerry" Velez on congas. For Jimi, Woodstock signified the start of a musical transition, one band was fading while morphing into another, it was fluid yet fully formed. It was the beginning of a period of musical experimentation that was risky from a commercial perspective, and one that Mike Jeffery was no doubt watching closely.

Jimi at Woodstock has been analysed and watched for decades. It is quite rightly referred to as the music performance that defined the 1960s. The new band were still unfamiliar with each other at this time, with Jimi introducing more musicians to his act, moving away from the familiar power trio. What is interesting however was that even though Jimi had more musicians on stage, you can only actually hear the trio of performers, that being Jimi, Billy Cox and Mitch Mitchell. The percussion and the rhythm guitar are faded so far down the mix they're barely audible; only on a few tracks can they be clearly heard, allowing Jimi to easily interact with them.

The reason for this was rumored to be some technical tampering behind the scenes. The new set up was still very much in its infancy, especially Jimi's desire to have an expanding presence to his band. Prior to the performance the mix was purposely tuned so that it was solely centered around the previous trio, heavily focusing on the sound of his guitar work. So visually it is an expanded ensemble, but sonically the power trio he was moving away from, largely remained.

'Message To Love' kicked off the set, energising the crowd with a recognizable riff and stellar lead work. Jimi matched his voice's pitch with his guitar at one point, creating a stunning effect. 'Hear My Train A Comin' follows, which moves into 'Red House', showcasing Jimi's improvisation within blues, and 'Lover Man' with its precise vocals and impressive rhythms. 'Foxy Lady' followed, which was now a crowd pleaser, and a track Jimi enjoyed playing live, it featured a tighter rhythm section and a more restrained solo than previous versions, this moved into 'Jam Back At The House', which closed the first section.

The second half opens with solid renditions of 'Izabella and Fire', both benefiting from the new rhythm section. 'Voodoo Child' stands out with extended Wah guitar riff and intense improvisation, this made it a truly epic performance. 'The Star-Spangled Banner' is famously chaotic and raw, while 'Purple Haze' remained close to the studio version. 'Hey Joe' concluded the show, with a stellar rendition of this rock classic.

It was simply dazzling to watch him play at Woodstock: Jimi was totally in control of what he was doing but still improvising or playing song patterns from memory. Previously, there were recordings made from rehearsals in New York, and there were also recordings of a performance they gave at the Tinker Street cinema in Woodstock. These surprisingly show the band struggling to play together as a cohesive unit. After such a struggle with rehearsals for the new set up, it's amazing the Woodstock performance would be so good. Jimi and the strength of his onstage presence was captivating from the onset.

The set from Gypsy Sun and Rainbows was a loose affair, which was precisely where Jimi wanted to be. It was unpolished and improvised, giving Jimi many incredible opportunities to branch out into various solos.

One of these solo's, however, would hit the headlines and be watched and admired continuously, even to this day. The one track of the whole performance, the performance within the performance, was of course Jimi's take on the national anthem, 'Star Spangled Banner'. It is arguably this that made Woodstock famous. This was what everyone was talking about after Jimi left the stage.

Despite the controversy that followed, or the interpretation of 'Star Spangled Banner', it wasn't the first time he had played it, he had been adding it to his sets for quite a while. It is fair to say however, that the Woodstock interpretation is widely regarded as the most controversial. This was due in part to the festival setting, and what it represented, the love and peace environment it cohesively defined. It was performed into the rising sun, at the height of counterculture during a summer of love. It is fresh in the wake of political activism surrounding Vietnam, and civil rights. It signified antiestablishment, perfectly performed through sound and vision.

Nothing matched the timing of Woodstock for 'Star Spangled Banner': Jimi's incomparable skill of making the guitar launch into different effects; the firing guns, dropping bombs and rockets soaring, all brought the whole ethos of the festival to a complete and fitting finale. America was raging, political change was everywhere and the counterculture movement was at its hedonistic peak. The 1969 summer of love was continuing and the anti-war, pro-peace movement was in unison for all. With one instrument, Jimi criticised politics, created musical war and condemned Vietnam through a bizarre twist of national pride. All penetrated through the county's most sacred tune. It stands as the most bizarre and wonderful musical conflict in history.

Although 'Star Spangled Banner' grabbed the headlines as a finale, it wasn't the last track. Another rarity for Jimi was that he performed an encore. He almost never performed encores, but at Woodstock, despite the sun rising and the vanishing crowd, he did. On recordings, he can be heard considering 'Valleys of Neptune', which he never performed publicly, before or after Woodstock. He opted, instead, for 'Hey Joe'.

If there were any doubts about Jim's potential or his fame, Woodstock eliminated them entirely. Any previous reservations about his status were silenced after his performance at Woodstock. He was undeniably recognised as the greatest guitarist of his time. But of course, with this increased notoriety came opportunities for money to be made, including anyone connected to him.

Mike continued in his pursuit of cash above anything else after Woodstock. Jimi had hangers on all over the place and was becoming desperately unhappy. Mike was simply a businessman, cash was all that mattered, there was simply no understanding of music, or interest in it for creative purposes, he had no time for the process or artistry. For Jimi it was just one gig to the next; airplanes, cars, buses: a performance on a TV show, an interview, a photoshoot. He literally had no means to slow anything down, it was a complete whirlwind for him. He knew he needed to make a change; he was at a crossroads.

It was around this period that Jimi started to make plans to sever his ties with Mike. He openly told friends he had had enough, and he wanted out. Essentially Jimi wanted to gain some control over his affairs, and his life in general. He was concerned about money, and more to the point, where it was. He was aware of course that this was handled by Mike and others, but the fact remained he knew he had earned a massive amount, but at times was also broke. On many occasions he resulted to borrowing from friends and associates. He was starting to ask questions as to where his money was. He was also concerned about his taxes and questioned if they were being properly paid.

Although things were bleak for him at this time, there was one aspect of business that he was excited about. The acquisition of his own studio. A sanctuary where he could create in freedom, and at his own pace. Plans were put in place that would eventually become Electric Lady Studios. The purchase was not as smooth as it seemed, and the set-up went far over the initial budget, rumored to be over $300,000. To pay for the ongoing work, Mike booked Jimi in for a relentless tour, he dangled the carrot here, Jimi was told the cash generated would be used to pay for the outgoing cost of the studio.

On the setup of Electric Lady, engineer Eddie Kramer recalled; *"Jimi was jamming in New York at any studio he could get his hands on, he loved creating new sounds. He could barely breathe; he was in such a hurry to get it all out. And thank God he did, because what he created then was the basis for all the music we were going to do next."* Jimi's pursuit to expand his band and jam with every musician around was an ongoing thing, he never stopped searching for new musicians to jam with, to bounce off, he was constantly searching for new inspiration and interplay.

For years, Jimi desperately wanted his own club, his own creative home. Somewhere the jam sessions he loved to host could all come under one roof, all 'in- house'; His house. He decided to purchase his own place where he could play in front of people whenever he wanted and with whomever he liked. A venue was found, a recently closed and freshly boarded club located on West 8th Street called The Generation. It wasn't new to Jimi; he had played at practically every decent club in New York, here he had previously jammed with BB King and Sly Stone. To create the aesthetics

Jimi hired a 22-year-old recently qualified architecture graduate John Storyk.

John knew Generation, and was ambitious, around a year before he met Jimi, he had just finished college and had driven to Manhattan in search of his own musical fortune. He was also a musician and played saxophone and piano for a Blues band, he recalled *"We'd listen to Blues guys like Junior Wells, James Cotton and Muddy Waters at a club in New York."* Although he had a passion for playing, like many young musicians, money just wasn't coming through. He looked for a day job and eventually landed one in an architecture office. He found it quite dull and was unable to expand any of his young creativity. While looking for something more fulfilling, he saw an ad while in line for an ice cream looking for free carpentry labour for an experimental night club, downtown. John liked the advert , *"Yes, I did inhale"* he recalled later.

Something about the ad appealed to John, he answered it and met with the owners. He volunteered his services on the condition he could redesign the club.

From Jimi's perspective his only instructions were to paint everything white, give the space as much sensuality as possible, and no sharp edges. Everything must run smoothly from one space to the next, it was ambitious for the time, John added *"He had this idea that at the back of the club would be a control room that could record the music played in the club. It doesn't sound particularly complicated today. But in 1968/69, that sort of thing wasn't happening."*

Once the young architect presented his ideas to Jimi things progressed quickly. Jimi loved the plans John had made, and things were on track to continue. That was until Eddie suggested to Jimi that a studio would be a far more prudent use of the space, both financially, pleasing Jeffery, and creatively, pleasing Jimi. His new club in progress was costing a lot of money to set up, in addition it was estimated that Jimi was clearing $200,000 per year in costs just for studio time, a staggering $1.8m today. Eddie recalled saying to Jimi *"Let's build you the best studio in the world, where you would not be disturbed, a womb-like structure where you could feel at home."* He and his manager (Michael Jeffery) looked at me and said, 'Good idea'."

John Storyk was retained to create the design space, as he had already done a great job in bringing Jimi's initial vision to life when the space was to be a club. As engineer, Eddie would oversee the audio aspects for the studio. John realised quickly that the transition from a club to a recording studio wasn't as simple as he first thought; *"Everything we know now about studios didn't exist then,"* John said. *"There was no manual you could follow."* Eddie also remembers the challenges involved: *"The major* studios were these horrible boxes. They were uninspiring places to make music. The idea of even putting a couch or a plant in a studio was not happening. The control rooms tended to be small, designed to accommodate the producer, not the artist. At the time, the artist would just come into the studio, do their takes and go, they didn't go into the control room because they didn't produce their own records. Electric Lady was meant to rebalance the power dynamic, putting the artist in charge, an emerging idea at the time. It was incredibly rare for artists to have their own studios then, that idea was way ahead of its time."

The studios also tended to be cold environments. It was a place where an artist wasn't meant to stay in for too long, the notion of it being comfortable, or a place to relax in, was completely alien in the 1960s. Electric Lady would be a warm, inviting space, Jimi wanted it to feel almost feminine, safe and somewhere you could relax, somewhere to chill. The curves were still in the instruction with no sharp edges, as was soft carpet to make the space appear to flow and enfold. It was all about the flow, everything fluidic and seamlessly rolling into one. No columns were permitted just an inspiring sinuous space to create in. Color was also a key element for Jimi, even though the initial instruction was to make the walls white, he wanted the ability to project onto them, to change them as the mood hit him, Eddie remembered the importance of color within Jimi's music, and not from a visual perspective; *"When Jimi said, 'Hey man, give me some green' or 'Give me more purple,' it was code, I knew when he said 'green' it meant more reverb. 'Red' meant more distortion. Having the ability to dial in different colors to match whatever he was thinking was a great blessing."* It wasn't just the redefining of the area that made the studio work, it was also its basic shape, even more interesting, was the ceiling.

The ceiling, largely ignored on first inspection, actually had a decisive consequence. The new studio Jimi was creating was located underneath a movie theater, the 8th Street Playhouse. As a result it had a floor that sloped down, the slope of the floor was matched by the ceiling, it sloped in parallel to it. To visually exaggerate the effect, John created a flying saucer design on the ceiling. The shape itself gave a unique audio to Electric Ladyland. *"The real magic of the room is the ceiling,"* John said. *"I thought the shape would absorb mid and high frequencies. Little did I know that what we actually wound up making was a low frequency membrane absorber. That's the science that made this a great rock'n'roll room."* John reflected back years later on the ceiling and how fortunate he was in the design work. *"It wasn't until many years later that I realised we got a little lucky, especially with the ceiling, I went back and found out why the room worked so well, and it's because of the ceiling, which looks like a flat propeller. It was partly aesthetics, and partly a half-baked notion that I shouldn't have a parallel ceiling. I also remembered reading a little bit about membrane absorbers. They'd been used at RCA Studios and the great Kultura Studios in Moscow. I didn't completely understand the science and took a stab at how to build it. We used very lightweight plaster and the ceiling turned out to be a giant membrane absorber, which keeps the low frequency reverb time down in the room. I'm not going to lie. I had very little science to back up what I was conceiving, but Eddie and I took a shot at it and it worked out."*

It wasn't until many years later that he realised it gave Electric Lady, a desirable large studio, the characteristic of tailing down the low frequency reverb time. It tightened up the sound, as opposed to concert halls, where you'd want it to tail up and bloom. Talking specifically about the studio sound John said. *"It's not Jimi Hendrix's spirit in the walls, the colored lighting, the fact you have to slide in a tiny door on Eighth Street, or the river that flows under the studio. All interesting stories, but the science is in the ceiling... although we all still wonder if Jimi is still with us sometimes."*

Although the construction of Electric Lady was unique, and a wonderful example of the vision of Jimi Hendrix and his creativity, the construction was plagued with issues. One of the costliest was the river that John referenced in his interview. Upon construction the team discovered a water table left over from the Minetta Creek that ran just below the floor. Minetta Creek was one of the largest natural watercourses in Manhattan. It was fed from Fifth Avenue and 21st Street, and also Sixth Avenue and 16th Street. They both flowed and came together near Fifth Avenue and 11th Street. The creek was filled in by the mid-19th century, although it persisted as an underground stream throughout the 20th century. The name Minetta Creek's is thought to have originated from the Native American term 'Manette', meaning 'Devils Water'.

The Devils water was exactly that for Jimi, the underground stream caused countless floods during the construction and caused major delays at a huge cost. In the end, the studio's construction took twice as long as expected, in fact it took a full year, from May 1969 to the next spring. The cost at the time peaked at over $1m, the equivalent of around $8.7m today. The decision was made to open up the studio, to recoup some of the cost, so it wasn't just a sanctuary for Jimi but a fully functioning studio that could be booked and used to full effect. This was logical, Jimi was at this point one of the most important and admired musicians in the world, he had great influence when it came to those wanting to record with him or simply be around him.

Another aspect unique to Electric Lady was that it didn't own the space it occupied. To this day, the owners pay rent. *"It may be the worst real estate deal in New York history"*, John said. Eddie added *"For Jimi it was well worth it. Once he could start using the studio, he was the happiest I'd ever seen him. He was completely in his element. Jimi was especially excited about the new configuration of his band, which featured himself, the drummer Mitch Mitchell and the bassist Billy Cox. Jimi's direction was to take some of the funk and blues elements from* his *Band of Gypsys, but with Mitch in the group, Mitch had been listening to Buddy Miles (from Band of Gypsys) and you can hear it in his playing. It's way funkier and less showy."*

Jimi was delighted with his new acquisition; he had an opening party on 26th August 1970. Sadly however, despite his forward plans for his studio, Jimi would only spend around 10 weeks recording in Electric Lady, most of which during the final phases of its construction. Shortly after its completion he left New York. Sadly, he would never return…

Chapter 20

Fly on, my sweet angel

"I'm the one that's got to die when it's time for me to die, so let me live my life the way I want to."

Shortly after Woodstock there were bizarre rumours circulating that Jimi was abducted and held for ransom by mafia gunmen; the reports suggested that he was held in captivity for two days in New York and a ransom was issued to his managers. Some of Jimi's unsavory contacts soon identified and caught up with the abductors, and they allegedly had the beating of their lives. The story goes that Jimi himself was too stoned to remember any of it. Unsurprisingly this story remains speculative and unproven, but another theory was that Mike had staged the whole event to prove himself as the right guy for Jimi going forward. He had heard the talk of Jimi wanting to break free from him and, being the character he was, wanted to prove he had the capability to protect him. The theory that they were actually Mafia members is also unlikely.

From Jimi's perspective he was increasingly convinced that Mike was stealing from him, furthermore he saw Mike as someone that was stifling his creativity for his own financial gains. As time went on the reputation of Mike Jeffery, that of a shady character who should never be trusted, was for Jimi, proving to be the case. Whether the abduction reports were true, exaggerated, or completely fabricated, it does shine a light into the seemingly chaotic management and hangers on that surrounded Jimi; and the reason he was trying to leave and move away, attempting to cut ties and make a fresh start.

After the success of Woodstock, Jimi's management tried continuously to convince him to reform the original band: it was better and more profitable in their opinion. Jimi, however, was sticking to his vision of a free-flowing band, it became another irritant for him, another conflict of interest as his creative vision was at odds with the commercial aspect that Mike wanted to maintain. The commercial side of pop was of course huge at this time, and managers simply wanted their bands in the charts. There was a story around this time where Jimi was at Mike's house one afternoon. Mike had a huge vinyl collection running down a complete wall, Jimi walked along, looking for something to play, he found nothing. It was commercial pop, there was nothing that interested him at all from the hundreds of vinyl records proudly displayed. According to various accounts, Jimi was deeply distressed by the situation. It appeared that his manager was primarily focused on, and seemingly accumulating subpar pop records, which starkly contrasted with the innovative brilliance of the artist he represented.

In March 1970 the live album 'Band of Gypsys' was officially released. It was the first album without the original line up of The Jimi Hendrix Experience. It was recorded on Dec 31st 1969/January 1st 1970, at the Fillmore East in New York City with Billy Cox on bass and Buddy Miles on drums, frequently referred to as the Band of Gypsys. It's an album that captures Jimi primarily within a fusion of funk and R&B entwined with harder rock and free form jams; this approach would later morph into the genre of funk rock. It contains previously unreleased songs and was the last full-length Jimi Hendrix album released before his death.

Band of Gypsys

Side One
1. Who Knows (3rd show)
2. Machine Gun (3rd show)

Side Two
1. Changes (4th show)
2. Power to Love (4th show)
3. Message of Love (4th show)
4. We Gotta Live Together (4th show)

The album was nothing short of polarising, its focus is on jam-oriented songs, a place where Jimi loved to be. His tones and phrasing throughout the recording are nothing short of spectacular, it gives the listener a chance to listen again to Jimi, to enjoy his talent, to appreciate and to ponder the unrivalled skill and effortless gift that he had. Often when Jimi was live this aspect was somewhat lost, particularly on some of the audience that were watching him for the first time. Here he can be appreciated, and you can fully understand why the best guitarists and musicians of the time were in absolute awe of him.

Buddy Miles can be heard scat singing, and provides great backing vocals, it works well behind Jimi. What makes the record so outstanding is the interplay with the Band of Gypsys, from the opening groove of 'Who Knows' you can hear how telepathically locked in Jimi, Billy and Buddy are. Jimi was searching at this time for a more cohesive sound incorporating more of a funk and R&B oriented direction, and it's achieved. The band sound fresh and unique, within their own sub-genre, it has a style of guitar playing that is not heard elsewhere. The guitar solos, of course are a natural highlight, Jimi extends with ease on 'Power to Love & Machine Gun'. He stages his skill for straight rhythm & lead guitar playing on every tune, such as in 'Changes', this time without the usual gimmicks or eclectic sounds. The whole band rocked, it's a wonderful example of a night with Jimi Hendrix, in perfect unison.

Jimi also produced the album but found it difficult to get it completed the way he wanted to. He also had to hand it over to fulfill the previous contract, despite its brilliance he was again left frustrated with the final outcome. It was another idea by Mike to get Ed Chaplin's away from Jimi, to produce a live album and simply give him that. It would be relatively inexpensive to produce, and if they put in some new tracks, it would also fulfil the contract. Billy Cox claimed that this was the reason the band came into existence in the first place, *"At the time I was there I think Mitch was in England, He was asked to do it, but I think he wanted to stay in England. Buddy was easily available, so me, Buddy and Jimi rehearsed for a couple of weeks and that was The Band of Gypsys".*

Shortly after its release, 'Band of Gypsys' reached the top ten of the album charts in the US and UK, as well as appearing in charts in several other countries. The influence of the album was huge and it paved the way for the funk rock developments of the 1970s, being noted as a key inspiration by rock musicians and bands for decades after its release.

On November 27th, 1969, Jimi celebrated his 27th birthday in New York. Unbeknown to the music world, it would be his last; The Rolling Stones were also in New York at this time. Jimi joined them during their concert at Madison Square Garden. After the performance… the party continued. The Rolling Stones tour of the United States in 1969 (with Ike & Tina Turner, BB King and Terry Reid as opening acts) has been described by music critics as *'the first legendary rock and roll tour in history.'* It was also hyped as *'the biggest rock event of the year.'* It was the first tour with Mick Taylor, who replaced Jimi's friend Brian Jones, who died in July '69, aged 27. Ironically Janis Joplin performed with the Turners during an improvised performance of 'Land of 1000 dances', she also would not see her 28th birthday, passing away aged 27 on October 4th, 1970. Brian Jones, Janis Joplin and Jimi would all begin the fascination with the notorious 27 Club.

Prior to the concert, Jimi arrived well in advance and enjoyed the party, he chatted, smoked and drank, enjoying the pre party and improvising notes with his guitar, his inseparable companion. Eddie Kramer reflected on the birthday celebration; "*I got a phone call. It was very strange for me to get a call from Jimi. 'Hey man, Do you want to come see the Rolling Stones at Madison Square Garden tonight?' I said, 'Yes, Jimi, that would be great, thank you very much.' And he concluded, 'See you backstage.'* "That's how it all happened. I grabbed my camera bag and met up with him. The Stones and Jimi were friends, and it was wonderful. In the locker room, talking to all the guys. I have that beautiful photo of Mick and Jimi sitting on the bench, with the cinder block wall and the hangers behind it. These two icons, magnificent rock personalities, sitting together...just chatting." In the locker room, Jimi also talked and joked with Keith Richards, they had a mini jam session alongside Mick Taylor, he also recalled the moment: "*He came to the concert, I think he was living in New York at the time... during the period with his band The Gypsys. He came backstage and we improvised a little with our guitars in the locker room. I very rarely saw Jimi Hendrix without a guitar. He was always playing the guitar.*"

When the concert ended, Jimi and the Rolling Stones and others continued the celebration at a private party. Devon was with Jimi as the party continued but rumors followed that she actually left with Mick Jagger, and Jimi was too downtrodden at the time to care. Mick became the inspiration for the posthumous song, 'Dolly Dagger', after an incident that happened, coincidentally, during this party. The story is said that Mick accidentally cut his finger, and when he asked about a Band-Aid, Devon Wilson, Jimi's girlfriend for the evening, ran up to him and told him it wasn't necessary. In front of Jimi, she sucked the blood from his finger. Hence this Jimi Hendrix Lyric from Dolly Dagger; "*She drinks the blood of a jagged edge. She Drinks, baby.*"

Monika Dannemann was still on the scene, and was a completely different character to Devon Wilson, some even said she was naïve in comparison to the street wise Devon. Devon was now heavily using cocaine and heroin, previously she had been a supplier for Jimi, but many around Jimi stated that he was actively trying to clean himself up. His opinion of Devon was becoming more pitiful, he felt sorry for her, rather than a girlfriend or genuine companion. Jimi was hesitant for Monika to come to New York with Devon on the scene, he didn't want any form of confrontation between the two, they both were, even though very different personalities, striving to be the number one girl in his life.

It was after his appearance at Woodstock that Jimi started to work on various demos, some of these would be used in the aforementioned settlement from the legal disputes that were occurring. The new material, which was largely driven by Billy Cox's and Buddy Miles' musical approaches, started a new direction for Jimi. Jimi loved new directions, new challenges and was keen to evolve his sound. Mike Jeffery on the other hand saw things differently. He actively tried to move Jimi away from these tendencies, constantly pushing for more commercial approaches. It was distressing for Jimi and did nothing to aid his downbeat outlook on his future. Jimi's lyrics also changed during this period, becoming more humanistic in themes. He adopted new directions in guitar improvisation and his tonal effects became more dominant.

It was in May 1970 that the Woodstock soundtrack was released. The full title of the album was *'Woodstock: Music from the Original Soundtrack and More'*. On side 6 of the album Jimi was featured. His contributions were listed as:

- *Medley (Performed by Jimi Hendrix)*
- *Star Spangled Banner (Traditional arrangement, Jimi Hendrix)*
- *Purple Haze (Hendrix)*
- *Instrumental Solo (Hendrix)*

As expected, the album was a sonic celebration of the event, a memento to the greatest festival of all time. The benchmark to it all. *'Woodstock: Music from the Original Soundtrack'* was a live album of selected performances from the festival. It was originally released on Atlantic Records' Cotillion label as a triple album on May 11th 1970. Producer Eddie Kramer was the sound engineer during the three-day event. A second collection of recordings from the festival, *'Woodstock Two'*, was released a year later.

The album was far more than a mere soundtrack. The first recording to capture the music made at Woodstock reclaimed a magical moment that was frozen in time. It effectively illuminated one of the great phenomena of the '60s, a historic event of unparalleled proportions that gathered the tribes and gave voice to half a million young people who proclaimed not only their independence, but their cultural credence as well. Thus, the Woodstock generation was born.

The music on those three slabs of vinyl was essential of course, not just for posterity but also for the tiny and often consequential soundbites. Small bits of dialogue and aural effects that grasp hold of the spirit of that incomparable gathering, wrapping it all in a nostalgic haze that remains every bit as affecting today as it was at the time it took place.

This was also a triple album, and these were very rare in 1970, but the sheer volume of quality, and of course the magnitude of the event itself, couldn't be contained any other way.

Jimi's struggle at the immense pressure he was under continued on, to him things were getting worse. At this time, he was dealing with two pending lawsuits; one was a paternity case and the other the recording contract dispute, which was due to be heard by a UK High Court within a month or so. It was now no secret that he desperately wanted to leave the clutches of Mike, the feeling of mistrust about how his affairs were run was becoming intolerable, and Mike new this. Whether he cared much however is up for debate, but true to form he carried on regardless. He booked Jimi on another full tour of the US, with hardly any breaks at all through May, June and July. Jimi had no consultation for this and was simply made to do it. He was trapped, and without cash coming in needed the concerts to simply keep the band functioning, as well as other costs that he was told were still outstanding.

Jimi was suffering from fatigue; he was in poor health, overworked and exhausted, physically, emotionally and creatively. On top of this he had severe lack of sleep and felt increasing paranoia towards those around him. He was also getting increasingly frustrated and disenchanted with the music industry itself, in particular the lack of control over his creativity and releases. At this time, Mike also informed Jimi that after the US tour he had booked him into another major festival that was being planned, at the Isle of Wight.

Monterey and Woodstock would be forever cemented in the legacy of Jimi Hendrix, and rightly so, but The Isle of Wight Festival, one of his final shows on British soil, would be just as memorable. It would be Jimi's first visit to England in nearly eighteen months. The festival had a reputation for being a shambolic affair, but in the festival-pinnacle peak of 1970 it was a sought-after event for the weird and wonderful, a free-spirited festival for the flower power generation to flock too. Despite the issues that Jimi had, this one event was something he was looking forward to. For him it was a simple one off, he then planned to head back to New York to finish his new album, which he had written tracks for and was keen to progress with.

After Jimi had completed his US tour he planned to go back to England. Prior to travelling he called Monika to ask her to find him a place in London, a place where he could be left alone. At this point in time, with all the pressures that surrounded him, this was very important to Jimi. He was originally booked at The Londonderry Hotel, a place where he could conduct meetings and interviews. But alongside that Monika found another place, and it was perfect; The Samarkand Hotel, in Lansdowne Crecent, Notting Hill Gate, London. It had a private garden that had a small gate that went straight into a London Park. It was also a short walk from Holland park and Hyde park. Jimi could be alone and unbothered here should he wish. On the first evening there Jimi and Monika went to the Speakeasy and stayed the night together at The Samarkand. There was no relaxation for Jimi, he was on a tight schedule of interviews that were pre-booked for him. Monika recalled that in the three days in London he had hardly slept. The next day he flew to the Isle of Wight.

The small Isle of Wight community were overwhelmed with festival goers, who had travelled across to the small island situated off the southern coast of England. It was a great proposition and a fitting one for Jimi. The first Isle of Wight Festival was in 1968 and it was to this point ostensibly another counterculture event. This festival was scheduled to be the largest yet, by a long way. With the excitement that was gathering in the weeks before, it attracted far more fans than were anticipated. The small island was swamped with unexpectedly high attendance levels. The location of the event was not easy to get to once you landed on the island. From the mainland of England you would arrive at the north of the island, and festival goers were then forced to travel the length of it to arrive. Locals were so inconvenienced by the amount of people that descended on their small communities that they switched sign posts on the many twisty country lanes, causing chaos as festival goers tried to navigate across the island. There was huge opposition to the event and this grew year on year. Here, as the build up to the 1970 event took place, the locals and opposition groups were far more organised in trying to ban and prevent the event from happening.

After this event they were successful in their pursuit of a ban. The following year the UK Parliament added a section to the Isle of Wight County Council Act 1971. This prevented any overnight open-air gatherings of more than 5,000 people on the island without a special license from the council. It effectively closed the festival altogether after,1970. The event was eventually revived in 2002.

The Isle of Wight performance has long been rumored as presenting Jimi in a very poor state. Tired, disillusioned, stoned out of his mind and actually sick of live playing. On the other hand, certain fans claim that what some people view as a 'poor' state of playing is actually nothing but Jimi playing in a more refined and moderate style: simply put, Jimi was sick of his usual image, that of the tongue-waggler 'n' teeth-picker that casual fans regarded him to be. For this particular show he decided to refrain from the gimmicks and just play his guitar.

For this performance Jimi was back to the power trio. Taking place in August 1970, the performance from Jimi, Mitch Mitchell and Billy Cox is one of the final shows of note for Jimi Hendrix that he would ever perform in the UK before his untimely death on September 18th. Jimi had literally just finished another USA tour; took another flight, spent a few nights in London and headed straight to the Isle of Wight. On reflection Jimi's appearance at the Isle of Wight, because it would tragically be his last of any notable size, gave more kudos and gravitas to the performance. Jimi was both physically and emotionally exhausted, but he got through it. It also became hugely significant to the massive audience who watched him. There was expected to be around 150,000 people at the festival, but over 500,000 actually attended. Most of the crowd obviously witnessed him for the last time.

It's understandable that with everything that was going on in Jimi Hendrix's life at this time he was extremely anxious about performing. One of his girlfriends who was with him at the time, Kirsten Nefer, was worried about the imposing nature of the crowd: she said that *"He was so afraid of going on the stage, in front of all these people, all of a sudden he felt trapped you know, in this little caravan and getting his clothes on."* Jimi was growing out of fame, he needed a break and possibly a change in direction, but as with many who are in his position, the forward train kept rolling and Jimi was unable to get off or leave: he was completely trapped by his fame, and by his management and the commitments he had.

He was now a truly global icon and the weight of expectation on him was absolutely huge. Nevertheless, he composed himself and walked to the stage to perform again in front of half a million people. Jimi arrived by helicopter at around 8.30pm on the evening of the festival. One friend named Vishwa noted on greeting Jimi that he seemed extremely tired, but more than that, he appeared down, very depressed in his persona. Jimi was fashionably late to do his set; he walked on stage in the early hours of the morning.

Although clearly vulnerable and afraid backstage, on stage Jimi Hendrix was a different animal. Here he owned it; the lawsuits, the managers directing him and controlling him, and the immense pressure and expectations he was under simply went away. Here, for now, he was free, and his performance at the 1970 Isle of Wight Festival proved that. It was one of his most legendary sets, among a string of countless other iconic sets.

Jimi walked on stage and addressed the festival crowd- Monday Aug 31 1970.

"Yeah ... Thank you very much for showing up, man, you all look really beautiful and outta sight ... And thanks for waiting. It has been a long time, hasn't it? ... That does mean peace not this ... Peace ... OK give us about a minute to tune up, all right? Give us about a minute'

One fan, who was just sixteen at the time, recalled the festival. He travelled with his brother to the Isle of Wight; along the way they had their sleeping bags stolen. They spent three nights just sleeping under the stars, waiting for the event to start. It would be worth it. The below is a beautifully written account of Jimi's set that morning by one of the brothers.

Shortly after 2.00 a.m. the eyes of those lucky to be awake and standing are centred on one individual walking towards the front of the stage. Jimi Hendrix is dressed in a colourful garment with long trailing sleeves. He is cradling a black and white fender Stratocaster. There is no crush or discomfort: just lights, colours, darkness, people waking, coughing and rubbing their eyes. I try to wake my brother. Gradually, he opens his eyes and sits motionless. I tell him Jimi Hendrix is on stage. My brother rubs both his eyes and attempts to stand with some difficulty.

A calm cold beauty descends as I gaze at this amazing human being and his backdrop of daisy-chained Marshall stacks. For a moment I'm fearful of tumbling, being crushed, or losing my brother, as people start to move closer to the stage. I think of some of the inventive music and guitar solos Jimi has created. The first time I heard 'Purple Haze' is ingrained in my memory. How could someone compose such a sublimely inventive and haunting song? The opening riff using tritones is unforgettable. I can hardly grasp that I'm going to witness Jimi Hendrix in concert for the first time.

Music, to my mind, is an emotional roller-coaster to be experienced live: to be captured with your eyes and ears, and if it fails to change your emotions and feelings then move on to music that does. A live performance cannot be captured on vinyl, video, CD or DVD, etc. Such mediums fail to convey the potpourri of images, colours, sounds, vibrations and volume which make your inner being glow. As Jimi speaks, sings, plays his guitar, the crowd watch in silence mesmerised by his magical charisma, stage presence, mercurial rhythms and soaring solos. I cheer and shout - like most people - after each song. My tiredness replaced by immense energy (I can't remember the last time I rested or slept).

The frost melts as Jimi plays Spanish Castle Magic. It sounds like a hot bright light breaking through the black, blue and white formations created by the stage lights. Jimi's guitar playing reaches a higher level: soaring, electrifying, intense. His vocals are full of sensuality and power, and during the final solo his guitar sound becomes surreal - distortion and feedback combine to create an expansive dreamy sound. While it is evident there are technical problems with Jimi's amplification, pedals and guitars (mostly going out of tune) his voice, phrasing and guitar playing are, at times, exceptional and soul-stirring. He establishes rhythms that are startling and utterly original. Jimi sings 'All Along the Watchtower' passionately. His soloing is enhanced by feedback and infectious interplay with Billy Cox on bass.

I believe Jimi is blessed to have Mitch Mitchell on drums and Billy Cox on bass as his rhythm section. They bring out the best in Jimi. Mitch shows he is an imaginative and multi-dimensional drummer, and Billy plays fluid and tight, with a deep intuitive skill, matching Jimi pattern for pattern. Jimi's playing is remarkable as it takes different twists and turns.

The patterns weaved by Jimi and Billy Cox are hypnotic during Machine Gun and once again Jimi creates some outstanding runs and sounds. Jimi plays soft, raw, loud, continually bending and moving in the direction of the sound he is trying to create. At times it appears to be a struggle and there is a haunting tension and passion in his playing. Then the rhythm changes and the trio synthesise again to paint a different musical landscape. Adorning a Flying V Jimi plays a powerful yet turbulent rendition of Red House. I watch and listen as Jimi deliveries his guitar phrases and vocals with a wrestling intensity. It is great to hear new numbers: Freedom, Dolly Dagger and Hey Baby (Land of the New Rising Sun).

Jimi pulled a blistering version of Voodoo Child (Slight Return) out of the bag. His guitar sounded heavily distorted, and the notes rained down sprinkled with Jimi's unique creative powers. For Jimi, the band and some of the audience - who were awake and standing - the show may have been uneven. All I know is that Jimi's performance at the festival shook and moved me and that for a while I was wrapped in its warmth and magic.

I was shocked - similar to millions of people worldwide - when news of Jimi's death was announced on September 18, 1970, and facts surrounding his physical and emotional health were released. I still believe Jimi's performance was the defining moment of the festival. His set showed an innovator and experimenter reaching out to his audience with his musical genius. For those fortunate to come of age during the 1960s Jimi Hendrix raised the bar and brought unparalleled power, sensuality and sustained resurrection to guitar playing, song writing and performance. He exuded a contagious charisma and spirit rarely witnessed by any musician, past or present. No one but Jimi Hendrix knows what his state of mind was during his last month on this earth. I believe, however, he had new horizons to explore musically, emotionally and spiritually. It is often forgotten that while Jimi was a guitar virtuoso, and an instrumentalist of profound influence, he was also an incredibly gifted, first-rate songwriter. Jimi's musical genius will continue to astound future listeners' as long as music exists and his memorable riffs, songs and lyrics will reverberate wherever sound can be heard.

After his performance Jimi retired backstage and slumped in his caravan, he was exhausted. He wanted some peace, and needed it, both physically and mentally. There was simply no time for that, a helicopter was waiting to take him directly to Southampton, to catch a flight to Stockholm.

It was revealed later that a few days before the festival, while he was at The Londonderry Hotel in Central London, Jimi was unexpectedly very ill. Although the room's heating was turned up to the maximum Jimi could not stop shivering. It was an unusual episode and one that those close to him had not seen before. His illness continued, and he couldn't shake it. Immediately after his performance at The Isle of Wight, his management refused to change plans. He was already booked on a tour of Scandinavia, an area Jimi was huge in.

After a couple of gigs Jimi arrived in Arhus, Denmark. During this time, he was repeatedly complaining about the cold he couldn't get rid of. In fact, Jimi was feeling so ill that he forgot his lyrics and unusually performed badly, he simply couldn't continue feeling like he did. Shortly after the set had started, around three songs in, he quit. He promised to give all the crowd their money back. Suffering from what looked like exhaustion and a high temperature he was helped back to his dressing room. There was cause for concern.

A local reporter interviewed Jimi for a Danish newspaper, she noted that he seemed, *"Exhausted and scared, I mean that's how he appeared to me, scared, like a frightened child."* Jimi also said something extremely prolific: He told the reporter that he didn't think he would reach 28: *"The moment that I feel that I don't have anything more to give musically, that's when I won't be found on this planet unless I have a wife and children. Because if I don't have anything to communicate through my music, then there is nothing left for me to live for."*

After a couple more concerts in Germany, Jimi flew back to London on the 6th September, staying at the Cumberland. Devon had followed him there, something that annoyed Jimi, it was reported that he didn't want her there. He didn't contact Monika at this time, she only knew Jimi was back in London after she saw Eric Barrett with Billy Coc at The Speakeasy. Jimi also spoke about having a change of heart about returning to New York as he had previously planned to do. Monika claimed Jimi now wanted to settle in England, as the frenzied pace of New York was driving him insane. He also stated, *"I'm so glad the mini skirt hasn't gone out of style, there's no place like London."*

Jimi loved London, and compared to other musical hubs around the world it was a place he felt comfortable in. It was of course the city where he had his musical breakthrough, and unlike places such as New York, was relatively safe in comparison. That said, there were reports from inside

Jimi's camp that he feared for his life when his inner circle became aware of him wanting to change his management, change his musical direction, and move on.

Jimi visited Ronnie Scotts on September 15th, 1970; to jam with Eric Burdon, he had a new band named War and Jimi wanted to jam with him. Jimi, however, was still unwell and after a couple of songs left the stage. This was the last time Jimi played in public.

On September 16th, 1970, Jimi spent time with Monika Dannemann. She had been at Ronnie Scotts the previous evening and left with Jimi when he cut short his performance with Eric Burdon. In the afternoon she took some photos of Jimi. 29 photos were taken of him sitting in the gardens of the Samarkand Hotel in Notting Hill, London. Alongside Jimi was a small bistro table, a China tea service with a single rose, and of course his Fender Stratocaster. These would be the last photos taken of Jimi Hendrix. In addition, Monika Dannemann herself would be reported to be the last person to see him alive. She would later sign two statements on Jimi's death, one to the police and one to the inquest, which would be highly controversial.

There were some conflicting stories at this point, Eric Clapton claimed he was supposed to meet Jimi at the Lyceum to see Sly Stone play, he claimed he had purchased, and carried along with him, a left-handed Stratocaster. Mitch stated that a jam was arranged at the Speakeasy, and he spoke to Jimi around 7pm at a flat owned by Gerry Stickells. Mitch claimed Jimi confirmed he would be there, but unusually, never showed. Chas claimed, however, that Jimi was with him until the early hours of Thursday morning; he claimed Jimi had given a location for them to meet, with a plan for Chas to manage him again. Jimi's contract with Mike actually expired the following month, in October, so some view this as a credible claim.

Jimi's desire to move forward, to plan new bands, and to go in a different direction were met with a stern resistance. Despite Jimi's pleas, his management were unmoved: Jimi was to stay exactly where he was. Although there wasn't long left Mike had Jimi locked into a contract and he was, from a professional standpoint, trapped within it. From Mike's perspective if Jimi was to move on, to sever ties completely, then he would get as much money out of him as possible.

Kathy Etchington recalled Jimi the day before he tragically died; *"It was the Thursday afternoon, he died the following morning, I saw him in Kensington Market, and he seemed fine, he came up to me and squigged me around the waist. He said I'm staying at The Cumberland Hotel; do you want to come for a drink later? in fact I didn't go. Later my friend called me up, she said 'Jimi's dead, I just heard it on the radio'. According to her*

I didn't say anything, I put the phone down, I didn't say a word. I tuned into the radio, they were beginning to report it, Hendrix dead at 27. I was really upset; I still remember it now. It did cross my mind that if I had gone round there it might not have happened, If only I had done this, if only... Theres no point in dwelling on that. I didn't go, and it happened. I've never visited the grave, because I prefer to remember him as he was."

Despite Kathy remembering Jimi as being fine, he was obviously in a bad way. Reports stated that the contract that was due to expire had Mike Jeffery earning an alleged 40% of all Jimi's earnings. It was a vast amount by any standards, and of course Jimi had no way of actually knowing if the percentage he was receiving was actually higher or lower than this in any way. On his return to London, Jimi was now using barbiturates to help him sleep, and amphetamines to function through the day. This became a normal way of life as he tried to cope with the pressures and demands that were now pulling him in all directions. Cocaine was his drug of choice however, and this was the one for which he was most dependable. Things were not good.

On the evening of September 17th, 1970, Jimi went to a party. He was reported to be drinking red wine. It was hosted by a record company executive and Jimi spent time with record producer Alan Douglas. During the evening Jimi approached Alan to see if he would be interested in managing him after he had severed ties with Jeffery. If the various reports were correct then Jimi had approached Alan as well as Chas, so this indicates he was shopping around for alternative management.

Jimi was never known to be a big drinker, but on this occasion, he reportedly drank, which for some was uncharacteristic. During the evening it was reported that he was flirtatious with many women; Monika Danneman, like many women within Jimi's inner circle viewed him as her boyfriend; she claimed afterwards that they planned to get engaged, but this was questioned later, and friends were skeptical. She was described as obsessive towards him, a fantasist, and Jimi had no plans at this stage in his life to settle down. On this evening at the party she became increasingly jealous of Jimi and the girls that were surrounding him. Jimi, however, was reported to be in good spirits as the night went on, despite the turmoil in his career.

Moving into the early hours of September 18th, 1970, it was claimed that Jimi returned to his hotel with Monika and then left shortly afterwards alone, leaving Monika back at the hotel. He then ventured out to another party. Here he met the usual entourage of women that he often hung around with. Devon Wilson was at this party. It would later be reported, after investigation, that she supplied Jimi with amphetamine. At this time in the

1960s this was known on the street as 'Black Bombers', Jimi allegedly mixed the drug with the red wine in the early hours of the morning. At this time there was little known about drugs and alcohol and taking them together was not thought of as a particular risk, on the street anyway. Around 3am Jimi left the party. He was reported again to be optimistic and in good spirits, he then returned to the Samarkand Hotel in Notting Hill.

From this point onwards, when Jimi returned to the Samarkand Hotel, it is not known exactly happened to him, or the events that led to his tragic death. The last person reportedly to see him was Monika Danneman and crucially her account of what happened from here onwards is all anyone actually has of the final hours of Jimi's life. And later this account would be questioned.

Monika claimed she made Jimi a meal that he didn't eat and she fell asleep around 4am. Between 9am and 10am, on the morning of September 18th, she woke up and went out for around 10 minutes, leaving Jimi alone. When she returned, she noticed vomit on the corner of Jimi's mouth and tried to wake him. He was unresponsive; She later claimed at this point he was still breathing. She could see also that he had vomited over his clothes.

In a panic she called his friends, who quickly persuaded her to call an ambulance. This call for the ambulance was officially logged at 11.18am. On arrival the paramedics checked Jimi over and he was admitted to St Mary Abbots Hospital. It was also reported they carried him upright to the ambulance, which would have been unusual if that was the case. At the hospital Monika was adamant that Jimi was alive, a nurse had told her he would be fine and not to worry, and he was taken in to the waiting doctor and the team.

Jimi was seen and treated by Dr John Bannister, who at the time was unaware that the man he was trying to resuscitate was in fact Jimi Hendrix. On arrival he stated that Jimi was in fact not breathing, so they started to pump his chest to try and resuscitate him. There was no response. Dr Bannister stated that they tried to turn him but that he was very stiff, a sign that rigor mortis had already set in.

One thing the doctor did state that would arouse suspicion was that there appeared to be a huge amount of fluid in Jimi's lungs, later identified as red wine. The doctor estimated this to be at least two or three bottles. The amount of wine that was found did not match the alcohol levels in Jimi's system. As a result, the inquest declared his death as 'suspicious'. As with all cases of famous people who have died in various circumstances there is always speculation, and different accounts will always exist.

Jimi Hendrix was officially pronounced dead at 12.45pm on September 18th, 1970.

Once the news broke the music world fell into complete shock. The autopsy report was obviously looked at in detail. It has even been studied and discussed many times since Jimi's untimely death and has many theories. Many questions still remain into how and why Jimi Hendrix died at just 27 years of age. The official report stated he died from asphyxiation on vomit while intoxicated; however, the coroner returned an open verdict and this is where, as with all these situations, various conspiracy theories started to arise, especially surrounding Monika Danneman's account of what happened.

All substances were examined to determine if he had overdosed. The symptoms he experienced during his tour, where he felt very ill, were also investigated. During this time, there was an influenza pandemic in Europe. However, influenza, LSD, and heroin were ruled out as causes of Jimi's death, as none of these substances were present in his system. Additionally, no cocaine was found in his system, and the alcohol levels detected were not high enough to cause him to choke on his own vomit. There was however a significant quantity of amphetamine that was found in his urine.

It was well known in Jimi's inner circle at the time leading to his death that tensions between him and Mike were at an all-time high. For many, Mike Jeffery was instantly someone of suspicion around Jimi's final hours. There followed reports that the day before Jimi's death he had called his American lawyers. He had informed them that he had made the decision to leave his management. He had allegedly asked them to draw up papers and immediately annul the management contract. In addition, he wanted to take Michael Jeffery to court for embezzlement.

At this time Jimi was Michael Jeffery's only legitimate source of income. In a bizzare twist however Jimi's lawyers were also the lawyers for Mike, so there was a huge conflict of interest. Mike would have known Jimi wanted to leave, and it is worth assuming that Mike would have been made aware that Jimi had made official legal plans. There were also reports that Mike had an insurance policy if Jimi died. If Jimi was to leave, financially his manager had nothing, he would be bankrupt. But if Jimi died, he would receive a substantial payout, allegedly around $2 million, which in 1970 was a vast amount of money. However, all these theories and allegations were unproven and remain as pure speculation and opinion; no one was ever charged with any crime resulting from the death of Jimi Hendrix.

It was well known that Michael Jeffery managed all of Jimi's cash, in fact all the cash accumulated from the Jimi Hendrix Experience went through Michael Jeffery. He worked the same way when he was the manager of the Animals, which led the group to question where their money had actually gone, this ultimately split the band up completely.

Jimi and his band only got to see a fraction of what they actually made; the money went through an offshore company that Michael Jeffery set up, Yamata. It was basically a tax haven. All the tour money, record sales, publishing, royalties, everything, went into Yamata. The company was ran in silence, under the radar, and didn't submit any accounts. This meant that Jimi and the band had no way of keeping track of what was happening with their money.

There were efforts later to recover funds from Yamata. Sums were estimated to be between $2 and £5 Million, but by the time the recovery was actioned it had allegedly disappeared. Law suits and the pursuit of money allegedly owed to band members and associates of Jimi Hendrix continued for many years after his death. It goes back to the basic notion that the contracts that musicians and singers signed in the 1960s and 1970s were completely unfit for purpose. Another aspect was of course, the vast amount of posthumous releases after the death of Jimi Hendrix, there were literally hundreds distributed through various sources, and many that didn't deserve to be, unworthy of carrying his name. Exactly where and who the royalties went to for these releases is another tangled web in the contractual chaos that surrounded Jimi, when he was alive and recording.

On top of the recreational drugs and alcohol Jimi had taken it transpired he had taken an amount of sedative to help him sleep. Empty blister packs were found at the scene that indicated that Jimi could have taken 9 or 10 tablets, which would, if correct, have been fatal. In addition, Jimi had written some lyrics the night before which were also found, and the words that were written led many to draw the conclusion that his death was suicide. This theory indicates that it was a suicide note, in the form of a poem.

The poem read:

"...the story of life is quicker than the wink of an eye, the story of love is hello and good-bye, until we meet again. Jimi Hendrix September 17th, 1970."

Again, this was speculation and no real evidence exists for this; it is a theory that is highly unlikely. The sleeping drug that was in Jimi's system, which the autopsy report highlighted, was Quinalbarbitone. This was a very powerful amphetamine sedative used in the 1960s as a sleeping tablet. Again, little was known at the time around these kinds of drugs, especially regarding any recommended dosage. Monika herself was on a prescribed German sleeping tablet called Vesparax, which has the main ingredient of Quinalbarbitone, the same sedative to be found in Jimi. Because Monika herself was prescribed these tablets from her own doctor, Jimi could, in many people's opinions, have taken them thinking that they were safe. The German version of these tablets, unbeknown to Jimi, was many times stronger than its UK equivalent at the time.

These type of drugs were viewed in the 1960s as something to take to help you relax and fall asleep, and no danger would have even been in Jimi's mind if he had indeed taken 9 or 10 of these tablets, as indicated by the empty blister packets on the floor. The normal prescribed dose was half to one tablet, and if he had taken 9 of these, he would have taken far more than the recommended dosage, which would have been catastrophic. In the UK, during the year Jimi died there were over 1000 people who died in a similar way. This adds weight to the theory many had that his death was nothing but a very tragic accident. However, many inconsistencies exist; especially in the reports that Monika Danneman gave as to what happened to Jimi in his final hours.

Kathy Etchingham later investigated the reports that Monika Danneman gave. She revealed huge inconsistencies in her statements and account of the events leading up to Jimi's death. Monika did not, for example, inform the police that Jimi had previously gone to a party, just that they stayed in and talked. There were also reports that two attractive girls had approached Jimi while he was in the car with Monika and asked him to go to a party with them. He agreed and took down their address. This again was not reported.

Kathy also found further issues with the statement given. Monika was increasingly unhappy with the attention Jimi was getting; as his inner circle stated, and she basically wanted him for herself. On the evening in question she became increasingly jealous. This resulted in her having a huge public row with Jimi at the party; it was reported that she screamed at him for over half an hour. Again, this was not mentioned in her statements. Also, Monika collected Jimi from the final meeting he had in the early hours of the morning; reports from inside this meeting state that Jimi did not want to leave and tried to get rid of her. Eventually, after she refused to leave, Jimi left and the pair were seen arguing down the street. Jimi eventually walked away on his own, but obviously at some point made his way back to the Samarkand Hotel. Monika's statement reads that they had a very cosy, romantic evening indoors, which was clearly not the case. There was also no food anywhere in the room, whereas she claimed she made him a sandwich, which he did not eat .

The ambulance statements also gave material for suspicion and speculation. It was claimed that when the paramedic arrived Jimi was on top of the bed and was fully clothed. He was also completely saturated in vomit, not a trickle as Monika had said: they said it was everywhere and described it as a pool of vomit, and that it was horrific. It was described as dark red, red wine, it was also in his hair, which was completely matted. They stated that he was covered in it, as if he had drowned in it.

What was even more alarming, considering the amount of wine that was all over him and what was pumped out of him later at the hospital, was the alcohol levels in Jimi's blood and urine: 5 milligrams per 100 milliliters in blood and 46 milligrams per 100 milliliters in urine. These are very low levels and do not seem to equate to the amount of wine found over him and present in his lungs. This gave rise to the speculation that he was murdered by waterboarding, but with red wine: the act of forcing large amounts of fluid into the mouth while pinned down, to make him effectively drown. The sleeping pills would have made him incapacitated to resist such an attack. The medical reports indicate that Jimi would have died very soon after this amount of wine had entered his body, indicating there was no time for it to be absorbed into his bloodstream. That said he was also reportedly alive in the ambulance on route to the hospital.

Suspicion here lay again with Michael Jeffery. He was reported to be heavily in debt, and owed a considerable amount of money to the IRS (Internal Revenue Service). It was also claimed he owed money to the Mob. Other reports stated he had a Power of Attorney for Jimi, meaning he was worth more to him dead than he was alive, and when you consider Jimi was about to leave him, and was possibly investigating him, this added more weight to this theory. No charges however were ever brought and many feel that this was a completely far-fetched theory. Although Michael Jeffrey was money obsessed and controlling, the idea that he was a murderer was too much for some.

Michael Jeffery would later die in a mid-air collision over Nantes, France, on 5 March 1973, eight days before his 40th birthday.

Regarding the ambulance, the reports claimed that on arrival they checked for signs of life and there were none: they knew he was dead. This again was disputed in the years ahead. They did not, however, obviously know it was Jimi Hendrix. Monika also claimed she sat with Jimi in the ambulance to the hospital, but this was untrue. She was reported later to have not been in the ambulance at all. All reports after the event from Monika Danneman give different and misleading explanations as to exactly what happened to Jimi Hendrix in his last hours.

There are so many conflicting reports given by Monika, with so many inconsistencies, that the only conclusion anyone could come up with was that she herself was covering something up. Or that she was protecting someone else from further investigation. She, like Mike, remains in many people's eyes deeply suspicious in the death of Jimi Hendrix. Monika wrote in her own book, published in 1995, *The Inner World of Jimi Hendrix*:

"There was a couple of reasons for such suspicion - one being that he had intended leaving Jeffery, the other that he was on the track of his manager's misappropriation of his money. I feel myself there is a slight possibility Jimi was murdered."

This is an extraordinary sentence, especially when you consider she was with him the entire evening. The inconsistencies of Monika feed further ongoing theories and speculations as to exactly what happened to Jimi Hendrix. She was described as a stalker, fanatical about Jimi, and would stop at nothing to have him as her own. Another assumption by many that resurfaces was that she gave Jimi the sleeping tablets herself so he wouldn't leave in the morning, not knowing that they would in fact kill him. It was an accidental death that she then tried to cover up because of the drugs that were in the room. A serious offence in 1970. But again this has never been proven and remains as pure speculation.

She later stated that they were planning to get married and have children. A statement that those close to Jimi believe to be complete fantasy. Monika was due in court to give further evidence on the death of Jimi Hendrix after her book was published, and she was due to give evidence under oath. This appearance however never happened. Monika Danneman committed suicide on April 5th, 1996, in East Sussex, England. She was 50. Her body was found in her car within her garage, filled with fumes.

To this day confusion still remains as to what actually happened. Inexplicably passing away in his sleep, Jimi Hendrix's death at age 27 saw him join the so-called '27 Club', sparking continued questions and persistent rumours. There are still individuals and journalists who continue to believe there was more to the death of Jimi Hendrix than was reported or written about in the years ahead. The same can be said for others who died at a young age in similar unusual circumstances.

Becoming part of the 27 Club accelerated the theories, it's a speculative forum that first came into the consciousness of the general public between 1969 and 1971 when Jim Morrison, Janis Joplin, Brian Jones and of course Jimi Hendrix all died within this period of time, all aged 27. Four of the biggest names in the music world had gone in just two years. This led to widespread studies and theories as to why this age was 'seen' as more common in the deaths of popular musicians.

Although studies have not been able to say with certainty that the age of 27 is any more likely to be the age of death for a famous musician than any other age, there is a link between other factors in the way these musicians led their lives. They all dealt with very familiar issues: fame, alcohol, drugs, depression, and immense public and personal pressure. They all had consistent and constant media attention and had to deal with being adored and criticised in equal measure. It's these contributing factors that are the highlighted as more than coincidence when looking at the theory.

The members of the 27 club may simply be just that, coincidence, but the factors that led to their tragic deaths are similar, and these factors undoubtedly involve a reoccurring pattern of events. Each of the legendary musicians had similar attributes, which ultimately led to their tragic early deaths. To speculate the theory further, The 27 club has since moved on from musicians and now incorporates many famous people including young actors and artists who lost their lives due to addiction, suicide or tragic accidents. It's a mythology and concurrence that resurfaces with each and every tragic case, and with every one of these, many different theories and speculations resurface, looking at the possible connections. It's therefore an ongoing, disturbing and fascinating study that highlights the statistical spike of musicians that die at 27 years of age, arguably the most famous, of course being Jimi Hendrix.

Speculation aside, the fact is that the greatest guitarist the world had ever witnessed left us at just 27 years old. Kathy Etchingham summed up the events leading to his death to a reporter, she recalled *"The death was all very dodgy, I don't think it should have happened. He was in the wrong place at the wrong time with the wrong people."*

Kathy Etchingham would later publish her own book. Through Gypsy Eyes was released in 1998, which she wrote with Andrew Crofts, about her life, the 1960s, and of course Jimi Hendrix. In 1997, she was involved in arranging the English Heritage blue plaque on the wall of Jimi Hendrix's former home at 23 Brook Street, Mayfair.

She later stated, *"I want him to be remembered for what he was - not this tragic figure he has been turned into by nitpickers and people who used to stalk us and collect photographs and evidence of what we were doing on a certain day. He could be grumpy, and he could be terrible in the studio, getting exactly what he wanted - but he was fun, he was charming. I want people to remember the man I knew."*

Arguably the most influential musical performer of the twentieth century was gone. Although there is much speculation and ongoing suspicion surrounding Jimi's death, as highlighted previously, it does not in any way tarnish his incredible legacy, whatever the truth to his death actually was. Jimi Hendrix's body was flown to Seattle and buried in a somewhat private ceremony on October 1st, 1970. His grave was selected to be near to his mother's, located at Dunlap Baptist Church in Rainier valley, within the Dunlap neighborhood of Seattle.

There was nothing Jimi Hendrix could not do with an electric guitar. Endlessly inventive, visionary, explosive, he was the complete package. Not only was he the greatest electric guitar player that ever lived, but he was also a wonderful, underrated singer, he had the looks. Women loved him, men loved him, he was the ultimate sexually exotic rock star; and the first of a kind. Of all the ill-fated members of the 27 club, Jimi Hendrix is undoubtedly the one who leaves the largest hole in a 'what could have been' musical void. He had so much more to give.

When he died it left a gap that even to this day, as far as the guitar is concerned, has not been filled. He was the ultimate power with the instrument, a prodigy on stage and a life force of immense talent. He coped with the relentless bar he had set himself, always living with the pressure to deliver something extraordinary.

Jimi Hendrix is incomparable. Following his passing, the numerous music lovers who had attended his live performances, regardless of whether they had been part of a vast audience or close to him, lauded his talent. It became an esteemed distinction for any music enthusiast to proclaim that they had once witnessed Jimi Hendrix perform.

Jimi Hendrix reinvented the guitar; he redefined it. He had an ability to effortlessly change forever how rock music should be presented. We sadly only had the tip of the iceberg in what Jimi Hendrix could have delivered to the music world. A music world that would be forever in debt, to the legacy that he left. I guess he was right:

Castles made of sand fall in the sea, eventually.

Jimi Hendrix Timelines.

The following references provide key timelines in the life and music of Jimi Hendrix. The times and dates on the below may differ, but the listing comes from various sources. The timeline of events begins with Jimi's arrival in London, in 1966.

1966.

24 Sept – Jimi arrives in London – Scotch of St. James, London, he plays a small solo during the evening. His first in UK.
26 Sept – Jimi Auditions for backing group at Birdland, London.
27 Sept – Scotch of St. James, London – Jimi plays briefly with The VIPs. Connected formerly to Mike Jeffery,
28 Sept – The Cromwellian London: Jimi is introduced to Brian Auger & The Trinity, who Jimi jams with.
29 Sept – Jimi jams with Alexis Korner. Auditions at Birdland & meets Noel. Chas arranges French tour with Johnny Halliday.1 30 Sept – Polytechnic of Central London – Guest appearance with Cream
3 Oct – Noel Redding is recruited as Bass Player for Jimi,
5 Oct – Mitch recruited as Drummer following a coin toss. Band jam with Roosevelt Sykes and others at Les Cousins London .
6 Oct – Aberback House, London. Initial rehearsals for the new band
7 Oct – Aberback House, London – continued rehearsals
8 Oct – Jimi, Noel and Mitch pay a visit to the Marshall Amplification factory based in Milton Keynes England.
10 Oct – Aberback House, London – continued rehearsals
11 Oct – The band sign contracts with Chas Chandler and Mike Jeffrey
12 Oct – Flight to France followed by rehearsals at the Olympia
13 Oct – Cinéma Novelty, Evreux, France – 1st concert of The Jimi Hendrix Experience, supporting Johnny Hallyday.
14 Oct – Cinéma Rio, Salle Poirel, Nancy, France supporting Johnny Hallyday.
15 Oct – Salle Des Fetes, Villerupt, France supporting Johnny Hallyday.
16 Oct – Tchoo Tchoo Club, Plessis-Robinson, Hauts-de-Seine, Paris..
17 Oct – L'Olympia, Paris – rehearsals
18 Oct – L'Olympia, Paris France supporting Johnny Hallyday.
19 Oct – The Experience fly back to London
20 Oct – Jimi and Chas see The New Animals, Geno Washington and

Georgie Fame at The Astoria, London
22 Oct – Rehearsals, London
24 Oct – Knuckles Club, London, jam with Deep Feeling (Dave Mason and Jim Capaldi are band members)
31 Oct – Knuckles Club, London – rehearsals
2 Nov – De Lane Lea Studios, London – *Stone Free, Can You See Me* + Aberback House, London – rehearsals
3 Nov – Aberback House, London – rehearsals
8 Nov – Big Apple Club, Munich, Germany (2 shows) + photo session
9 Nov – Big Apple Club, Munich, Germany (2 shows)
10 Nov – Big Apple Club, Munich, Germany(2 shows)
11 Nov – Big Apple Club, Munich, Germany (2 shows)
25 Nov – Bag O' Nails, London. Press reception show – Chas sold four guitars to pay for the Press show.
26 Nov – Ricky Tick, Hounslow
27 Nov – 24th Birthday
30 Nov – Jimi sees The Young Rascals at Blaise's
06 Dec – Jimi moves into a spare room at Chas's flat at 24, Montagu Square, London
10 Dec – The Ram Jam Club, London
11 Dec – Jimi meets his old employer Little Richard at a London hotel
13 Dec – CBS Studios, Performance for Wembley for "Ready Steady Go"
15 Dec – CBS Studios – *Foxy Lady, Can You See Me, 3rd Stone From The Sun*
16 Dec – Chislehurst Caves Bromley Kent – UK release of Hey Joe/Stone Free – + photo session in London
21 Dec – De Lane Lea Studios, London
22 Dec – Guildhall, Southampton
23 Dec – Ricky Tick, Hounslow
26 Dec – The Upper Cut, London
29 Dec – BBC TV, Lime Grove Studios, London for "Top Of The Pops" – Hey Joe
31 Dec – Hillside Social Club, Folkestone

1967

1 Jan – Hillside Club, Folkestone: rehearsal.
2 Jan – Two shows at the
4 Jan– Bromel Club, Bromley Court Hotel, Bromley
5 Jan – Interview with Rave Magazine
6 Jan – Photo session for Fabulous 208 magazine

7 Jan – New Century Hall, Manchester + Twisted Wheel Manchester – Jimi sees The Spellbinders in concert
8 Jan – Mojo A Go-Go, Tollbar, Sheffield
9 Jan – Interview with Keith Altham + photo session at the 7½ Club London
10 Jan – Interview with Nick Jones for Melody Maker
11 Jan – Bag O' Nails London + same day: De Lane Lea Studios, London, live shows.
13 Jan – 7½ Club London live performance
14 Jan – Beachcomber Club, Nottingham live performance
15 Jan – The Country Club, live performance
16 Jan – 7½ Club London show
18 Jan – 7½ Club London + earlier: BBC, Lime Grove, London for "Top Of The Pops" – Hey Joe + 7½ Club London
19 Jan – Speakeasy, London
20 Jan – Haverstock Hill Country Club, London
21 Jan – The Refectory, Golder's Green, London
22 Jan – Astoria, Oldham
24 Jan – Marquee Club, London
25 Jan – The Orford Cellar, Norwich
26 Jan – Photo session by Paul Popper at the Montagu Square flat
27 Jan – Chislehurst Caves, Bromley
28 Jan – The Upper Cut, London + earlier: photo session by Petra Niemeier at the Montagu Square flat
29 Jan – Saville Theatre, London (parts of gig and rehearsal filmed for Hey Joe promotional film)
30 Jan – BBC Broadcasting House, London for "Pop North" – Hey Joe, Rock Me Baby, Foxy Lady
31 Jan – Saville Theatre, London ◊ – mimed film session for a "Hey Joe" promotional film by Peter Clifton.
1 Feb – New Cellar Club, South Shields
2 Feb – Imperial Hotel, Darlington + photo session
3 Feb – Ricky Tick, Hounslow + earlier: Olympic Studios, London – *Purple Haze*
4 Feb – Flamingo Club, London + The Ram Jam Club
5 Feb – Jimi sees Cream at The Saville Theatre, London
6 Feb – Star Hotel, Croydon
7 Feb – Olympic Studios, London – *Purple Haze*
8 Feb – Bromley Club, Bromley + earlier: Olympic Studios, London – *Purple Haze, Fire, Foxy Lady*
9 Feb – Locarno, Bristol
10 Feb – Plaza, Newbury

11 Feb – Blue Moon, Cheltenham
12 Feb – Sinking Ship Clubland, Stockport
13 Feb – BBC studios, London for "Saturday Club" – Foxy Lady, Stone Free, Hey Joe, Love Or Confusion
14 Feb – The Civic Hall, Gray's
15 Feb – Dorothy Ballroom, Cambridge
17 Feb – Ricky Tick, Thames Hotel, Windsor
18 Feb – York University, York
19 Feb – Blarney Club, London
20 Feb – The Pavillion, Bath + earlier: De Lane Lea Studios, London – *I Don't Live Today*
21 Feb – Interview for The New Musical Express, Soho
22 Feb – The Roundhouse, London + BBC Playhouse Theatre for Top Of The Pops.
23 Feb – The Pavilion, Worthing
24 Feb – Leicester University, Leicester
25 Feb – Corn Exchange, Chelmsford
26 Feb – Cliffs Pavilion, Southend-On-Sea
27 Feb – Photo session by Brian Fleming for the cover of *Are You Experienced*
1 Mar – Orchid Ballroom Purley Surrey + earlier: De Lane Lea Studios, London – *Like A Rolling Stone*
2 Mar – The Marquee Club, London for "Beat Club" (German TV)
3 Mar – Flight to Paris
4 Mar – Le Cadran, Paris
5 Mar – Twenty Club, Loison-sous-Lens, France + Twenty Club, Mouscron, Hainaut, Belgium
6 Mar – RTB Studios, Waterloo for "Vibrato" (Belgian TV) – Hey Joe mimed
7 Mar – Universal Studio, Waterloo for (Belgian TV) – Hey Joe, Stone Free mimed
8 Mar – Flight to England
9 Mar – Skyline Ballroom, Hull + earlier: London photo session by Gered Mankowitz
10 Mar – Club A Go-Go, Newcastle-Upon-Tyne
11 Mar – International Club, Leeds
12 Mar – Gyro Club, Troutbeck Hotel, Ilkley
13 Mar – Flight to Amsterdam
14 Mar – Bellevue Studio, Amsterdam – Fan Club TV show (Hey Joe/Stone Free mimed) + informal photo session
15 Mar – Photo session outside Montagu Square flat
16 Mar – Speakeasy, Margaret Street, London – launch party for Track

Records.
17 Mar – Star-Club, Hamburg Germany + interview at Danny's Pan Club – Purple Haze/51st Anniversary released in the UK
18 Mar – Star-Club Hamburg Germany (2 shows) + earlier: Studio 1, NDR Funkhaus, Hamburg, Germany (2 shows)
19 Mar – Star-Club, Hamburg Germany + interview for Bravo at The Antenna + photo session in the gardens of Hotel St. Paul.
21 Mar – Interview for Radio Luxembourg
23 Mar – Guild Hall, Southampton
25 Mar – Starlight Room, Boston (England)
26 Mar – Tabernacle Club, Stockport
27 Mar – BBC Studios, Manchester for "Dee Time" – Purple Haze
28 Mar – Assembly Hall, Aylesbury + earlier: BBC studios, London for "Saturday Club"
29 Mar – Delane Lea Studios, London – *Manic Depression*,
30 Mar – 'BBC studios, London for "Top Of The Pops" – Purple Haze (live vocal)
31 Mar – The Astoria, London (1st guitar burned) – (2 shows) – start of Walker Brothers package tour
1 Apr – Gaumont, Ipswich (2 shows)
2 Apr – Gaumont, Worcester (2 shows)
3 Apr – Olympic Studios, London
4 Apr – Olympic Studios, London
5 Apr – Odeon, Leeds (2 shows)
6 Apr – Odeon, Glasgow (2 shows)
7 Apr – ABC, Carlisle (2 shows)
8 Apr – ABC, Chesterfield (2 shows)
9 Apr – The Empire, Liverpool (2 shows)
10 Apr – Olympic Studios, London – *Third Stone From The Sun* + BBC Playhouse
11 Apr – Granada, Bedford (2 shows)
12 Apr – Gaumont, Southampton (2 shows)
13 Apr – Gaumont, Wolverhampton (2 shows) + a jam with The Californians at The Kingfisher, Wolverhampton
14 Apr – Odeon, Bolton (2 shows)
15 Apr – Odeon, Blackpool (2 shows)
16 Apr – De Montfort Hall, Leicester (2 shows)
17 Apr – BBC TV Studios, London – for "Late Night Line Up"
19 Apr – Odeon, Birmingham (2 shows)
20 Apr – ABC, Lincoln (2 shows) + photo session in hotel gardens
21 Apr – City Hall, Newcastle-Upon-Tyne (2 shows)
22 Apr – Odeon, Manchester (2 shows)

23 Apr – Gaumont, Hanley (2 shows)
24 Apr – Jimi attends a Donovan concert at the Saville Theatre
25 Apr – Colston Hall, Bristol (shows) + earlier: Olympic Studios, London – mixing
26 Apr – Capitol, Cardiff (2 shows)
27 Apr – ABC, Aldershot (2 shows)
28 Apr – Adelphi, Slough (2 shows) + UFO club, London (jam with Tomorrow)
29 Apr – Winter Gardens, Bournemouth (2 shows)
30 Apr – Granada, Tooting London (2 shows) (end of Walker Brothers package tour)
1 May – Hey Joe/51s Anniversary released in the UK
4 May – BBC TV Lime Grove studios, London for "Top Of The Pops" – Purple Haze + Olympic Studios.
5 May – Olympic Studios, London – *If 6 Was 9, Mr Bad Luck* – The Wind Cries Mary/Highway Chile released in the UK
6 May – The Imperial Ballroom, Nelson
7 May – Saville Theatre, London
8 May – Speakeasy, London – jam with Brian Auger & Trinity
9 May – Olympic Studios, London – *Burning Of The Midnight Lamp*.
10 May – BBC TV Lime Grove studios, London for "Top Of The Pops" – Wind Cries Mary
11 May – Theatre d'Issy Les Molineaux (TV studio) Paris for "'Music Hall de Paris"/"Tilt Magazine"
12 May – The Manor House, London – "Are You Experienced" – UK release
13 May – Imperial College, London
14 May – Belle Vue, New Elizabethan, Manchester
15 May – Neue Welt, Berlin, Germany
16 May – Big Apple, Munich Bayern, Germany (2 shows)
17 May – Interview at the Hotel Intercontinental Frankfurt.
18 May – Offenbach, Hessen Germany for *Beat, Beat, Beat* TV show (5 songs)
19 May – Gothenburg, Sweden
20 May – Karlstad, Sweden
21 May – Copenhagen, Denmark
22 May – Helsinki, Finland
23 May – Klubb Bongo, Malmo, Sweden
24 May – TV Huset studios, Stockholm for "Pop side"; Stora
25 May – Interview for Swedish radio, Stockholm. Broadcast on 'Pop'67 Special', 28/05/1967 Stockholm Sweden
27 May – Star Palace, Kiel, Germany (2 shows)

28 May – Jaguar-Club, Herford, Germany
29 May – Tulip Bulb Auction Hall, "Barbeque 67", Spalding
31 May – Speakeasy, London – jam with Eric Clapton, Jack Bruce, José Feliciano and Edge
1 Jun – Rehearsals at The Saville Theatre
4 Jun – Saville Theatre, London
5 Jun – Olympic Studios, London
14 Jun – Jimi sees The Doors at The Scene Club, NYC
15 Jun – Flight to San Francisco
18 Jun – Monterey International Pop Festival, Monterey
20 Jun – Fillmore Auditorium, San Francisco (2 shows)
21 Jun – Fillmore Auditorium, San Francisco (2 shows)
22 Jun – Fillmore Auditorium, San Francisco (2 shows)
23 Jun – Fillmore Auditorium, San Francisco (2 shows)
24 Jun – Fillmore Auditorium, San Francisco (2 shows)
25 Jun – The Panhandle, Golden Gate Park + Fillmore Auditorium, San Francisco (2 shows)
26 Jun – Radio Interview LA
27 Jun – Jam at Stephen Stills' house in Malibu
28 Jun – Houston Studios, LA
29 Jun – Houston Studios, LA
30 Jun – Houston Studios, LA
1 Jul – Earl Warren Showgrounds, Santa Barbara
2 Jul – Whiskey A Go Go, Los Angeles
3 Jul – Scene Club, NYC
5 Jul – Rheingold Festival, Central Park, NYC
6 Jul – Mayfair Studios, NYC – *Burning Of The Midnight Lamp*
7 Jul – Mayfair Studios, NYC – *Burning Of The Midnight Lamp*
8 Jul – Coliseum, Jacksonville
9 Jul – Convention Hall, Miami (supporting The Monkees)
11 Jul – Coliseum, Charlotte (supporting The Monkees)
12 Jul – Coliseum, Greensboro (supporting The Monkees)
13 Jul – Forest Hills Stadium, NYC (supporting The Monkees)
14 Jul – Forest Hills Stadium, NYC (supporting The Monkees)
15 Jul – Forest Hills Stadium, NYC (supporting The Monkees)
16 Jul – Forest Hills Stadium, NYC (supporting The Monkees)
17 Jul – Studio 76, New York City – 1st session with Curtis Knight
18 Jul – Gaslight Club, NYC +Mayfair Studios, New York City – *Stars That Play With Laughing Sam's Dice*
19 Jul – Mayfair Studios, New York City – *Stars That Play With Laughing Sam's Dice*
20 Jul – Salvation Club, NYC + Mayfair Studios, New York City – *Stars*

That Play With Laughing Sam's Dice
21 Jul – Cafe A Go Go, NYC (2 shows)
22 Jul – Cafe A Go Go, NYC (2 shows)
23 Jul – Cafe A Go Go, NYC (2 shows)
25 Jul – Jam at The Generation Club with B.B King, Al Kooper and Ted Nugent
26 Jul – Jam at The Gaslight with John Hammond Jr and Eric Clapton
27 Jul – Jam at The Gaslight with John Hammond Jr and Eric Clapton
28 Jul – Jam at The Gaslight with John Hammond Jr
29 Jul – Session at Mayfair Studios and jam at The Gaslight with John Hammond Jr
3 Aug – Salvation Club, NYC
4 Aug – Salvation Club, NYC
5 Aug – Salvation Club, NYC
7 Aug – Salvation Club, NYC
8 Aug – Salvation Club, NYC + 2nd session with Curtis Knight, Studio 76, New York City.
9 Aug – Ambassador Theatre, Washington
10 Aug – Ambassador Theatre, Washington – Cancelled (Mitch had appendix trouble)
11 Aug – Ambassador Theatre, Washington
12 Aug – Ambassador Theatre, Washington (2 shows)
13 Aug – Ambassador Theatre, Washington (2 shows) – benefit for "Keep The Faith For Washington Youth Fund"
15 Aug – Fifth Dimension Club Ann Arbor Michigan (2 shows)
17 Aug – Promo film made at Falcon's Lair (Rudy Valentino's mansion)
18 Aug – Hollywood Bowl, Hollywood (supporting The Mamas & The Papas)
19 Aug – Earl Warren Showgrounds, Santa Barbara
21 Aug – Back to the UK – Heathrow Airport
22 Aug – BBC TV Lime Grove Studios for "Dee Time" – Burning Of The Midnight Lamp
23 Aug – "Are You Experienced" – US release
24 Aug – BBC TV Lime Grove Studios for "Top Of The Pops" – Burning Of The Midnight Lamp
25 Aug – Photo session by Terence Donovan a the Upper Berkeley Street flat
26 Aug – Jimi sees Zoot Money's new band at The Spreakeasy
27 Aug – Saville Theatre, London
28 Aug – Photo session in Hyde Park
29 Aug – Nottingham Blues Festival, Sherwood Rooms, Nottingham
30 Aug – Jimi visits The Inn Club, London

31 Aug – Arrival in Berlin – live radio show and photo session in funfair
1 Sept – Jimi goes to Barry Gibb's 21st birthday party than on to The Playboy Club
2 Sept – ZDF TV studios, Berlin – Can You See Me, Burning Of The Midnight Lamp
3 Sep – Gothenburg, Sweden (2 shows) + visit to The Roastery Club
4 Sep – Tivoli Gardens, Stockholm, Sweden
5 Sep – Studio 4 Stockholm, Sweden – full concert performance
6 Sep – Vasteras, Sweden (2 shows)
7 Sep – Club Filips, Stockholm – jam with Hansson and Karlsson + En Till Club, Stockholm, Sweden
8 Sep – Sweden (2 shows) + TV studio
9 Sep – Karlstad, Sweden (2 shows)
10 Sep – Stora Salen Lund, Sweden
11 Sep – Dans In, Grona Lund, Tivoli Gardens, Stockholm Sweden
12 Sep – Gothenburg, Sweden
13 Sep – Return to London
14 Sep – Top Of The Pops appearance
15 Sep – Bluesville Club 67, The Manor House, London – jam with Eric Burdon & The New Animals
16 Sep – Europa Hotel, London – Jimi receives the trophy for "World's Best Musician" (Melody Maker Awards)
18 Sept- Monday radio show, London + Hyde Park photo session2021 Sep – Interview for Intro magazine
23 Sep – Jimi sees Frank Zappa and The Mothers Of Invention at the Royal Albert Hall
24 Sep – Jimi sees Traffic at The Saville Theatre
25 Sep – "Guitar-In", Royal Festival Hall, London – photos with Jeremy Thorpe MP (Liberal Party)
26 Sep – Interview for Newsweek. Chandler and Jeffrey fly to New York for a meeting with Ed Chalpin
1 Oct – Olympic Studios, London – *Little Miss Lover, One Rainy Wish*
2 Oct – Olympic Studios, London – *Little Miss Lover, One Rainy Wish, You Got Me Floatin*
3 Oct – Olympic Studios, London – *Little Miss Lover, You Got Me Floatin*
4 Oct – Olympic Studios, London – *Untitled Jimi Demo #1, Ain't No Tellin', Bold As Love*
5 Oct – Olympic Studios, London – *Bold As Love, Castles Made Of Sand, Little One*
6 Oct – Playhouse Theatre, London for BBC Radio's "Top Gear"
7 Oct – The Wellington Club, Dereham

8 Oct – Saville Theatre, London
9 Oct – L'Olympia, Paris
10 Oct – Paris: "Portrait de Marie Laforêt."
12 Oct – Paris: filmed for TV shows "Dim, Dam Dom" and "Discorama"- Hey Joe, Burning Of The Midnight Lamp (mimed)
13 Oct – ATV Elstree Studios, Herefordshire for "Good Evening" – Little Miss Lover + Interview with Jonathan King
14 Oct – Olympic Studios, London – *Little Wing, South Saturn Delta* (riff) + Interview with Melody Maker
15 Oct – Starlight Ballroom Crawley Sussex
17 Oct – Playhouse Theatre, London for BBC Radio's "Rhythm And Blues" Blues breakers
18 Oct – Jimi goes to the premier of the film "How I Won The War" (featuring John Lennon) a the London Pavillion
19 Oct – Interview with Fabulous 208 magazine
22 Oct – Hastings Pier, Hastings
23 Oct – Delane Lea Studios rehearsal session
24 Oct – Marquee Club London
25 Oct – Olympic Studios, London – *Wait Until Tomorrow, Little Wing, Electric Ladyland, South Saturn Delta*
26 Oct – Olympic Studios, London – *Ain't No Tellin*
27 Oct – Olympic Studios, London – *EXP, Castles Made Of Sand, Spanish Castle Magic*
28 Oct – California Ballroom, Dunstable, Bedfordshire + earlier: Olympic Studios, London – *Spanish Castle Magic, Little Wing*
29 Oct – Olympic Studios, London – *Up From The Skies, Bold As Love*
30 Oct – Olympic Studios, London – *Wait Until Tomorrow, She's So Fine, Spanish Castle Magic*
31 Oct – Olympic Studios, London – mixing session
1 Nov – Olympic Studios, London – mixing session
2 Nov – Olympic Studios, London – mixing session
4 Nov – Leeds University – Cancelled
7 Nov- Chas Chandler's apartment a test pressing of "Axis: plus+ photo session
8 Nov – The Union, Manchester University
10 Nov – Ahoy Hallen, Rotterdam + earlier: Vitus TV Studios, – Foxy Lady, Catfish Blues, Purple Haze
11 Nov – New Refectory, Sussex University, Brighton
12 Nov – Regent Sound Studio, London. Photo session at The Sweeny Todd Barber Shop, London
13 Nov – Olympic Studios, London – Sweet Angel + photos at hairdresser
14 Nov – Royal Albert Hall, London (2 shows) .

15 Nov – Winter Gardens, Bournemouth (2 shows) + interview with Jonathan King for Good Evening (ATV).
16 Nov – Photo session with David Montgomery for The Sunday Times
17 Nov – City Hall, Sheffield (2 shows)
18 Nov – The Empire, Liverpool (2 shows)
19 Nov – The Coventry Theatre, Coventry (2 shows)
22 Nov – Guild Hall, Portsmouth (2 shows)
23 Nov – Sophia Gardens Pavillion, Cardiff (2 shows)
24 Nov – Colston Hall, Bristol (2 shows)
25 Nov – Opera House, Blackpool (2 shows) – some songs filmed
26 Nov – Palace Theatre, Manchester (2 shows)
27 Nov – Queen's College, Belfast (2 shows) – Jimi's 25th birthday
1 Dec – Central Hall, Chatham (2 shows) "Axis Bold As Love" – UK release
2 Dec – The Dome, Brighton (2 shows)
3 Dec – Theatre Royal, Nottingham (2 shows)
4 Dec – City Hall, Newcastle-Upon-Tyne (2 shows)
5 Dec – Green's Playhouse, Glasgow (2 shows) – last date of "package" tour.
6 Dec – Jimi goes to a party for The Foundations
7 Dec – Jimi as Santa photo session (or 14th) + Jam with Noel Redding.
8 Dec – ATV Studios, Elstree for "Good Evening" – Spanish Castle Magic
9 Dec – Interview with Tom Lopez (a.k.a. Meatball Fulton)
10 Dec – Jimi sees The Moody Blues at The Speakeasy
11 Dec – Interview with Disc & Music Echo
12 Dec – Jimi jams with Fairport Convention at the Speakeasy
14 Dec – Photo session with Dezo Hoffman (used for the Smash Hits album cover)
15 Dec – The Playhouse Theatre, London for BBC Radio's "Top Gear"
16 Dec – Filming for Top Of The Pops
18 Dec – Interview for Melody Maker
19 Dec – Bruce Fleming's studio, London (acoustic Hear My Train A Comin')
20 Dec – Olympic Studios, London – *Crosstown Traffic, Dream, Touch You/Dance, Dream*
21 Dec – Olympic Studios, London – *Crosstown Traffic, And The Gods Made Love* + interview by Linda Eastman
22 Dec – 'Christmas On Earth Continued', London Olympia, Kensington
23 Dec – Jimi attends a Christmas party for children at The Roundhouse (where he dresses up as Father Christmas)
24 Dec – The Speakeasy – jam with Sam Gopal Dream

25 Dec – Jimi goes to Noel's birthday party
26 Dec – Jimi spends Christmas with Bruce Fleming and his family
27 Dec – The Speakeasy – jam with Eric Burdon, Dave Mason and Harry Hughes (Clouds)
28 Dec – Olympic Studios, London – *Little One, Sweet Angel*
29 Dec – Olympic Studios, London – *Little One*
30 Dec – Olympic Studios, London – *Dream*
31 Dec – Speakeasy, London – New year's Eve party

1968

1 Jan – Rehearsal at the Hillside Club. Interview with the BBC at Broadcasting House, London.
2 Jan – Railway Hotel, West Hampstead – jam with John Mayall and Al Sykes
3 Jan – Flight to Gothenburg, Sweden
4 Jan – Circus, Gothenburg (2 shows) – Jimi arrested for smashing up a Hotel Opalon room.
5 Jan – Sports Hall, Sweden
6 Jan – Interview with Casten Grolin for Ekstra Bladet.
7 Jan – Copenhagen Zealand Denmark (2 shows)
8 Jan – Stora Salen, Stockholm Sweden (2 shows)
9 Jan – Return to Gothenburg
11 Jan – Interview with Expressen
15 Jan – Axis Bold As Love released in the USA
16 Jan – Municipal Court, Gothenburg – Jimi is fined 8918 crowns for the Hotel Opalon incident
17 Jan – Flight back to London
18 Jan – Hanover Grand Hotel – a reception party for the group Grapefruit
19 Jan – Interview for The London Herald (unpublished)
20 Jan – Photo session for Top Pop magazine. Jimi records with McGeough & McGear with Paul McCartney producing
21 Jan – Olympic Studios, London – *All Along The Watchtower*
22 Jan – Jimi jams with Sam Gopal's Dream at the Speakeasy, London
23 Jan – Interview with Richard Robinson for Hullabaloo at Upper Brook Street
24 Jan – Interviews at the Upper Berkeley Street flat
25 Jan – Band rehearsal at Middle Earth Club, Covent Garden, London
26 Jan – Olympic Studios, London – *Tax Free, All Along The Watchtower*
27 Jan – Interview with Disc & Music Echo
28 Jan – Olympic Studios, London – *Mushy Name, Tax Free*

29 Jan – Olympia, Paris (2 shows) (2nd show)
30 Jan – Flight to New York
31 Jan – Interview at The Copter Lounge, Pan Am Building Manhattan New York
1 Feb – Fillmore Auditorium San Francisco (2 shows)
2 Feb – Winterland Ballroom, San Francisco (2 shows) + club jam with Mick Taylor and Jack Casady
3 Feb – Winterland Ballroom, San Francisco (2 shows)
4 Feb – Winterland Ballroom, San Francisco (2 shows) *(stated as The Fillmore West for this date)*
5 Feb – Sun Devil's Gym, Arizona State University, Tempe
6 Feb – V.I.P. Club, Tucson
8 Feb – Sacramento State College, Sacramento
9 Feb – Anaheim Convention Centre, Anaheim (2 shows)
10 Feb – Shrine Auditorium, Los Angeles
11 Feb – Robertson Gym, Santa Barbara
12 Feb – Seattle Centre Arena, Seattle
13 Feb – Ackerman Union Grand Ballroom
14 Feb – Regis College, Fieldhouse, Denver
15 Feb – Municipal Auditorium, San Antonio
16 Feb – State Fair Music Hall, Dallas
17 Feb – Will Rogers Auditorium, Fort Worth
18 Feb – Music Hall, Houston, Texas (2 shows)
20 Feb – Scene Club, NYC – jam with members of Electric Flag, Soft Machine and The Tremolos
21 Feb – Electric Factory Philadelphia (2 shows)
22 Feb – Electric Factory Philadelphia (2 shows)
23 Feb – Masonic Temple, Detroit
24 Feb – CNE Coliseum Arena, Toronto
25 Feb – Chicago Civic Opera House, Chicago (2 shows)
27 Feb – The Factory Madison (2 shows)
28 Feb – The Scene Milwaukee (2 shows)
29 Feb – The Scene Milwaukee (2 shows)
1 Mar – Jimi and Noel visit the Scene Club
2 Mar – Hunter College, NYC (2 shows)
3 Mar – Vets Memorial Auditorium, Columbia
6 Mar – Recording of 1983 and Somewhere + jam with The Hollies at The Scene Club
7 Mar – The Scene, NYC – jam session with Jim Morrison
8 Mar – Marvel Gym, Brown University, Providence
9 Mar – State University of New York, Stony Brook, Long Island, New York

10 Mar – International Ballroom, Washington Hilton Hotel (2 shows) The Scene, NYC
13 Mar – New York Sound Centre, New York City – *My Friend, 1983, Little Miss Strange, Somewhere*
14 Mar – New York Sound Centre, New York City – *My Friend*
15 Mar – Attwood Hall, Clark University (2 shows)
16 Mar – Lewiston Armory, Lewiston
17 Mar – Cafe Au Go Go, New York City – jam with Elvin Bishop, Herbie Rich, Harvey Brooks and Paul Butterfield
18 Mar – Jam with Steve Stills at Sound Centre
19 Mar – Capitol Theatre, Ottawa (2 shows)
21 Mar – Community War Memorial, Rochester
22 Mar – Bushnell Memorial Hall, Hartford
23 Mar – Buffalo Memorial Auditorium, Buffalo
24 Mar – IMA Auditorium, Flint
25 Mar – Otto's Grotto, Cleveland – jam with Good earth
26 Mar – Public Music Hall Cleveland
27 Mar – Teen America Building, Lion's Delaware Co. Fairgrounds, Muncie
28 Mar – Xavier University Fieldhouse, Cincinnati (2 shows)
29 Mar – Chicago University, Chicago + jam with Paul Butterfield Blues Band at The Cheetah Club
30 Mar – University of Toledo, Fieldhouse, Toledo
31 Mar – Arena, Philadelphia
1 Apr – Flight to Montreal. Jimi goes to see Chubby Checker play.
2 Apr – Paul Sauve Arena, Montreal
4 Apr – Civic Dome, Virginia Beach – assassination of Martin Luther King
5 Apr – Symphony Hall, Newark, NJ + jam with Buddy Guy at The Generation Club
6 Apr – Westchester County Centre, White Plains
7 Apr – Generation Club, New York City – Jimi attends a Buddy Guy concert and later jams with Roy Buchanan
8 Apr – Generation Club, New York City – Jimi attends a second Buddy Guy concert and jams with Guy.
9 Apr – Generation Club, New York City – jam with BB King, Al Kooper, Paul Butterfield and Elvin Bishop among others
13 Apr – Interview with Beat Instrumental
15 Apr – Jimi sees B.B.King at the Generation Club and jams with him and Elvin Bishop &, Paul Butterfield.
17 Apr – Interview with Life Magazine
18 Apr – Record Plant, NY – *Long Hot Summer Night*

19 Apr – Troy Armory, Troy
20 Apr – Record Plant, New York City – *Little Miss Strange* (Noel alone)
21 Apr – Record Plant, NY – *Little Miss Strange, South Saturn Delta, Three Little Bears*
22 Apr – Record Plant, NY – *1983*
24 Apr – Record Plant, NY – *Little Miss Strange, Gypsy Eyes*
28 Apr – Record Plant, NY – *Little Miss Strange*
29 Apr – Record Plant, NY – *Gypsy Eyes, Tax Free, Little Miss Strange* (Noel)
30 Apr – Record Plant, NY – *Gypsy Eyes*
1 May – Record Plant, NY – *Gypsy Eyes, House Burning Down, Tax Free,*
2 May – Record Plant, NY – *Three Little Bears, Cherokee Mist* (feedback/electric sitar version),
3 May – Record Plant, NY – *Voodoo Chile (Slight Return)* – filmed + Town Hall, NYC – jam with Joe Tex
4 May – Record Plant, NY – *Little Little Girl*
5 May – Record Plant, NY – *House Burning Down, Voodoo Chile (Slight Return), Walking Through The Garden*
10 May – The Fillmore East Auditorium, NYC (2 shows)
17 May – Record Plant, NY – *Gypsy Eyes*
18 May – Miami Pop Festival, Gulf Stream Race Track, Hallandale, Miami (2 shows)
19 May – Thee Image Club, Miami – jam with The Blues Image
20 May – The Wreck Bar – jam with Noel, Frank Zappa, Arthur Brown and Jimmy Carl Black
22 May – Record Plant, NY – *1983*
23 May – Piper Club Milano Italy
24 May – Teatro Brancaccio Rome/Roma Lazio Italy (2 shows)
25 May – Teatro Brancaccio Rome/Roma Lazio Italy (2 shows)
26 May – Bologna Emilia Romagna Italy (2 shows)
29 May – Flight to Zurich
30 May – Zurich Switzerland
31 May – Zurich Switzerland
1 Jun – Flight to England
4 Jun – Rehearsal for 'It Must Be Dusty', ITV Elstree Studios
5 Jun – 'It Must Be Dusty'. ITV, Elstree Studios, Studio D, Borehamwood – Voodoo Chile (Slight Return) , Mocking Bird
7 Jun – Flight to New York
8 Jun – Guest at Fillmore East, NY with Electric Flag – (South Saturn Delta, Hey Joe with Buddy Miles vocal)
10 Jun – Record Plant, NY – *Rainy Day session, Voodoo Chile, 1983,*

House Burning Down
11 Jun – Record Plant, NY – *Inside Out (*proto Ezy Ryder riff)
13 Jun – Record Plant, NY – *House Burning Down, Gypsy Eyes* + jam with Jeff Beck at the Reality House Rehabilitation Center
14 Jun – Record Plant, NY – *South Saturn Delta* (with horns),
15 Jun – Jam with Jeff Beck and Eric Clapton at The Scene Club
16 Jun – Jam with Jeff Beck Group at the Day top Music Festival, Staton Island
17 Jun – Record Plant, NY – *Gypsy Eyes*
18 Jun – Record Plant, NY – *Gypsy Eyes*
22 Jun – Jam with Larry Coryell at The Scene Club
28 Jun – Record Plant, NY – *Rainy Day, Dream Away/Still Raining Still Dreaming*
29 Jun – Record Plant, NY – *And The Gods Made Love*
1 Jul – Record Plant, NY – *And The Gods Made Love* + jam with Graham Bond Organisation
3 Jul – Record Plant, NY – *All Along The Watchtower*
4 Jul – Flight to England
6 Jul – Woburn Music Festival Woburn Abbey Bedfordshire
8 Jul – Interview with Melody Maker
18 Jun – Sgt. Pepper's, (Rock and Roll Set) Palma Majorca, Spain
19 Jul – Flight back to London
22 Jul – Interview with Black Music magazine
24 Jul – Record Plant, NY – *Gypsy Eyes*
26 Jul – Record Plant, NY – *House Burning Down, Long Hot Summer Night*
27 Jul – Interview with Hullabaloo magazine
28 Jul – Flight to L.A.
29 Jul – Record Plant, NY – *Long Hot Summer Night*
30 Jul – Independence Hall, Lakeshore Auditorium, Baton Rouge (2 shows)
31 Jul – Municipal Auditorium, Shreveport
1 Aug – City Park Stadium, New Orleans
2 Aug – Municipal Auditorium, San Antonio
3 Aug – Moody Coliseum, Southern Methodist University Dallas
4 Aug – Sam Houston Coliseum, Houston
5 Aug – Flight to New York
6 Aug – Jam with Alvin Lee and Larry Coryell at The Scene Club
7 Aug – Record Plant, NY – *Long Hot Summer Night* (+ Central Park photo shoot by Dave Sygall and Linda Eastman)
10 Aug – Auditorium Theatre Chicago Illinois (2 shows)
11 Aug – Colonial Ballroom Davenport

12 Aug – Record Plant, NY – *Room Full Of Mirrors* with Paul Caruso
16 Aug – Merriweather Post Pavilion, Columbia
17 Aug – Atlanta Municipal Auditorium, Atlanta (2 shows)
18 Aug – Curtis Hixton Hall, Tampa
20 Aug – The Mosque, Richmond (2 shows)
21 Aug – Civic Dome Virginia Beach (2 shows)
23 Aug – The New York Rock Festival, Singer Bowl, Flushing Meadow Park, Queens, NY
24 Aug – Bushnell Memorial, Hartford
25 Aug – Carousel Theatre, Framingham
26 Aug – Kennedy Stadium, Bridgeport
27 Aug – Record Plant, NY – *Gypsy Eyes, Come On*
30 Aug – Lagoon Opera House, Salt Lake City
31 Aug – Jimi attends an Everly Brothers concert in Salt Lake City
1 Sep – Red Rocks Park, Denver
2 Sep – All Along the Watchtower/Burning of the Midnight Lamp released in the US
3 Sep – Balboa Stadium, San Diego
4 Sep – Memorial Coliseum, Phoenix
5 Sep – Swing Auditorium, San Bernardino
6 Sep – Seattle Centre Coliseum, Seattle
7 Sep – Pacific Coliseum, Vancouver + interview
8 Sep – Coliseum Spokane, Washington
9 Sep – Memorial Coliseum, Portland
11 Sep – Photo session, Beverly Hills, for Life magazine
12 Sep – Interview for KMET radio station
13 Sep – Oakland Coliseum, Oakland
14 Sep – Hollywood Bowl, Hollywood
15 Sep – Memorial Auditorium, Sacramento
18 Sep – Jam at the Whiskey A Go Go, LA – Jimi, Mitch, Noel, Buddy Miles, Eric Burdon and Graham Bond – filmed
24 Sep – Chas legally separates himself from Jimi, selling his share to Jeffery
28 Sep – The Factory, Hollywood – Party for Donovan–
3 Oct – Flight to Honolulu
5 Oct – Honolulu International Centre, Honolulu + after show jam at Thomas Square "Art-Park Festival"
6 Oct – Photo shoot with Ron Raffaelli
7 Oct – Photo shoot with Ron Raffaelli
8 Oct – Flight to L.A.
10 Oct – The Winterland, San Francisco (2 shows)
11 Oct – The Winterland, San Francisco (2 shows)

12 Oct – The Winterland, San Francisco (2 shows)
14 Oct – TTG Studios, LA – Eire Apparent "Sunrise" sessions
15 Oct – TTG Studios, LA – Eire Apparent "Sunrise" sessions
16 Oct – TTG Studios, LA – Eire Apparent "Sunrise" sessions, "Electric Ladyland" – US release
17 Oct – TTG Studios, LA – Eire Apparent "Sunrise" sessions
18 Oct – TTG Studios, LA – *Midnight, Izabella,* Burning of the midnight Lamp released in the UK
20 Oct – TTG Studios, LA – *The Messenger*
21 Oct – TTG Studios, LA .
22 Oct – TTG Studios, LA – *Look Over Yonder*
23 Oct – TTG Studios, LA – *New Rising Sun, Peace In Mississippi*
24 Oct – TTG Studios, LA – *Peace In Mississippi*
25 Oct – TTG Studios, LA – *Slow Walking Talk* (session with Robert Wyatt), "Electric Ladyland" – UK release
26 Oct – Civic Auditorium Bakersfield California
27 Oct – TTG Studios, LA – Jam session
29 Oct – TTG Studios, LA – *Here He Comes (Lover Man), Gloria*
30 Oct – Promo clip filmed in Laurel Canyon
31 Oct – Studio work with Eire Apparent
1 Nov – Municipal Auditorium, Area Kansas City
2 Nov – Minneapolis Auditorium, Minneapolis
3 Nov – Kiel Auditorium, St. Louis
4 Nov – Flight to New York
6 Nov – Record Plant, NY – production for Cat Mother & The All Night Newsboys
7 Nov – Photo session for Seventeen magazine
8 Nov – Interview with Beat Instrumental magazine
9 Nov – Melody Maker interview, The Experience will break up in the new year.
10 Nov – A planned appearance on the Ed Sullivan Show is cancelled because of a camera crew strike
11 Nov – Jam with Fleetwood Mac at The Scene Club, NY
15 Nov – Cincinnati Gardens, Cincinnati
16 Nov – Boston Garden, Boston
17 Nov – Woolsey Hall, Yale University New Haven Connecticut (2 shows)
22 Nov – Jacksonville Coliseum, Jacksonville
23 Nov – Curtis Hixon Hall, Tampa
24 Nov – Miami Beach Convention Hall, Miami
27 Nov – Rhode Island Auditorium, Providence, Rhode Island
28 Nov – 'An Electronic Thanksgiving', Philharmonic Hall, NYC (2

shows)
30 Nov – Cobo Arena, Detroit
1 Dec – Coliseum, Chicago 13 Dec – Jam at The Scene Club, NY. 18 Dec – Café A Go Go, NY
20 Dec – Fillmore East , NY – jam with the James Cotton Blues Band
24 Dec – Jimi attends a poetry evening at St. Mark's Church, The Bowery, NY
26 Dec – Jimi tears ligaments his leg after slipping in the snow
28 Dec – Utrecht pop festival in The Netherlands – cancelled by Jimi due to leg injury

1969
1 Jan – Record Plant
2 Jan – Flight to London. Jimi moves into 23, Brook Street, London with Kathy Etchingham
3 Jan – Interview at Jimi's flat
4 Jan – BBC Television Centre, London for "A Happening For Lulu"
5 Jan – Polydor Studios, London – Eire Apparent session for "Sunrise"
6 Jan – Interview with the Daily Mirror at Jimi's flat
7 Jan – Interview with Hugh Curry at >Jimi's flat for the Canadian Broadcasting Company
8 Jan – Gothenburg Sweden (2 shows) – Interview for Pop 69 Special TV show
9 Jan – Stockholm, Sweden (2 shows)
10 Jan – Copenhagen Denmark (2 shows) + interview for Danish radio
11 Jan – Hamburg Germany (2 shows)
12 Jan – Dusseldorf, Germany (2 shows)
13 Jan – Cologne Germany (2 shows) + interview for Beat Club TV show
14 Jan – Munster Germany
15 Jan – Munich, Germany (2 shows)
16 Jan – Nuremberg Germany (2 shows)
17 Jan – Frankfurt Germany (2 shows) + a loose jam at the K52 club with members of The Riot Squad.
18 Jan – Interview and impromptu acoustic Hound Dog filmed
19 Jan – Stuttgart Germany (2 shows)
20 Jan – Flight to Strasbourg
21 Jan – Wacken Halle, Strasbourg France
22 Jan – Vienna Austria (2 shows)
23 Jan – Berlin
24 Jan – Flight back to London

25 Jan – Jimi goes to see The Pretty Things at The Roundhouse.
30 Jan – Flight to New York to discuss converting The Generation Club into a recording studio (future Electric Lady Studios)
4 Feb – Jam at The Scene Club with Johnny Winter (Jimi on bass).
7 Feb – Interview with The Sunday Mirror at Jimi's flat.
11 Feb – Record Plant, NY – production session with Buddy Miles
12 Feb – Flight back to London
13 Feb – Jimi attends launch party for Mary Hopkin's "Postcard" album
14 Feb – Olympic Studios, London – *Slow Version, Blues Jam, Ezy Ryder (riff)/Star Spangled Banner*
15 Feb – Jimi collects World Top Musician award at the Seymour Hotel, London
16 Feb – Olympic Studios, London
17 Feb – Olympic Studios, London – rehearsals for Royal Albert Hall concert.
18 Feb – Royal Albert Hall, London + Speakeasy
19 Feb – Interview with Richard Green for NME
22 Feb – Olympic Studios, London – *Go My Own Way, Hound Dog Blues, Message To Love, Valleys Of Neptune, Gypsy Blood*
23 Feb – Speakeasy, London – jam with Dave Mason and Jim Capaldi
24 Feb – Royal Albert Hall, London + Speakeasy – jam with The Gods.
25 Feb – Interview with Melody Maker. Band meeting with Jeffery and Chandler (at the latter's house).
26 Feb – Olympic Studios, London – *Valleys of Neptune, 12 Bar Blues Jam With Horns, Noel's Tune*
27 Feb – Interviews with Ray Coleman (Disc & Music Echo) and Alan Smith (N.M.E)
28 Feb – Speakeasy
3 Mar – Aborted interview with Caroline Coon for Oz magazine.
4 Mar – Interview with Jane de Mendelssohn for International Times (part one).
5 Mar – Interview with Jane de Mendelssohn for International Times (part two). Interview with Record Mirror too?
6 Mar – Speakeasy, London – jam with Billy Preston around this date
7 Mar – Interview with John Grant for N.M.E. around this date
8 Mar – Ronnie Scott's Club, London
10 Mar – The Speakeasy – jam with The Gods
13 Mar – Flight to New York
15 Mar – Around this date – Mercury Studios (or The Record Plant): session with the Buddy Miles.
18 Mar – Early morning jam at Small's Paradise, Harlem with Lonnie Youngblood and The Blood Brothers + Record Plant, NY

19 Mar – More jams with Youngblood's band at Small's Paradise and The Record Plant.
25 Mar – Record Plant, NY – jams with Mitchell, Jim McCarty, John McLaughlin, Dave Holland, Buddy Miles
28 Mar – Pop Expo '69 festival at The Palladium, Hollywood
29 Mar – Jimi gets a Corvette Stingray in LA
30 Mar – Around this time: a jam with Slim Harpo at Thee Experience club (or The Whiskey A Go Go) in Hollywood
1 Apr – Olmstead Studios, NY – *Midnight, Bleeding Heart*
2 Apr – Olmstead Studios, NY – *Hear My Train A Comin, Midnight*
3 Apr – Olmstead Studios, NY – *Midnight/Trash Man, Peace In Mississippi* jams
4 Apr – Olmstead Studios, NY – *Trash Man, Crash Landing* (proto Power Of Soul)
5 Apr – Record Plant, NY – *Ships Passing Through The Night* (proto Night Bird Flying)
6 Apr – Record Plant, NY – *Ships Passing Through The Night, Lullaby For The Summer* (proto Ezy Ryder)
7 Apr – Record Plant, NY – *Hear My Train A Comin, Stone Free, Lullaby For The Summer*
8 Apr – Photos session (mirrored room) with Raymundo de Larrain for Life magazine . Record Plant: *Stone Free*
9 Apr – Record Plant, NY – *Hear My Train A Comin, Stone Free*
10 Apr – Jimi perhaps sees Ten Years After and The Nice at the Fillmore East
11 Apr – Dorton Arena, Raleigh
12 Apr – Spectrum, Philadelphia + interview for Distant Drummer magazine
13 Apr – Stepping Stone/Izabella released in the US
14 Apr – Record Plant, NY .
15 Apr – Band rehearsal at the Scene Club, NY
16 Apr – Band rehearsal at the Scene Club, NY
17 Apr – Record Plant, NY
18 Apr – Ellis Auditorium Amphitheatre, Memphis
19 Apr – Sam Houston Coliseum, Houston
20 Apr – Memorial Auditorium, Dallas interview with Rick Vittenson
21 Apr – Record Plant, NY – jam with Billy Cox
22 Apr – Record Plant, NY – jam with Cox and Buddy Miles – *Mannish Boy*
24 Apr – Record Plant, NY – jam with Cox and The Cherry People
25 Apr – Flight to L.A. and party for Donovan at The Factory
26 Apr – LA Forum, Los Angeles

27 Apr – Oakland Coliseum, Oakland
29 Apr – Hollywood – cowboy/Hell's Angels photo session with Ed Thrasher
1 May – Interview with Sharon Lawrence at The Beverly Rodeo Hotel
2 May – Cobo Arena, Detroit
3 May – Maple Leaf Gardens, Toronto (also that day: heroin bust at Canadian customs)
4 May – Syracuse War Memorial Auditorium, Syracuse
5 May – Court appearance in Toronto
6 May – Record Plant, NY – Mixing October 68 Winterland recordings
7 May – Memorial Coliseum
9 May – Charlotte Coliseum, Charlotte
10 May – Charleston Civic centre, Charleston
11 May – State Fairgrounds Coliseum, Indianapolis
12 May – Flight to New York
13 May – Record Plant, NY – jam with unknown musicians – *Keep On Groovin'*
14 May – Record Plant, NY & .
15 May – Record Plant, NY – with Cox and Layne
16 May – Civic Centre, Baltimore
17 May – Rhode Island Auditorium, Providence /Record Plant, NY with Cox and Mitchell – *Stone Free*
18 May – Madison Square Garden, NYC
19 May – Interview with Newsweek
20 May – Record Plant, NY – jam for Timothy Leary album.
21 May – Record Plant, NY – party/jam with Cox, Miles and others.
22 May – Record Plant, NY – with Cox and Miles – *Message From Nine To The Universe* (with Devon Wilson rap)
23 May – Seattle centre Coliseum, Seattle
24 May – Sports Arena, San Diego
25 May – Santa Clara Pop Festival, Santa Clara County Fairgrounds, San Jose
30 May – Waikiki Shell, Honolulu
31 May – Waikiki Shell, Honolulu
1 Jun – Waikiki Shell, Honolulu
8 Jun – Studio 3, Wally Heider Recording, Hollywood – Mixing session for a Jimi Hendrix Experience live album
9 Jun – Studio 3, Wally Heider Recording, Hollywood – Mixing session for a Jimi Hendrix Experience live album
10 Jun – Studio 3, Wally Heider Recording, Hollywood – Mixing session for a Jimi Hendrix Experience live album
13 Jun – On this day or the day after: jam with The Blues Image at Thee

Experience nightclub
15 Jun – Beverley Rodeo Hyatt House Hotel Beverley Hills: Interview with Nancy Carter
17 Jun – Interview with Rolling Stone
19 Jun – Court hearing at Toronto Court House, Canada
20 Jun – Newport '69, Devonshire Downs, Northridge
22 Jun – Newport '69, Devonshire Downs, Northridge – on stage jam with various musicians.
23 Jun – Jam with Johnny Winter and Buddy Miles at Thee Experience club
24 Jun – Jam with Eric Burdon, Jack Casady and Noel Redding at Thee Experience club
27 Jun – Wichita State University, Kansas – Cancelled due to poor ticket sales
29 Jun – Denver Pop Festival, Mile High Stadium, Denver (last performance of The Jimi Hendrix Experience).
30 Jun – Noel leaves the band
2 Jul – Around this time: jams and auditions with Willie Weeks.
3 Jul – This week: Jimi and various musicians spend weeks at a house near Shokan and Boiceville NY
7 Jul – ABC TV Studios, NY for "The Dick Cavett Show" – Hear My Train A Comin' with ABC house band.
10 Jul – NBC TV Studios, NY for "The Tonight Show" 12 Jul – Jimi visits Manny's Musical Instruments, NY and buys equipment
31 Jul – Holiday in Morocco
1 Aug – Holiday in Morocco
2 Aug – Holiday in Morocco
3 Aug – Holiday in Morocco
4 Aug – Holiday in Morocco
5 Aug – Holiday in Morocco
6 Aug – Holiday in Morocco
8 Aug – Jams/rehearsals at Shokan House, NY
9 Aug – Jams/rehearsals at Shokan House, NY
10 Aug – Tinker Street Cinema, Woodstock – jam with several musicians
11 Aug – Jams/rehearsals at Shokan House, NY
14 Aug – Rehearsals at Travor Hollow Road Shokan New York with new group: Gypsy Sun & Rainbows
17 Aug – Woodstock Music & Art Fair, Bethel – programmed evening performance cancelled
18 Aug – Woodstock Music & Art Fair, Bethel♦
19 Aug – Interview with Jimi for Network New York, New York City
21 Aug – Jams/rehearsals at Shokan House, NY

22 Aug – Jams/rehearsals at Shokan House, NY
23 Aug – Jams/rehearsals at Shokan House, NY
24 Aug – Jams/rehearsals at Shokan House, NY
25 Aug – Jams/rehearsals at Shokan House, NY
28 Aug – Hit Factory, NY – *Message To The Universe, Lover Man, Izabella, Jam Back At The House*
29 Aug – Hit Factory, NY – *Message To The Universe, Izabella, Machine Gun*
30 Aug – Hit Factory, NY – *Sky Blues Today, Mastermind, Jimi's Jam*
3 Sep -Interview for United Block Association at Frank's Restaurant, Harlem New York City New York
4 Sep – Hit Factory, NY – *Jam Back At The House, Mastermind*
5 Sep – Harlem, NY (benefit concert) + Hit Factory, NY – *Burning Desire*
6 Sep – Hit Factory, NY – *Valleys Of Neptune, Lord I Sing The Blues For Me And You, Lover Man, Trying To Be*
8 Sep – Auditions for new musicians at The Salvation Club, NY (approximate date – perhaps many days of auditions)
9 Sep – ABC TV Studios, NY for "The Dick Cavett Show" – interview + Izabella, Machine Gun with Mitchell, Cox and Sultan.
10 Sep – Salvation Club, NY – informal jam with Cox, Mitchell, Lee and Sultan
11 Sep – NYC – jam on bass with Mountain (approximate date – 9th to 11th)
13 Sep – Jams at the Shokan house with Mike Ephron (on electric clavichord) and Juma Sultan
15 Sep – Record Plant, NY – *Sky Blues Today, Villanova Junction, Burning Desire* (Larry Lee quits)
17 Sep – Interview with the New Musical Express
20 Sep – Cancelled concert: Municipal Auditorium, Atlanta. Interview with Rolling Stone magazine
21 Sep – Cancelled concert: Jai-Alai Fronton, Miami. Interview with Rolling Stone magazine
22 Sep – Cancelled concert: St. Bernard Civic Auditorium, Chalmette. Record Plant, NY
23 Sep – Record Plant, NY – *Valleys Of Neptune, Message To Love, Jam Back At The House, Drinkin Wine, Izabella*
24 Sep – Record Plant, NY – *Power Of Soul, Stepping Stone*
25 Sep – Record Plant, NY – *Keep On Groovin', Sky Blues Today, Room Full Of Mirrors*
26 Sep – Record Plant, NY – *Message To Love, Valleys Of Neptune, Night Bird Flying, Stepping Stone*

27 Sep – Cancelled concert: Will Rogers Coliseum, Fort Worth.
28 Sep – Cancelled concert: HemisFair Arena, San Antonio.
29 Sep – Cancelled concert: University Of Texas, Austin
30 Sep – Record Plant, NY – jam with Steve Stills, John Sebastien, Duane Hutchings, Miles, Mitchell (Jimi on bass)
1 Oct – In October, Mitchell leaves for England (plans exist for him to reunite with Jimi the spring)
2 Oct – In October: Record Plant session
20 Oct – Record Plant with Stephen Stills, John Sebastien and Buddy Miles (first session with Alan Douglas)
24 Oct – Sound centre Studios – session with The Organisms
28 Oct – Sound centre Studios – session with The Organisms
3 Nov – Around this date: jam (on bass guitar) at Ungano's with Leslie West and Tim Davis (Steve Miller Band)
6 Nov – Jam at Ungano's with B.B. King, Joe Cocker, Elvin Bishop, Buddy Miles and others.
7 Nov – Record Plant, NY
18 Nov – Record Plant, NY Nov – Record Plant, NY 26 Nov – Jimi goes out on the town with Mick Jagger
27 Nov – Jimi sees The Rolling Stones at Madison Square Garden's + Jimi's 27th birthday party (Jagger attends)7 Dec – Jimi is arrested at Toronto airport for possession drugs. Spends the night in jail.
8 Dec – Toronto Court House – drug possession trial
9 Dec – Toronto Court House – drug possession trial
10 Dec – Toronto Court House – drug possession trial – Jimi cleared of all charges: The drugs were legal.
12 Dec – Interview by Sue Clark
15 Dec – Record Plant, NY
18 Dec – Record Plant, NY
19 Dec – Record Plant, NY23 Dec – Record Plant, NY – *Honey Bed, Come Down Hard On Me, Night Bird Flying*
25 Dec – Jimi spends two days at Deering Howe's Hotel Navarro penthouse suite in New York for Christmas.
27 Dec – Rehearsals at Baggy's Studios, NY
28 Dec – Rehearsals at Baggy's Studios, NY
29 Dec – Rehearsals at Baggy's Studios, NY
31 Dec – The Fillmore East, NY (2 shows)

1970

1 Jan – The Fillmore East, NY (2 shows) – Ungano's, NYC – after show jam with Elvin Bishop, Buddy Miles and others
7 Jan – Record Plant, NY – *Cherokee Mist, Astro Man, Stepping Stone, Room Full Of Mirrors*, mixing
14 Jan – Juggy Sound Studios, NY – reviewing Fillmore recordings
15 Jan – Juggy Sound Studios, NY – reviewing Fillmore recordings
16 Jan – Juggy Sound Studios, NY – reviewing/mixing Fillmore recordings + Record Plant
17 Jan – Record Plant, NY – mixing
19 Jan – Juggy Sound Studios, NY – mixing Fillmore recordings + Record Plant, NY – Burning Desire, mixing
20 Jan – Record Plant, NY – *Message To Love, Earth Blues, Stepping Stone, Ezy Ryder*, mixing
21 Jan – Juggy Sound Studios, NY – mixing Fillmore recordings + Record Plant
22 Jan – Record Plant, NY – mixing
23 Jan – Record Plant, NY
28 Jan – "Winter Festival For Peace", Madison Square Garden, NY .– Only two songs played. End of the Band Of Gypsys
30 Jan – Jimi goes to see Jack Bruce & Friends at The Fillmore East, NY.
2 Feb – Juggy Sound Studios, NY – mixing Band Of Gypsys album
3 Feb – Record Plant, NY – *Power Of Soul*
4 Feb – Interview with John Burkes of Rolling Stone magazine.
5 Feb – Juggy Sound Studios, NY – mixing Band Of Gypsys album
11 Feb – Record Plant, NY – mixing
12 Feb – Record Plant, NY – mixing
14 Feb – Juggy Sound Studios, NY – editing, mixing
15 Feb – Juggy Sound Studios, NY – mixing Band Of Gypsys album + Record Plant, NY – mixing
16 Feb – Juggy Sound Studios, NY – mixing Band Of Gypsys album + Record Plant with Buddy Miles
17 Feb – Juggy Sound Studios, NY – final mixing, editing of Band Of Gypsys album
18 Feb – Sterling Sound, NY – mastering of BOG album
19 Feb – Sterling Sound, NY – mastering of BOG album
3 Mar – Jimi sees Rubber Duck at The Revolution Club
10 Mar – Flight to London
15 Mar – Island Studios, London – session with Stephen Stills – *Old Times, Good Times*
16 Mar – Interview with Keith Altman at the Speakeasy

17 Mar – Olympic Studios, London – session with Love – *The Everlasting First, Ezy Ryder jam*
18 Mar – Speakeasy, London -after hours jam with Stephen Stills
19 Mar – Flight back to New York
23 Mar – Sound centre, NY – session with Noel Redding and his group Fat Mattress
24 Mar – Record Plant, NY – *Bleeding Heart* (with drummer Steve Angel), *Midnight Lightning, Earth Blues*
25 Mar – BAND OF GYPSYS released
15 Apr – Interview with Keith Altman at Jimi's New York flat
18 Apr – Flight to L.A.
1 May – Milwaukee Auditorium, Milwaukee
2 May – Dane County Memorial Coliseum, Madison
3 May – St Paul's Civic Centre, St Paul
4 May – Benefit for Timothy Leary ("Holding Together"), Village Gate, NY – three songs played.
8 May – University Of Oklahoma Field House, Norman (2 shows)
9 May – Will Rogers Coliseum, Fort Worth
10 May – San Antonio Hemisfair Arena, San Antonio
11 May – Woodstock: Music from the Original Soundtrack and More released
14 May – Record Plant, NY
15 May – Record Plant, NY
16 May – Temple University Stadium, Philadelphia
22 May – Cincinnati – Jimi is ill so show is cancelled
23 May – St. Louis – Jimi is ill so show is cancelled
24 May – Evansville – Jimi is ill so show is cancelled
30 May – Berkeley Community Theatre, Berkeley (2 shows)
1 Jun – Early June: Jimi checks out his (and Jeffrey's) new Electric lady Studios and on one occasion jams with Richie Havens
5 Jun – Memorial Auditorium, Dallas
6 Jun – Sam Houston Coliseum, Houston
7 Jun – Assembly centre Arena, Tulsa
9 Jun – Mid-South Coliseum, Memphis
10 Jun – Roberts Municipal Stadium, Evansville
12 Jun – Band Of Gypsys album released in the UK
13 Jun – Civic Centre, Baltimore
15 Jun – Electric Lady Studios, NY
16 Jun – Electric Lady Studios, NY
20 Jun – Swing Auditorium, San Bernardino
21 Jun – Ventura County Fairgrounds, Ventura
23 Jun – Mammoth Gardens, Denver – CANCELLED

24 Jun – Electric Lady Studios, NY
25 Jun – Stanley Theatre, Pittsburgh – CANCELLED.
26 Jun – Electric Lady Studios, NYY
27 Jun – Boston Garden, Boston
29 Jun – Electric Lady Studios, NY – *Drifting*
30 Jun – Electric Lady Studios, NY – mixing, overdubs of *Freedom, Drifter's Escape* and other tracks
1 Jul – Electric Lady Studios, NY
2 Jul – Electric Lady Studios, NY – *Ezy Ryder, Belly Button Window*
4 Jul – Atlanta International Pop Festival, Middle Georgia Raceway, Byron
5 Jul – Miami Jai Alai Fronton, Miami
6 Jul – Jam with local musicians at The Blue Room, St. Petersburg, Florida (approximate date)
11 Jul – Jam with local musicians at Tampa Men's Garden Club Tampa, Florida (approximate date)
12 Jul – Jam with local musicians at Club 300, Treasure Island, Tampa, Florida
14 Jul – Electric Lady Studios, NY – *Come Down Hard On Me, Bolero, Midnight Lightning*
15 Jul – Electric Lady Studios, NY – *Dolly Dagger*
17 Jul – New York Pop, Downing Stadium, Randall's Island, NY
19 Jul – Electric Lady Studios, NY – *Lover Man, Midnight Lightning, Dolly Dagger, Angel*
21 Jul – Electric Lady Studios, NY – *In From The Storm, Hear My Train A Comin*
22 Jul – Electric Lady Studios, NY – *In From The Storm* and mixing
23 Jul – Electric Lady Studios, NY
25 Jul – Sports Arena, San Diego
26 Jul – Sicks Stadium, Seattle
27 Jul – Electric Lady Studios, NY – *Drifting, Angel, Belly Button Window*
30 Jul – Haleakala Crater, Maui
1 Aug – Honolulu International centre, Honolulu♠
2 Aug – Jimi goes back to Maui for a 10 day holiday
3 Aug – Holiday on Maui
4 Aug – Holiday on Maui
5 Aug – Holiday on Maui
6 Aug – Holiday on Maui
7 Aug – Holiday on Maui
8 Aug – Holiday on Maui
9 Aug – Holiday on Maui

10 Aug – Holiday on Maui
11 Aug – Holiday on Maui
12 Aug – Holiday on Maui
14 Aug – Electric Lady Studios – mixing, planning
18 Aug – Electric Lady Studios – *Dolly Dagger* with The Ghetto Fighters
20 Aug – Electric Lady Studios – *In From The Storm, Slow Blues*, mixing
22 Aug – Electric Lady Studios – mixing, overdubs
24 Aug – Electric Lady Studios – mixing, overdubs
25 Aug – Electric Lady Studios – mixing, overdubs
26 Aug – Sterling Sound, NY – mastering of single Dolly Dagger/Night Bird Flying + opening party of Electric Lady Studios
27 Aug – Flight to London. Jimi rests at The Londonderry Hotel.
28 Aug – Interviews with numerous newspapers and music journals. Jimi goes to The Speakeasy in the evening
29 Aug – Press interviews at The Londonderry Hotel
30 Aug – Isle Of Wight – Jimi is billed for this date but doesn't come on until the early hours of the following morning.
31 Aug – Isle Of Wight Festival, Isle Of Wight
1 Sep – Gothenburg Sweden – Billy Cox gets spiked with a acid at a party after the concert
2 Sep – Vejlby Risskov Hallen, Arhus, Denmark – aborted after two songs (Jimi ill)
3 Sep – K.B. Hallen, Copenhagen, Denmark
4 Sep – Berlin Germany
5 Sep – Fehmarn Island – programmed performance cancelled
6 Sep – Fehmarn Love And Peace Festival, Germany – Jimi's last concert. Returns to London to stay at The Cumberland
8 Sep – Jimi looks after Billy Cox. They go to a restaurant on Fulham Road.
9 Sep – Either on this day or the next, a distraught Billy Cox flew back to the U.S.A. Jimi goes to Tramp discotheque.
10 Sep – Jimi goes to a party held by Mike Nesmith at the Park Hotel, Mayfair.
11 Sep – Dinner at Ginger Baker's house. BBC interview with Keith Altham at The Cumberland Hotel.
12 Sep – Jimi goes to see the Antonio movie "The Red Desert" in the West End of London.
13 Sep – Rotterdam concert cancelled. Jimi meets friend at his Cumberland Hotel suite in the afternoon.
14 Sep – Nefer leaves, and Jimi starts seeing Monika Dannemann and meets up with his other girlfriend Devon Wilson.
15 Sep – Jimi goes to see Eric Burdon at Ronnie Scott's, London.

16 Sep – A party for Judy Wong's birthday
17 Sep – Photos in garden behind Samarkand Hotel. Jimi meets up with various friends around London.
18 Sep – Jimi dies in the ambulance on route to St. Mary Abbot's Hospital, London (stated by the hospital on the day & inquest)

Album Discography:

The Jimi Hendrix Experience
1967 Are You Experienced, Label Polydor/Track
1967 Axis: Bold as Love, Label Polydor/Track/Reprise/Barclay
1968 Electric Ladyland, Label Polydor/Track/Reprise/Barclay

Jimi Hendrix/Band of Gypsys
1970 Band of Gypsys, label Polydor/Trac

Posthumous Discography

Jimi's posthumous discography includes recordings released after September 18, 1970. The list of Albums within this category is often discussed, with lots of discussion to what should be included and what shouldn't. Jimi's jammed with hundreds of bands and performers over the years, and many of these jam sessions were recorded. Whether they ever intended to be released and attributed to Jimi Hendrix is highly debateable. Especially when many of the recordings were at varying stages of completion, and differing quality in audio. Therefore, many albums exist that have been released in various formats.

In 1995 Experience Hendrix was set up, owned and operated by The Hendrix family. It took control of future releases. There have been over 15 Hendrix albums that have appeared on the main US albums chart. Several of these have also achieved major chart success in more than 18 countries around the world. There are also hundreds of other albums that have been released over the years, many of live performances, that have been attributed to Jimi Hendrix. Below is a list of just some of these releases.

Posthumous Studio Albums:

1971 A cry of Love, Label Reprise/Track
1971 Rainbow Bridge, Label Reprise
1972 War Heroes, Label Reprise/Polydor
1974 Loose Ends, Label Polydor
1975 Crash Landing, Label Reprise/Polydor
1975 Midnight Lighting, Label Reprise/Polydor
1980 Nine to the Universe, Label Reprise/Polydor
1995 Voodoo Soup, MCA
1997 First Rays of the New Rising Sun, Label MCA
1997 South Saturn Delta, Label MCA
2010 Valleys of Neptune, Label Legacy/Sony
2013 People, Hell and Angels, Label Legacy/Sony
2018 Both side of the Sky, Label Legacy/Sony

Posthumous Live Albums

1971 Woodstock 2, Label Cotillion/Atlantic

1971 Experience, Label Ember
1971 The First great Rock Festivals of the Seventies/Isle of Wight: Atlanta, Label Columbia/CBS
1972 Hendrix in the West Label Reprise/Polydor
1972 More Experience, Label Ember
1973 The Jimi Hendrix Concerts, Label Reprise/CBS
1986 Jimi Plays Monterey, Label Reprise
1986 Johnny B. Goode, Label Capitol/Capitol/EMI
1986 Band of Gypsys 2, Label Capitol
1987 Live at Winterland, label Rykodisc
1988 Radio 1, Label Rykodisc/Castle
1987 Live and Unreleased The Radio Show, Label Castle
1991 Stages, Label Reprise/Polydor
1991 Live isle of Wight '70, Label Polydor
1994 Woodstock, label MCA /Polydor
1996 Message to Love. The Isle of Wight Festival 1970, Label Legacy/Castle
1998 BBC Sessions, Label MCA
1999 Live at Filmore East, Label MCA
1999 Live at Woodstock, Label MCA
2002 Blue Wild Angel. Live at the isle of Wight, Label MCA
2003 Live at Berkeley, Label MCA
2007 Live at Monterey, Label MCA
2011 Winterland, label Legacy/Sony
2013 Miami Pop Festival, Label Lagacy/Sony
2015 Freedom: Atlanta Pop Festival, Label Legacy/Sony
2016 Machine Gun, The Filmore East First Show, Label Legacy
2019 Songs for Groovy Children: The Filmore East Concerts, Label Legacy/Sony
2020 Live in Maui, Label Legacy/Sony
2022 Los Angeles Forum, April 26th, 1969, Label Legacy/Sony

Anthologies, Compilation and Retrospective Albums

1975 Re Experienced, Label Polydor
1978 The Essential Jimi Hendrix, Label Polydor
1979 The Essential Jimi Hendrix Vol 2, Label Reprise/Polydor
1981 Stone Free, Label Polydor
1983 The Singles Collection, Label Polydor
1984 Kiss the Sky, Reprise/Polydor
1989 The Essential Jimi Hendrix Vol One and Two, Label Reprise
1990 Cornerstones 1967-1970, Label Polydor
1990 Lifelines The Jimi Hendrix Story, Label Reprise
1992 The Ultimate Experience, Label MCA/Polydor
1993 The Experience Collection, Label MCA
1994 Blues, Label MCA/Polydor
1997 Experience Hendrix; The Best of Jimi Hendrix, Label MCA
2000 The Jimi Hendrix Experience, Label MCA
2001 Voodoo Child. The Jimi Hendrix Collection, Label MCA/Universal
2003 The Singles Collection, Label MCA
2003 Martin Scorsese Presents the Blues: Jimi Hendrix, Label MCA
2010 Fire: The Jimi Hendrix Collection, Label Lagacy/Sony
2010 West Coast Seattle Boy: The Jimi Hendrix Anthology, Label Legacy/Sony

Dagger Records

Based in Seattle, Dagger records started releasing Albums in 1998. Working with Experience Hendrix L.L.C and MCA records, Dagger Records releases official bootlegs and rare studio recordings. It has released over 12 albums to this point, the albums below are not attributed or released to any retail outlets, they are only available through Dagger online, the below is just a small portion with many more becoming available to order direct, or from Authentic Hendrix.

    1998   Live at the Oakland Coliseum, April 27, 1969, live at Oakland Coliseum.

    1999   Live at Clark University March 15, 1968, live at Clark University in Worcester

    2000   Morning Symphony Ideas, Studio demos recorded between 1969 and 1970

    2001   Live in Ottawa March 19, 1968, live at Capitol Theatre in Ottawa, Canada

    2002   Baggy's Rehearsal Dec 18/19, 1969, Band of Gypsys rehearsals in New York

    2003   Paris 1967/San Francisco 1968 Oct 9, 1967, live Olympia in Paris

    2004   Hear My Music Feb-April 1969 jams and unfinished songs. London and NY.

    2005   Live at Isle of Fehmarn Sept 6, 1970, live Open-Air Love & Peace Festival

    2006   Burning Desire Nov 1969- Jan 1970 Band of Gypsys studio jams RP NY

    2008   Live in Paris & Ottawa 1968 Jan 29, 1968, live in Paris & March 19, 1968.

    2009   Live at Woburn July 6, 1968, live at Woburn Music Festival in Woburn, UK

    2012   Live in Cologne January 13, 1969, live at Sporthalle, Cologne, Germany

A Lasting Legacy

Jimi Hendrix Park

In 2006, Seattle's Parks and Recreation Department renamed a 2.5-acre park in the Central District as Jimi Hendrix Park to celebrate the life and music of the Seattle-born artist. This park is adjacent to the old Colman School, which has housed the Northwest African American Museum since 2008.

The park was officially opened on Saturday, June 17, 2017, with a day of concerts honouring Jimi Hendrix on the park grounds. The event took place under a shelter designed to resemble a butterfly wing. Every aspect of the park pays tribute to Hendrix's work and legacy — including the shape of the park itself. The walkways form the outline of a guitar, with 12 "frets" in the instrument's neck illustrating the timeline of Hendrix's life. At the park's entrance, Hendrix's signature is carved into a concrete wall, leading to a green space adorned with purple flowering plants. Hendrix's lyrics are inscribed along the edges of the walkways. The park is designed to accommodate musicians and performers, featuring a paved area under the shelter specifically for concerts.

Janie Hendrix remarked, *"I don't think there's very many musicians that Jimi didn't inspire."*

What others say..

Over the years, Jimi Hendrix encountered numerous musicians and influential artists. His exceptional talent and genius left a lasting impression on all who met him. Whether it was his unparalleled stage presence or his off-stage generosity and kindness, everyone had something positive to say about him.

Below are some of the comments and tributes to the life and career of Jimi Hendrix from those who knew him, remembered him, played with him, or were simply inspired by him.

David Crosby: *One of the reasons Jimi's still such an important figure is because he was so complex. This was a guy who'd been in the 101st Airborne Division. You have to remember he wasn't just some one-dimensional being. He was somebody who'd been quite aways in his life and he had real depth to him. Which is something you can hear if you listen to the songs – he wasn't just a good guitar player. He was actually a brilliant songwriter and a great singer and had something to say.*

Kirk Hammett: *In terms of the overall package, it was so complete with Jimi. He had everything going: the look, the sound, the songs, the technique, the attitude. It's amazing how much music he created in that brief four-year window that he was around. It's just amazing.*

Don Felder: *The first time I heard Jimi Hendrix I had no idea who it was, but it was magical. His style, his tone, his vibrato, his voice – everything was unique. And those people with a unique approach to playing, writing and singing are the ones that go on to be legendary. Jimi Hendrix was one of the greatest players and most innovative musicians to come along in our generation.*

Ernie Isley: *When Eric Burdon and The Animals first came to the United States in 1964 and happened to do some shows with my older brothers, they were saying, "You know the Isley Brothers with that one-two punch of Shout and Twist And Shout. They've got a very dynamic live thing that they're doing. Who's the guitar player they've got? Not the right-handed guy, the guy that's left-handed?". That was Jimi Hendrix. Chas Chandler, who was a member of The Animals, turned out to be Jimi's first manager*

Bradley Pierce (promoter): *The first real disco on the East Side of Manhattan was Ondine's in the beginning of 1964. They used to have house bands, but I used to bring in groups from elsewhere because London, San Francisco and Los Angeles were where it was happening. In New York we* had the Lovin' Spoonful and the Young Rascals but that was about it. So, I imported groups from California. The Doors came first and then Buffalo Springfield. I booked Jimi locally. Actually Olivier [Coquelin, owner of Le Club in New York] recommended him to me. He told me about this group, Curtis Knight & The Squires, but mainly about their guitarist, Jimi Hendrix. Curtis was basically imitating James Brown, but he wasn't really that good. I told Jimi he should get himself into another group. I told him that if he quit Curtis Knight he could come and play at Ondine's, and I'd feed him and pay him something.

Graham Nash: *I first met Jimi in 1965, when he was playing guitar in Little Richard's band. It was the first time The Hollies had been to America, and we played at the Paramount Theatre in Times Square. We did about 10 days there on a bill that had around 20 acts on, five times a day. And that's when we first became aware of Jimi. Even in those days, and under those circumstances, he absolutely stood out.*

Micky Dolenz: *The first time I saw him play was at a club in New York City called the Café Au Go Go. He was playing guitar for John Hammond. Somebody had brought me down there and they said, "You gotta come hear this guy play guitar with his teeth!". That's all I was told. I remember seeing John Hammond on stage and there was this black guy, this young kid playing guitar with his teeth.*

Bill Wyman: *I saw Jimi first at a club in Queens in New York when he was just known as Jimmy James. It was bizarre because he was doing things the average person wasn't doing, though I knew they'd been done before: playing guitar round the back of your head and biting strings. Charlie Patton used to play guitar between his legs back in the 20s. T-Bone Walker did it all through the 40s and 50s too. So it wasn't new, but it was new to a different audience. He'd already been around and paid his dues in bands with Little Richard and Ike Turner. Jimi was a nice guy. All the Stones got on very well with him.*

Bob Kulick: *In 1966, I was 16 and my band, the Random Blues Band, played at the Café Wha? club in Greenwich Village. One day we were told this guy was coming down to audition and the name of his band was Jimmy James & The Blue Flames. So we watched as this guy came in and started to set up his gear. He was asking about using two amp cabs together and we all looked at each other like, "What? How do you do that?". On stage he had all these pedals and I thought, this should be interesting. He had a very interesting look. He looked like a star. The band started playing what sounded like a prototype of a* Third Stone From The Sun *kind of song, and* within one minute you knew that the guy wiped the floor with everybody we'd ever seen play. By the end of his set when he played solos with his teeth that nobody could play with their hands, we knew this guy was a sensation.

Bill Wyman: *When we got back from America, I bumped into The Animals at the Scotch of St James, where we all used to meet up with The Beatles and The Hollies and various bands. Chas [Chandler] said to me: "We're off to the States next week". I said: "If you're in New York, go and see this guy called Hendrix. He's fantastic". So they went, Chas met him and then signed him and brought him over. But Jimi had to come here to become famous.*

Robert Wyatt: *I remember Chas Chandler coming into the office and – I can't do the wonderful Geordie accent – he said, "I've just found this fucking guitarist. He plays the guitar with his fucking teeth! He's unbelievable and we're gonna get him!"*

Andy Summers: *I was living with Zoot Money at his house in Fulham, Gunterstone Road. There ought to be a blue plaque on that house for the number of people who passed through in the 60s. It was like the party house for the London scene, every night. I'd heard about Hendrix before I met him because we were quite tight with The Animals, and Chas Chandler – who I was sharing a girlfriend with at the time – called me and said that he'd found this fantastic blues guitarist in New York and he was going to bring him over, and he wanted me to come and see him play. The apocryphal story is that when Chas and Jimi arrived at Heathrow, they came into London to go and jam at a party somewhere and they passed by Zoot's and my flat on the way. That's true, but I wasn't there. They searched all round my room looking for my guitars, which I think I'd hidden under the bed. In the end Zoot had a left-handed acoustic guitar which is what they went off with.*

Jeff Dexter *(DJ and club promoter)*: *I first met Jimi the night after he arrived at the Cromwellian Club. He was charming, very polite, well-spoken, flabbergasted to be in London and didn't look anything like the wild Jimi Hendrix in all his gladrags. It took a couple of days to get him dressed up, but everyone was making a fuss about him. I didn't really get it, because to me he just seemed like another American in town. Then he mentioned that he'd played with Joey Dee & The Starliters [Hendrix was in the band briefly in late 1965] and that's when my ears pricked up. I thought that if he'd played with them then he must be great. They were a big influence on me, so I was more interested initially in talking to him about Joey Dee &*

The Starliters. Then we moved onto Bob Dylan. It had been the summer of Blonde On Blonde and, for anybody who cared about music and poetry and what was really happening, that was the event of the year. That album was inspirational for lots of us.

Dave Mason: *I first saw Jimi Hendrix at [Mayfair club] the Scotch of St James. It was just after Chas Chandler had brought him over and he took him round those little clubs. He got up and jammed with this band and I just happened to be there. At that point nobody knew about him. Chas was doing something very unusual and very smart in that he purposely introduced him to the London inner circle of musicians by bringing him down to some of those clubs and saying, "Go sit in". And that's how I first saw him. There were plenty of British guitarists on the scene: Eric Clapton, Jeff Beck, Peter Green. But there was no Hendrix. I watched him jump on stage with somebody and do everything that they could do and then play with his teeth. He was a showman. The English guitarists were busy mastering the blues, but Jimi had already done that. He was past all that stuff. Andy Summers, I got to see him a few days later at [Kensington club] Blaises where he was jamming with Brian Auger. He was up on stage wearing a white buckskin suit with these incredibly long fringes, a huge Afro and had this white Telecaster that, as I walked in, he was playing with his teeth. The guitar was wailing away, and I just stopped and stared. I was riveted, gobsmacked. And I think it was the same for all the musicians who saw Hendrix at that time. Even the established star names guitarists like Clapton and Beck. There was a whole paradigm shift. He seemed to come from a much more authentic, savage place. It wasn't some English guy trying to copy what they thought was going on in America, it was the real thing. And it had arrived on our shores. A lot of the English guys were so snobbish about the blues. But Jimi wasn't paying homage to any of the legends, he was doing his own thing. He'd taken it to another place. He had such an incredible feel for what he was doing, such a sound and such an attitude. There were no English reservations, that's for sure. Musically he played with a phrasing that was completely different. It was Hendrix – it wasn't BB King or Freddie King, it was him. He was much wilder and played more freely than anyone else. And that's what turned everyone on and got everyone talking. It was like, 'Have you seen the new model?'*

Brian Auger: *There was one night at Blaises [September 1966] We'd just finished our set and Jimi had sat in, and he was leaving the club. The club was in a basement, so there was a big flight of stairs down, and then his girlfriend ran in saying: "Brian, you've got to help Jimi! There's these* guys who are threatening him!*". This was a very strange thing to happen in London at that time, because it didn't matter what colour you were, man. So I told my roadie and a couple of guys from the band and we all went, a crowd of us, to the bottom of the stairs and looked up and there were these four huge South African guys – they looked like rugby players, all white guys – and they were shouting to Jimi: "Come up here, kaffir!". We basically told them to fuck off, and fortunately for us, they actually did. A cab drew up and they decided they'd leave. I'd never seen anything like that in London.

Arthur Brown: *Jimi's blackness was a thing. There was a lot of racial prejudice around – but then Otis Redding was the god of the Mods. Plus there was the Alexis Korner Marquee scene with all the black soul giants. And the Flamingo Club playing blues and Jamaican and calypso. There were prejudicial ideas, 'What's a black guy up to, compared to a white guy?'. But having the two white guys in the Experience meant he couldn't just be written off. There was unconscious racism around in the 60s, but Hendrix helped a lot of that turn around, certainly in the underground scene.*

Stephen Stills: *Jimi and I were hanging around together, hitting the clubs in England and going to the Bag O' Nails and taking over the stage. And it graduated to me and my friend Dan Campbell joining him. Maybe because Dan and I were both southerners, Jimi so missed talking to an American face that really understood black people. So he'd pour his heart out and we'd talk about everything under the sun. He'd steal away from his usual retinue and come talk to us.*

Ginger Baker: *We, Cream, were doing a gig in a theatre in London and Jimi turned up to sit in with the band at the Central London Polytechnic [October 1, 1966 – leading them through an incendiary version of Howlin' Wolf's Killing Floor, complete with behind-the-head picking and flamboyant splits – most of his moves copped from Eric's hero, the blues legend Buddy Guy. I was totally against it. I didn't want him to sit in at all because I didn't think it appropriate. We were fine without him. I didn't know who he was or anything and when he did sit in I was not at all impressed; he was doing all that playing guitar with his teeth and rolling about. I really don't know if Eric and Jack were impressed. I know Eric liked him. To me he was being the big showman, whereas Eric just stood there and played. He was a great player.*

Jack Bruce: *I was just having a pre-gig pint in a pub across the road and in comes this guy who turns out to be Jimi Hendrix. Now, we had* already heard about Jimi on the grapevine. Jimi came up to me and said: "Hi. I would like to sit in with the band". I said it was fine with me but he'd obviously have to check it out with Eric and Ginger. So we went across to the gig, and Eric immediately said yes and Ginger said: "Oh, dunno about that" [laughs]. So he came on and plugged into my bass amp, and as far as I can remember he just blew us all away.

Keith Altham (*journalist*): "*I gotta go and see Clapton,*" Jimi told me during an early interview, adding with a sly smile: "*I wanna see if he is as good as he thinks I am*".

Andy Summers: *Hendrix led the way into psychedelia in many ways. The London scene had been coming along and you had The Beatles, of course. Clapton was getting into Cream and Beck was doing various things, and then out of the fucking blue comes Jimi Hendrix. He fired everyone up. We all started writing songs and growing our hair longer. What a time to be a young musician.*

Neal Schon: *Jimi was so extraordinarily gifted. He was just seeing things so vividly. A lot of times when you're creating, you have to imagine things before you play them. And the only way I can imagine Jimi came up with a lot of his music was to vividly see it in his mind before he would play it. He would see the landscape and then create it. He was a definitive innovator of electric guitar, making sounds that nobody had ever heard before. And the music he made is timeless.*

Eric Burdon: *I wouldn't say anybody was a close friend of Jimi's. He was a strange guy, a loner. I think I got as close as anybody could do, though. As luck would have it, we were managed by the same people. But what started out as a really beautiful period of my life and a great friendship turned into a real tragedy. It's still something I think about on a bi-daily basis. Once a week, Hendrix creeps back into my life. Every guitar player who auditions for me wants to impress and play like Jimi. That gets on my nerves. It's difficult to find a guitar player these days that isn't influenced by Hendrix.*

Graham Nash: *Mitch [Mitchell] used to share my flat for a while in London. He had nowhere to live for a strange period at the beginning of the Experience and I had an apartment, so he just came to live with me for about a year. I'm not a jammer, but Jimi would come around a lot and we'd listen to music. Though most of all we'd play Risk. Nobody could beat him! Jimi would drop a few tabs of acid and that was it – nobody could beat him at Risk.*

Jeff Dexter: *I remember we went to the Bag O' Nails one night – Jimi had already got up and played a couple of times at the Bag. We sat down at the table to watch the band and chat with Al Needles, who was the disc jockey. Suddenly we got ordered off this table because we weren't the kind of people to spend money on champagne. A bunch of heavy spenders had come in, so they shifted us off to one side. Jimi said: "Don't worry, man, one day I'll come back and I'll buy that table!".*

Arthur Brown: *The vibe around him in London? People were gobsmacked. Certainly, all the guitarists were afraid. The extremes of sound – his use of wah-wah and the whole emotion he played with – was a brand-new thing. Everyone was put on their mettle. The generous ones were delighted, and the not so generous got jealous of him. He used to shop down Kings Road for all the outrageous clothes. He was vital to that whole scene. Plus he was so sexually available that he had a real energy. People who would have written off others as psychedelic namby-pambies saw his photos with his abdominal muscles and decided we don't mess with this guy.*

Graham Nash: *Jimi was very different from the outward image that the public knew. He was very intelligent and a shy, humble man in many ways. But he created this wild man sex object persona, who happened to play the most unbelievable guitar in the world. His image became almost a trap for him. And I think that in his later years he tried to just play music rather than play up to this wild-man image. I've heard talk about Jimi and I writing some songs together at one point, but that's completely untrue. That didn't happen. After wowing the London scene and a brief sojourn to France supporting Johnny Hallyday, the Experience knuckled down to make their debut album, Are You Experienced. It would be released in the UK on May 12, 1967.*

Eddie Kramer: *Jimi had already been in London for a few months when I met him. He'd already had a single out [Hey Joe]. He'd already played the Paris Olympia, so I really did know who he was. Everybody knew who he was and what he was doing – turning the music business upside down. I get a phone call from my lovely studio manager named Anna Menzies. She called me up and went [adopts tremulous posh English voice], "Oh, Eddie. There's this American chappie, with big hair and you should do the session because you do all that weird shit anyway". Because I had this reputation for doing a lot of avant-garde jazz, so she thought it would be a good fit. And she was right. We hit it off. They'd actually cut a few tracks, but when we started the sessions at the new Olympic Studios in Barnes, in January 67, it was a revelation for Jimi because a) it was a* fantastic studio, and b) not only did we hit it off in terms of an intellectual level, an emotional level and also a musical level and all that, but we were able to create different sounds for him that he wasn't able to get in the other studios. So we ended up overdubbing stuff on some of those tracks they'd originally cut. Then of course we dived right into the new album and started cutting new songs. We virtually finished up the record there at Olympic and mixed it there.

Mitch Mitchell: *As for the burning of the guitar, [Monterey] wasn't the first time that Jimi had done it. The first was at Finsbury Park Astoria in London, which later became the Rainbow. As usual in England, we got in trouble with everybody over it.*

Keith Altham: *I came up with the burning guitar idea in England, because Chas asked me what he could do to steal the headlines on the gloriously incongruous Engelbert Humperdinck-Walker Brothers-Hendrix package tour opening at Finsbury Park Astoria. It worked. And Jimi was not undyingly grateful, as a blazing conflagration was expected of him on every performance. And as he said to me before going on stage at Monterey: "I got an idea Keith – why don't you set fire to your typewriter tonight for a change?".*

Leslie West: *I was first aware of Hendrix when I plugged my guitar into an amp and someone gave me a copy of his debut album Are You Experienced and I said: "Boy, do I suck".*

Andy Summers: *I saw the Saville Theatre [June 67] gig where Jimi opened with Sgt Pepper's Lonely Heart's Club Band when the album had only been out for a couple of days. It was quite incredible. Brilliant. It just blew everyone away. And I remember seeing him later at the Hollywood Bowl where he came on and started with Sunshine Of Your Love. Which confounded everyone who assumed that there was this big rivalry between Hendrix and Cream. But Jimi was not like that. Mind you, he played it better than Cream. But then he seemed to be able to Hendrix-ify any song that took his fancy. He did it particularly with Dylan, first taking Like A Rolling Stone to another place and again, brilliantly, with All Along The Watchtower.*

Rick Springfield: *What Jimi Hendrix means to me is innovation and bravery. When I heard the first Jimi Hendrix Experience album I couldn't believe how heavy it was. This was still a time of mainly pretty pop all over the charts and Hendrix comes out of the gate with Fire!*

Ginger Baker: *We did lots of gigs that Jimi was also on, so we met up many times. There was a good one I remember at a festival in Lincoln at* the Tulip Bulb Auction Hall in Spalding [May 29, 1967]. At that time Polaroid cameras had just been invented – you could take pictures and instantly see them. Mitch Mitchell was running around and taking pictures of Jimi with various chicks at the Red Lion Hotel, where we were all staying [the Experience, Cream, Move, Pink Floyd]. He sprang to everybody and he had a reputation, there was just chicks everywhere climbing up knotted sheets to get to his room. In the summer of 1967 Jimi Hendrix returns to the United States with the Experience. On June 18 they play their definitive set at the Monterey Pop Festival.

Al Kooper: *I met Jimi at a soundcheck at the Monterey Pop Festival where I was the stage manager. We spoke in the wings and he invited me to play with him that night on Like A Rolling Stone, but I had to turn him down because I was working, and [promoter] Lou Adler would have got very mad at me if I'd ducked out. You don't want to fuck with Lou Adler. Every inch of me wanted to do it.*

Mitch Mitchell: *My overriding memory of Monterey is such a happy one. It was the first time I'd ever been to America. I can't tell you what a big deal that was for any English musician, really a dream come true. It was better than I imagined. The beauty of California, the sunshine, light and warmth after England was just magical. The American people showed us nothing but kindness and open friendliness that you just don't find anywhere else. Even the motorbike police at Monterey let people attach flowers to their caps and bikes. Not a thing that would happen in England.*

David Crosby: *Our paths would cross a lot of the time. We jammed with him, played with him and hung out with him. We loved him. We thought he was the genuine article, which of course he was. As flamboyant as Jimi was on stage, he was shy and quiet in person. He wasn't at all like the figure you saw up on there on a stage. But if one of his hands could touch the guitar, Lord have mercy! Because you just didn't want to get in the way. He was spectacular. I remember watching him play Foxy Lady at Monterey and it was almost too fucking good.*

Micky Dolenz: *I knew about Jimi before Monterey Pop, but I'm sitting there watching all these great acts at the festival – Ravi Shankar, The Who, The Byrds, Buffalo Springfield... The announcer said: "Here we have the Jimi Hendrix Experience!". Out come these three guys looking really cool, like circus performers wearing very psychedelic outfits. They start playing and I did a double take when Jimi started playing guitar with his teeth. I said to whoever I was with, "There's that guitar player that plays with his teeth!" I recognised him from seeing him in a little club in New York City.*

He was amazing at Monterey. I remember just being bewildered and in awe of his musicianship but also impressed by the showmanship because it was a very theatrical sort of performance. Like with The Who smashing guitars and drums. After the show, Jimi and a couple of other guys were in the one of the tents jamming until the wee hours of the morning on the last night. I was there watching all of that go down and remember being in awe.

DA Pennebaker (*documentary film maker*): *John Phillips of the Mamas & The Papas knew about Hendrix beforehand. At that time he was not known in America. John had told me about him and said, "This is a guy who plays blues and sets himself on fire" [laughs]. I said, "That's the kind of blues I guess I've never heard". I didn't know what to expect but I would soon find out at Monterey Pop Festival. In America, some underground radio stations were playing Hey Joe. But a lot refused to play it because it had to do with either suicide or murder. In those days people were very cautious about what kind of rock music they played on the radio.*

Mitch Mitchell: *For Jimi, Monterey was so special as well. He was going back home with a band he felt was something special, and playing with Jimi was always instinctive. He gave complete freedom, and I would have to say there was a very close link. We knew The Who were going to be a tough act to follow. Nobody would want to follow The Who on stage – they were just so great – but having said that we had faith in ourselves and felt we had something good too.*

Micky Dolenz: *At that time we were looking for an opening act for the upcoming Monkees tour. I told the producers of the television show: "We're looking for an opening act. I gotta tell ya, this act I saw at the Monterey Pop Festival was great!". Besides the music, which I loved, the reason I suggested Jimi was because he was very theatrical and so were the Monkees. I thought it would be a good mix.*

Mitch Mitchell: *Monterey really changed everything for us. We had nothing at all after Monterey, not one gig planned. But after Monterey we got loads of offers: the Fillmore, the Hollywood Bowl with the Mamas & The Papas, who were just terrific to us. It was really the start of everything. Besides we wanted to do well. Paul McCartney liked the band early on and suggested us for the gig. We didn't want to do anything but our best.*

Bradley Pierce: *I didn't hear from Jimi for some time, not until I was in California looking for a group to play at the opening of [New York nightclub] Salvation. I asked Jimi what he had been doing and he told me about his new group, the Experience, which I had never heard of because, although he was already big in Europe, he hadn't broken America yet. He* said I should come and see them at Monterey Pop. I knew that wherever Jimi was, that it would be exciting, however good the other two guys were. So I asked him there and then if he was free to play at Salvation when I opened. In the end, right after Monterey, he came and played two weeks at Salvation for nothing. I literally passed the hat in the club to get some money for them.

Micky Dolenz: *Chas Chandler must have also thought The Monkees tour was a good idea as, I assume, did Jimi, Mitch and Noel. Lo and behold they started opening for us. We were in awe of him. So much so that we very seldom got to the arenas much before we went on, but I remember going early many times to watch Jimi play. Mike [Nesmith] was totally blown away by him. Jimi was a great guy, quiet, naïve and gentle. We hung out a lot after the shows and in hotel rooms on the road. Steven Stills and Graham Nash showed up. After one of the shows, I remember being in a hotel room with Jimi, Peter Tork and Steve Stills was there and a bunch of guitars. I started strumming on a guitar along with those guys and they're playing all these amazing leads. I was just playing a rhythm guitar part. That song must have gone on for at least a half-an-hour. There was a whole bunch of people in the room – girls and roadies –and these guys are on fire jamming. I just stopped to go to the bathroom and they all stopped and they looked at me and said, "What did you stop for?", I said, "I didn't think anybody was listening".*

Bob Kulick: *The night the Jimi Hendrix Experience was fired from The Monkees tour he had a party in New York City and invited a bunch of us to hang out with him. Here was the conquering hero returning from England where he'd gone from Jimmy James & The Blue Flames and turned into the Jimi Hendrix Experience. It was a 'Holy shit! Oh my god!' moment. So we went up there and met Noel Redding and Mitch Mitchell. These guys were lit up. I hadn't seen the Jimi Hendrix Experience play yet but knew their record. I remember Jimi had a stack of 45s and a turntable. He wheeled us through all of the newest English music. The only artist that mattered to me that he played was Tales Of Brave Ulysses by Cream. We heard that song and saw the look on his face. Jimi immediately made the comment, "This guy is a better guitar player than me". That's what he thought of Eric Clapton, and Eric Clapton thought that way about Jimi.*

Micky Dolenz: *As for the crowd reaction to Jimi opening for The Monkees, it wasn't that they didn't dig it. They didn't boo Jimi off the stage. That's part of the urban myth. It just wasn't the music for a 10-year-old little kid. We loved it and I'm sure some of the older kids and parents dug* it. So it wasn't that they didn't dig it, they were just there to see The Monkees. It wasn't like the crowd were screaming, "You're terrible! Boo! Get off the stage!". It didn't matter who was up there. They were screaming "We want The Monkees. We want The Monkees! Micky! Davy! Peter! Mike!" even before the opening acts went on. It was embarrassing for me. Jimi sort of laughed it off until I think he just got fed up. His first record was breaking at the time, so I like to think he got some good exposure. I have no doubt Jimi Hendrix would have been Jimi Hendrix with or without the Monkees tour. We hung out a lot up until the last gig, which was in Forest Hills. Afterwards, we went to the Electric Circus club in New York right after that show.

Henry Diltz (*photographer*): Unfortunately, I didn't get to see Jimi perform on The Monkees tour as I showed up on the last date he played with them in Forest Hills, New York [July 19, 1967]. Ironically, I showed up just as he was coming off the stage. It was an afternoon show and later we all hung out at the hotel. Everybody was out in the hallway and I remember someone handing out little white pills, which I found out were psilocybin [natural psychedelic]. We all took them and got very high.

Nils Lofgren: I saw the Jimi Hendrix Experience play a lot and it was incredibly inspiring. I saw him for the first time in Washington DC in [August] 1967 and that's what inspired me to try a career as a musician. We idolised The Beatles and Hendrix but you didn't think you could ever do that for a living in Middle America.

Henry Diltz: I photographed Jimi when he headlined the Hollywood Bowl. They had a large wading pool right in front of the stage and the front row was behind that. They'd have coloured lights in the water with water squirting up at times so it was kind of a fountain pool. I was crouched at the edge, looking across at Jimi, taking photos and suddenly I was aware of someone jumping up on edge of the pool next to me. That person jumped into the pool and I thought, 'Wow, that's strange'. Suddenly a whole bunch of people jumped in. It was like those documentaries on wildebeests jumping into the river. At some point there were 20-30 people in the water wading up to the front of the stage with their arms flailing. Jimi bent over at one point to say something to them. I think he was concerned. Very quickly they stopped the concert because if a microphone or an amp fell into the pool those people would have been electrocuted. While much of 1967 was spent on tour, the Jimi Hendrix Experience managed to find time to sneak in sessions at Olympic Studios in London in May, June and

October to record their second album, *Axis: Bold As Love*. It would be released on December 1.

Rick Springfield: *Axis: Bold As Love is where Jimi demonstrated what you could do if you turned the guitar down and used tone. He turned the world on to Strats and showed what a melodic solo truly was. Hendrix changed music and guitar playing in particular forever. Not bad for the first two albums. I still don't know where those first two albums came from. They were magic. And he had the authenticity to make phrases like 'comin' to gitcha' sound so real, you never questioned that he was posturing or faking it.*

Trevor Burton: *The Move were recording at Olympic Studios and next door was the Jimi Hendrix Experience recording their second album. Roy [Wood] and I walked in to say hello because we knew them well by then. They were doing You Got Me Floating and Noel and Mitch weren't cutting the background vocals too good, so we asked Jimi, "Do you want us to have a go?". And he said, "Yeah!". I think we did it in two takes. Jimi was pleased with it. He sang his lead vocals live at the same time while we put down the background vocals.*

Eddie Kramer: *When you look at the progression of the albums and what Jimi was saying lyrically, musically, all of that stuff, you really get a sense that Are You Experienced starts the ball rolling. It's very raw, very in-your-face, very primitive. Then Axis... being the next stage of development where things are more experimental. I'm expanding the stereo imagery, the sounds are better. And the songwriting is much more experimental too. In the first part of 1968, the Experience found themselves back on the other side of the Atlantic for yet more gigs, including a Martin Luther King Jr wake and the Miami Pop Festival. In February, Jimi had the honour of having a certain part of his anatomy immortalised by Cynthia Plaster Caster...*

Cynthia Plaster Caster: *It was at the Conrad Hilton Hotel in Chicago, February 25, 1968. In between two concerts they were doing at the Civic Opera House that day. I wasn't a real big, humungous guitar aficionado, but I really got off on Jimi's guitar. We'd been experimenting with trying to figure out how to plaster cast anything, namely penises, after I'd gotten the idea from my art teacher two years prior. The only thing missing in the formula was what mould to use to make a negative impression. There were all these substances I was trying that were not very conducive to the prettiness of a penis, but I'd heard about dental moulds and that seemed to* be the best bet. I tried it a few times on a couple of friends because I wanted to be ready for Jimi Hendrix, and know how to do it.

DA Pennebaker: *I met Jimi later at a club in 8th Street in New York City where there was a wake being held for Martin Luther King who'd just been tragically killed. All hell was breaking loose in the city; they were tearing New Jersey apart and Harlem was blowing up. We set up an Ampex tape recorder in a booth in the back and were going to record everything and I was gonna film it. Jimi was there because he was one of the performers. It may be hard to believe but he did the sound recordings on my Nagra recorder while I shot the event. Jimi did my sound! We have a picture of him holding the slate in the film, which we've never released. It was a really grim day. The last song they played that night at the Martin Luther King wake was Dylan's All Along The Watchtower and it was dawn. Everybody got up on stage to perform it – Janis Joplin, Hendrix. It was a very powerful moment.*

Arthur Brown: *We did various festivals together - like Miami Pop Festival, some shows in Scandinavia and Germany, a whole series with Zappa, Hendrix and myself in America after the Fire success. At Miami Pop I took a ride in Jimi's helicopter and grabbed a ride on Noel Redding's motorbike. We hung out. That was the whole deal back then. We met at the Speakeasy for dinner and I'd sit with him. He was quite electric. He was ingesting various substances and the effect on ladies was extremely powerful. If a waitress walked by, then Jimi's hand would appear and he'd be touching her on the arm, or somewhere else. He was very available to ladies and they fancied him a lot.*

Billy Gibbons: *We toured with him most in 1968. It was a real mind-bender and eye opener, to say the least. As most now know, Hendrix, either consciously or subconsciously, made a decision to invent things to do with a Fender Strat that it had not necessarily been intended for. He did it very well, too. I was 18 at the time, and somehow the organisers saw fit to book us in the hotel room across the hall to his room. That was convenient to allow me to ask him the obvious question: "How do you do that?".*

Jack Bruce: *Hendrix had a positive effect on everybody, especially guitar players. He came to the sessions when we did White Room in New York and was very encouraging. He came up to me and said, "Wow, I wish I could write something like that". I said, "Jimi, what you've got to realise is that I probably nicked it off you!".*

Arthur Brown: *I used to play with him at the Scene Club in New York. I was there with the Crazy World when Chris Stamp brought him along to* see me. At other times it would be jams with all kinds of musicians, big names, or not so big. We would jam and he would play bass on those occasions. He didn't like singing. Even if I offered him the mic he wouldn't do it.

From those sessions he came up with the idea he had of us forming an actual band. We didn't come up with a name. It was going to be a band with tapes of Wagner in the background. He was aware that he'd had these commercial hits and as far as the audience were concerned he needed to move on musically. He wanted a stage show with a theatrical performance via me singing. He wanted huge projections on the screens and Vincent Crane on keyboards. The rhythm section was to be the Experience, so we'd elide the two bands. It was a continuum.

Nils Lofgren: *On one of my first New York adventures, I went to this famous nightclub called The Scene. After a show, I was hanging out and there was late-night jam session, where I somehow found myself up on stage at two in the morning, with a broken string and a bunch of other musicians. I suddenly realised Jimi Hendrix was at the back of the room, with this black bolero and his bullfighter-type clothes. At some point he got up and I could see through the smoky haze that he was coming towards the bandstand. Next thing I knew, he was standing right in front of me. Like an idiot, I didn't know what to say. Then he asked the bass player, who was standing next to me, if he could play bass. I was just freaking out. Here I was – 17, a broken string and I suck – and I'm going to play with Jimi Hendrix! To my amazement, the bass player turned him down: "Not now Jimi, I'm groovin'!". Jimi asked twice more if he could play bass, and the guy said no. So that was my near miss of jamming with Hendrix.*

Neal Schon: *I saw Jimi in concert in 1968 at Winterland in San Francisco. He played three nights – Friday, Saturday and Sunday –and I saw him on the Sunday. The Friday, I heard, was extraordinary. The Saturday I heard was very good but he was sticking the neck of the Strat into the speaker cabinets, and he wouldn't replace the cabinets. So when I saw him on the Sunday it sounded like a bunch of blown-up speakers. He looked amazing and he looked like he was playing amazing, but the cabinets had just had it. But the guy had incredible charisma like nobody else.*

Al Kooper: *Working on Electric Ladyland I didn't see any evidence that he'd fallen out with Noel Redding. I was only there for a three-hour session. We recorded Long Hot Summer Night from scratch. The song had never been done before. I got paid union scale. I played and he said, "Thanks man, catch you later on". In the room it was his band and I. It was* no stretch at all as a musician. Noel did play bass when I was in the room. Maybe that was replaced afterwards by Hendrix. Jimi sang the backing vocal tracks. I didn't leave the studio walking on air exactly, because we were pretty good friends prior to that. It wasn't like when I played on Bob Dylan's Like A Rolling Stone, when I did leave the studio walking on air. After the Jimi date I just wanted to avoid the rush hour on the subway because it was late afternoon, and I wanted to go home.

Ginger Baker: *Jimi paid us this incredible compliment on the Lulu TV show [January 4, 1969] when he stopped what he was playing, stopped his band, and did Sunshine Of Your Love. I didn't ever dislike him. It was just I wasn't impressed that first time he sat in with us. That was my first impression. Cream just weren't into showmanship at all, that's why I was horrified at the time. The audiences loved it, but Jimi's bag on stage was pulling as many chicks as he could. They used to congregate around Jimi like flies. They thought he was God Almighty. He had a fantastic reputation as a womaniser.*

Glenn Hughes: *I met him just the once. I was with my band Finders Keepers, before Trapeze. We were playing in London one night and I found myself in the famous Speakeasy nightclub. As I walked into the toilet, he was walking out. He held the door open for me. We chatted briefly and I remember him being genuinely sweet and kind. We did the brotherly handshake and "Hey man" thing. That's all I really needed... I was star-struck because the guy was royalty. I wasn't out to stalk him, we just happened to be going to the toilet at the same time. It's not much of an anecdote, but at least I met him.*

Stephen Stills: *Between Jimi and Neil [Young], they really tried to get me playing lead guitar. Jimi would say: "You can do this! If we play together, I want us both to play". He'd show me something and I'd have to remind him: "Jimi, your thumb is the size of my entire hand. I can't do that!". And he'd go: "Oh, yeah". He'd try and teach me things, explaining how I could play a certain way, then I'd see the whole scale and be free. Like it was so simple! It was hilarious. Some of it was just physically impossible to do. Then he'd say: "And the strength in that third finger will come. Keep trying to make the bend with that finger cos it leaves the others free". It was the best time. I also played bass a lot of the time when we were jamming, which I was pretty good at.*

Joe Cocker: *I was living in a place in the Valley in Los Angeles, and I got an invite from Mitch Mitchell who said Jimi wanted me to pay him a visit at his Hollywood pad because he liked my stuff. Since he was a hero* of mine I didn't need much persuasion. When I turned up Jimi greeted me inside although the sum total of his conversation was a mumbled "Hey, how are you, man. Glad you dropped by". After a while he decided he wanted to jam. At that time whenever he felt the urge to play at home he had the Irish guys from Eire Apparent on tap to back him up because he particularly liked their bass player Chris Stewart. So we all went into this tiny room full of equipment and he put on a total show with me as the sole member of the audience. The space was so small I literally had my right ear wedged against his amp, which is why I've now got tinnitus. Thanks for that, Jimi! He gave it everything though, played guitar upside down, between his legs, it was like a total performance. I was absolutely amazed. One thing was, he didn't ask me to sing. I was extremely stoned by the time I left his pad. I never felt I knew him. I don't think many people did. But I'm pleased to have that episode in my memory bank. A private concert from Hendrix? Unbelievable.

Leslie West: *I'd already met him at the Record Plant in New York in 1969. He was the first to hear the Mountain Climbing! album being mixed. It was quite a day for me. I was a nervous kid when he heard the record. And then a year later I'm in the club and he walks up to me just after Steve Miller had finished playing and says: "Do you wanna jam?". I'm like – are you kidding? I had a loft where I kept all my equipment, so we got into Jimi's limo and went down there. I couldn't get over him. Steve Miller missed out because he'd already left, but his drummer Tim Davis had hung around and he played drums. A lot of my friends are very jealous I got to play with Jimi and they didn't.*

Mick Brigden *(musician):* *One fabulous night Leslie brought Jimi up to our rehearsal studio. I watched them noodle away for a couple of hours and rolled them their joints. This was in a funky area on the East Side of Manhattan on the West 30s by the Lincoln Tunnel. It was around midnight and there was a bang on the door. I looked down from the second floor window and there was a stretch black Cadillac limo parked up with Leslie standing on the street. Leslie bowls in saying: "Hey Mickey, say hello to my friend Jimi", and coming out of the limo was Hendrix. He gave me his soft handshake and slides past me like a puff of smoke. I was in shock. Jimi Hendrix has come to visit me in the middle of the night? Fine. I'll remember this. Hendrix says: "We just want to jam, and hang out for a while. Can you set us up? Then we're going off to this club". I got together a quick array of Union Jack rehearsal amps for them while they got their thing together. They sat down and jammed while I sat on the bed. Both guys had* a traditional electric blues style so that's what they played. Jimi didn't play Foxy Lady or anything. It was blues progression jamming.

At the Denver Pop Festival on June 29, 1969, Jimi would play his last gig with the Experience. Already committed to play Woodstock, Hendrix put together a new band – Gypsy Suns & Rainbows – with old army buddy Billy Cox on bass, Mitch Mitchell on drums, rhythm guitarist Larry Lee and percussionists Juma Sultan and Jerry Velez.

Mitch Mitchell: *Woodstock for us – while it means so much to many people and I don't want to denigrate that in any way – was mud, tiredness, logistical problems on an epic scale and just difficult. Juma Sultan Jimi had been jamming with guys, auditioning guys every night. I knew all the musicians in the area. With Woodstock approaching, Jimi knew he had to tighten up, and he was committed to that contractually. Maybe a month before the festival, Jimi called in Billy Cox and Larry Lee, the guys that became Gypsy Suns & Rainbows. We started rehearsing every day. Mitch didn't come in until the tail end, and he was drunk most of the time and did not really rehearsal with us. That was the situation.*

Ernie Isley: *There was a show we were going to do in June of 1969, that we did at Yankee Stadium in New York. My older brothers wanted the Jimi Hendrix Experience to perform, and they asked him. His reply was, "Oh yeah man, cool. I'd love to do it, but let me talk to my people and I'll get back to you." And a few days went by and he called back and said, "Man, I'd love to do it, but there's this thing called the Woodstock Music and Art Fair in upstate New York in August and the promoter don't want me to play in the New York area before this Woodstock thing". Other than that, he would have been at the Yankee Stadium show.*

Henry Diltz: *The last time I photographed Jimi was at Woodstock. He went on stage Monday morning. The dawn was just breaking, and these colourful guys came out on stage. It was eye-opening because we'd been up all night and had been watching music for three days. Jimi had that white fringe jacket. The high point was the moment he launched into The Star-Spangled Banner solo on electric guitar. That was the best moment of Woodstock for me. It was awe-inspiring to hear this beautiful and piercing rendition of The Star-Spangled Banner with sound effects – airplane dive bombing, explosions and machine-guns. There was the Vietnam War, which we were all morally against, and here he was playing this patriotic song. You stopped and felt, "It's our song too. It doesn't belong to the government or the establishment, it belongs to all of us". There was a very tribal feeling there because it was the biggest assemblage of hippies and anti-war, peace-*

loving people. I happened to be standing about 10 feet away from Jimi when he was playing that song. I was speechless. It was so magnificent and moving and it's a memory I will never forget.

Kirk Hammett: *I just recently bought Live At Woodstock, and I've watched that clip over a hundred times, and every time I find something different: a nuance or little group of notes I hadn't noticed previously. I really like the three-song medley of The Star-Spangled Banner, Purple Haze and Villanova Junction. And I mean, seriously, his version of Star-Spangled Banner... there's absolutely nothing like it."*

Leslie West: *I saw him go on at Woodstock on Monday morning at seven o'clock. He was the unofficial headliner, and the reason why Mountain were on that festival at all was because we had the same agent, Ron Terry. Ron told the Woodstock folks if you want Hendrix you gotta take this new group called Mountain, so he kinda shoved us up their ass*

Tommy Ramone: *I worked from 1969 to 1970 as an assistant engineer at the Record Plant in New York City. I knew somebody at another studio who got me connected with the Record Plant. That period was a very interesting period for Hendrix. He had changed musicians – out were Mitch Mitchell and Noel Redding, and in on bass was his friend Billy Cox and Buddy Miles on drums. It was a whole different atmosphere. The producers were also different. He brought in Alan Douglas and his assistant Stefan Bright. I think Jimi was going through all kinds of changes and turmoil at the time. It was a strange atmosphere. Jimi was a perfectionist in the studio. He would never settle for second best. He was very hard-working and serious about his music. He would do all kinds of things to make a song happen. Some of the sessions I worked on were songs like Izabella, Freedom, Dolly Dagger, Stepping Stone, EZ Rider and Machine Gun. It was exciting to meet him, but what was even more interesting was how charming he was. In between songs he could be very playful. He always wanted to please you. He wanted to please me and I was just the assistant engineer!*

Steven Tyler: *I never met Jimi, but our paths crossed in the studio once. There was a Telefunken pencil mic I wanted to use, and the guy comes over and says, "You don't want to use that mic". And I go, "Why?", and he goes, "Hendrix used it". I said, "Well give it to me!" and he says, "You don't know how he used it". I said, "What do you mean?" and he said, "He was in that bathroom over there. We had a tape of him. He took that microphone, and he put it in a girl's pussy. We were taping it the whole* time". I listened to the whole session, and I was like, "Whoa". At the end, he goes, "What's your name again, honey?". I'll never forget it.

Brian Auger *In 1970, I was in New York, and I got a call from John McLaughlin and he said, "You should come down and listen to the mix of my album, I know you're going to really dig it". So I went along. Then the door opens and who should come in but Jimi and his girlfriend. We hadn't seen each other for a long time. But the thing that bothered me was that his skin tone, and that of his girlfriend, it was kind of a pallid grey colour. And I thought, "Whoa, he doesn't look too good here". We were talking and he asked me, "Listen, Bri, can you stay and make an album with me?". And I said, "I'd love to, man, but I have all these contracts that I have to fulfil, I just can't do it". And then Jimi pulls out of his pocket this silver paper, opens it up, and there's this brown heroin in there, and he takes a snort of that, gives it to his girlfriend, and then says, "Oh, sorry, Bri", and tries to hand it to me. This is one of those moments I'll never forget. I said to Jimi, "Hey Jim, I'm telling you, man, you'd better quit doing that stuff, as soon as you can, because it's gonna kill you". And he said this to me – I'll never forget it – he said, "You know what, Bri, I need a lot more people around me like you". That really touched me.*

Nils Lofgren: *I managed to sneak backstage one time at the Baltimore Civic Centre when Jimi was playing. I had snuck into a doorway and he came down a hallway all alone, on his way to the stage. I was just taken with how emaciated and sick he looked. He could tell I was a little startled by his appearance and he said, "Well, you know, I'm not feelin' so great. My manager's got me doing 64 shows in 65 days". As a teenager, I just thought, "Well, what kind of a manager is that?". Anyway, Jimi gave me a nod and made his way to the stage in this cloud of sadness and depression. I was really startled. It was the final years, when he was obviously getting frustrated with the whole business, and I think was way too hard on himself. He didn't have people looking after him.*

Jeff Dexter: *One of my defining memories of Jimi was when I was bringing him onto the stage at the Isle of Wight. His velvet trousers split as he came up the side. So I said, "Hang on there man", went to get some needle and cotton from my record box and sewed up his pants. I'm the only bloke who had my hand up his arse, while I sewed up his trousers! Then when he got onto the stage, he couldn't play his guitar properly because his new shirt had sleeves that were too voluminous, they hung down over his hands. So I got a bunch of safety pins and pinned up his sleeve. If you look* at the film you'll see safety pins holding up his sleeve. So he's really the first-generation punk to wear safety pins on stage!

Ginger Baker: *There was a gig we did with Ginger Baker's Air Force and with Jimi on the Isle of Fehmarn, off the coast of Germany, which was disrupted by the Hells Angels. It was the same day that I got busted in England so I was late arriving at the gig because I had to go to the police station. We had a plane I used to fly, Air Force craziness. The weather was terrible on the way over, violent storms, and when we got there we drove to the gig and it sounded like they were showing a Western film because there was all this gunfire and ricochets. It was the Hells Angels attacking people. So we repaired to the hotel, where there was a lot of craziness because on the way over with Jimi and the band they'd had a rare old time. We got very friendly. Jimi and I did have girlfriends in common. A very nice guy. Quite different to when he was on stage. He was very humble. I was very fond of him.*

Eric Burdon: *Quitting my band War all ties in to Hendrix's death. When we were on our way back from Paris, we passed through London and Ronnie Scott's club. And that's when Jimi died. That weekend, we were the last people he ever played with. It shook me up pretty bad. I went back to California for, I hoped, peace of mind. But it just got uglier and uglier. It was a pity to see a guy with whom I'd had lots of conversations about life and death end up like that. To see his body and the aftermath being tossed around like a basketball. I remember having endless discussions with Hendrix and John Steel from The Animals. We were convinced we weren't going to live that long. Maybe it's the Jesus complex. I tried to quit music a few times [after Hendrix died], but I always came back. I mean, what are you gonna do? It's too late to take up a profession in the medical world or be a bricklayer. That Jimi thing has never gone away. I just have to equate within myself that I was lucky to have been around at that point.*

Ginger Baker: *We became friends through Jimi's chicks, really, but we were also getting something together musically in 1970 after Blind Faith ended. He came over to my house in Harrow-on-the-Hill for dinner and we spent the whole day together working on stuff and then within a week he was dead. It was terrible. We were looking for him the night he died. Sly Stewart and the Family Stone were in town that evening and I'd got a big bottle, a marmalade jar size, full of cocaine hydrochloride, which a guy had nicked from a London hospital. Mitch saw the bottle and I told him there was another one going for 350 quid and Mitch went, "Oh man, Jimi will really go for that". So we all went to look for him. I was with my wife and*

Mitch and Sly Stone, and we couldn't find Jimi anywhere. We went to every possible haunt we could think of. We went to his flat, the Speakeasy, the Revolution and we just couldn't find him.

Leslie West: *I know exactly where I was when Jimi died. I was checking into the swanky Sheraton Cadillac in Detroit and when I signed in the lady says, "Another of you rock musicians died last night". Who? "The guitar player. The black guy". I said "Hendrix?". What a fuckin' waste…*

Betty Davis: *Jimi was very colourful. Very vibrant. He was electric – not just in his sound. He felt things on a deep, deep level. And he was like me, an introvert – he was an extrovert on stage and in his style, but Jimi was very quiet. He wasn't a big partier. He was very, very sensitive, and also very sensual. My favourite song is Foxy Lady: it's such a great way to describe a woman. I used to play Jimi really loud all the time in our apartment, so that's how Miles Davis was introduced to his music, just like I introduced him to Sly and Otis Redding. I remember I had Jimi and some people over our apartment for a Moroccan meal. Miles wasn't able to be there because he was working at a club. So, Miles called, and he said: "Put Jimi on the phone." And Miles asked him to go over to the piano and read the sheet music and tell him what he thought. And Jimi said: "I can't read music." The fact that Jimi couldn't read music, and he was that rhythmic, really impressed Miles. His understanding of what a musician was changed when he met Jimi.*

Electric Lady Studios

Shortly after the passing of Jimi Hendrix, Eddie Kramer and Mitch Mitchell found themselves in the control room of Studio A at Electric Lady Studios, listening to the recordings they had made that summer. These sessions were originally intended for the double album follow-up to *Electric Ladyland*. As they processed the news of their band leader and friend's untimely death, they were deeply moved by his guitar work and distinctive voice resonating through the studio. Just a few months prior, Hendrix, Mitchell, and bassist Billy Cox had created an exceptional masterpiece. Now, they found themselves questioning the absurdity of the situation and contemplating their future paths. They also wondered about the future of Jimi's cherished Electric Lady Studios, a place that had become the flagship of the his creative empire.

Their concerns proved unnecessary. Electric Lady Studios still stands today, over 50 years later, as a testament to Jimi's vision. It was a creative haven built by an artist for artists, a place where Jimi could create freely without concerns about time constraints or the sterile and restrictive environments prevalent in other studios of his era. In fact, within months of Jimi's passing, the elegant, arched cement walls of Electric Lady, located beneath the bustle of Greenwich Village, were more active than ever.

Initially, there was Jimi's legacy to address. *The Cry of Love*, the posthumous album compiled from the recordings Jimi was working on shortly before his death, was a priority, first however the studio needed to remain operational, which was no small feat given its $1 million cost. The final $300,000 required to complete the studio came from Reprise Records as an advance against Jimi's future royalties. Jimi had already made the first payment in August 1970, but his death just one month later cast uncertainty on the venture. However, word quickly spread, and artists soon flocked to the studio, recognising upon entry that this space was unlike any other they had encountered. The influx of artists that followed transformed Electric Lady Studios into a beacon for aspiring musicians, eager to record in the renowned studio created by Jimi himself.

Today, more than 50 years since Jimi Hendrix envisioned a studio he could call home, Electric Lady Studios has stood the test of time. It remains a place where artists can explore and realise their creative visions, free from the interference of label executives or business managers. Electric Lady is as busy and esteemed as ever. Upon entering its discreet yet enchanting doorway, descending into what still feels like Jimi's subterranean retreat, past the psychedelic murals and the hum of analog machinery, one can still sense Jimi's presence, inviting musicians of all genres to create and express their artistic visions.

It is a lasting legacy, and one that is especially appropriate for an artist of Jimi Hendrix's calibre.

Funeral and Final Goodbye

Jimi Hendrix's death had a profound impact on everyone who knew him. His passing further solidified his legacy as a legendary musician and the greatest guitarists of all time. On October 1, 1970, Seattle prepared for the funeral of one of its most renowned residents. The ceremony was a private and modest event held at Dunlap Baptist Church. In contrast to the chaos and energy that characterised Jimi Hendrix's career, the service was intimate and solemn. Family and close friends attended, while respectful fans and media gathered outside, separated by rope barriers. Inside, emotions were intense as family friend Patronella Wright sang spirituals, creating a reverent atmosphere. A poignant moment occurred when Freddie Maye Gautier read the lyrics from "Angel," serving as a touching tribute to the artist whose passion resonated through his music.

Angel came down from Heaven yesterday
She stayed with me just long enough to rescue me
And she told me a story yesterday
About the sweet love between the moon and the deep blue sea
And then she spread her wings high over me
She said she is gonna come back tomorrow
And I said, "Fly on, my sweet angel
Fly on through the sky
Fly on, my sweet angel
Tomorrow, I'm gonna be by your side"
Sure enough, this morning came on to me
Silver-winged, silhouetted against a child's sunrise
And my angel, she said unto me
"Today is the day for you to rise
Take my hand, you are gonna be my man, you are gonna rise"
And then she took me high over yonder
And I said, "Fly on, my sweet angel
Fly on through the sky
Fly on, my sweet angel

The service honoured not only the musician Jimi Hendrix but the individual, James Marshall Hendrix. The pallbearers included a combination of childhood friends and professional associates, such as Herbert Price, Jimi's chauffeur during his last summer in Hawaii. These details highlight the personal relationships that Jimi valued deeply.

The funeral brought together individuals from various phases of Jimi's short life, although the absence of Eric Burdon, was notable. Burdon did not attend, believing that Seattle was a city Jimi had mixed feelings about, and was not the appropriate place for his burial. This highlighted the complex relationship Jimi had with his hometown, while it significantly influenced his early years, it also caused him personal distress. Conversely, Mitch Mitchell and Noel Redding, his bandmates from the Jimi Hendrix Experience, were present, visibly mourning their friend. Jazz legend Miles Davis was also in attendance, honouring the young guitarist who had not only transformed rock but also influenced music as a whole. The presence of these prominent figures demonstrated Hendrix's wide-reaching impact across multiple musical genres, bridging blues, psychedelia, and jazz.

Although the initial idea for an all-star memorial concert was cancelled, music still played a role in honouring Hendrix after the service. At the Food Circus in Seattle Centre, Mitchell, Redding, Buddy Miles, Johnny Winter, and Miles Davis participated in an impromptu jam session. It was not comparable to Woodstock or Monterey Pop, but it served as a tribute to Hendrix's musical legacy. Although this gathering was not intended for the public, a Seattle radio station inadvertently broadcasted its location, attracting some fans to the venue. Despite the unplanned attendance, everyone respected the family's wishes, and the event proceeded as a respectful tribute.

Jimi Hendrix was interred at Greenwood Memorial Park in Renton, near Seattle, in a burial that held significant emotional weight due to its proximity to his mother, Lucille Hendrix, who had passed away during his teenage years. Although Jimi had complex feelings toward Seattle—where he endured a challenging childhood and initial struggles within the local music scene—the family selected this site to symbolically reunite him with his mother, imbuing his final resting place with personal significance. Despite returning to Seattle for performances, he never fully reconciled with the city, a sentiment reflected in Eric Burdon's decision not to attend the funeral. Burdon believed Jimi would not have wished to be buried in a location that evoked memories of his hardships.

In 2002, Jimi Hendrix's remains were relocated within Greenwood Memorial Park to a more elaborate granite memorial. This new site has since become a prominent destination for admirers from around the world, honouring Jimi Hendrix's life, his music, and his enduring legacy.

"When I die, just keep playing the records."
Jimi Hendrix
November 27th, 1942 - September 18th, 1970

About the Author

James Court is an author, writer and music biographer. His first biography was for Prince, released in 2018, Prince The Life The Genius The Legend. Following this he released Lenny Kravitz The Life The Genius The Legend in April 2019 and in the same year wrote a Madonna biography, the third book in The Life The Genius The Legend series.

His Aerosmith biography, titled Aerosmith A Band Like No Other, was released in 2019 and became his fourth release. Aerosmith was also made available as a large deluxe coffee table book with additional material and photography. Prince The Life The Genius The Legend was also converted to a large coffee table book, again with additional material and content. These releases were part of a new series of books entitled Rock the Coffee Table.

In 2020 James wrote and released The 27 Club, a book dedicated to the music legends that died at just 27 years of age: Amy Winehouse, Janis Joplin, Kurt Cobain, Brian Jones, Jim Morrison and Jimi Hendrix. Following on he released a book dedicated to the music of the 1980's, The 80's When Music Went Pop! was released in 2022. Jimi Hendrix Castles made of Sand is James's seventh release.

James has been nominated for *The Association for Recorded Sound Collection Awards for Excellence in Historical Recorded Sound Research*. He lives in Staffordshire, England.

All the books James has released to date are available on all platforms and in all formats, including direct from the publishers at www.newhavenpublishingltd.com

James Court Releases.

- Prince The Life The Genius The Legend
- Lenny Kravitz The Life The Genius The Legend
- Madonna The Life The Genius The Legend
- Aerosmith A Band Like No Other
- The 27 Club
- The 1980's: When Music Went Pop!
- Jimi Hendrix Castles Made of Sand

www.newhavenpublishingltd.com

www.ingramcontent.com/pod-product-compliance
Lightning Source LLC
Chambersburg PA
CBHW070726160426
43192CB00009B/1331